CONSCIOUS SPENDING
FOR COUPLES

CONSCIOUS SPENDING FOR COUPLES

Seven Skills for Financial Harmony

DEBORAH KNUCKEY

JOHN WILEY & SONS, INC.

Published by John Wiley & Sons, Inc., Hoboken, New Jersey.

Published simultaneously in Canada.

For general information on our other products and services, or technical support, please contact our Customer Care Department within the United States at 800-762-2974, outside the United States at 317-572-3993 or fax 317-572-4002.

Wiley also publishes its books in a variety of electronic formats. Some content that appears in print may not be available in electronic books.

Library of Congress Cataloging-in-Publication Data:

Knuckey, Deborah.
    Conscious spending for couples : seven skills for financial harmony / By Deborah Knuckey.
        p.   cm.
    ISBN 0-471-22140-6
    1. Married people—Finance, Personal.   I. Title.
HG179 .K5797 2002
332.024'0655—dc21   2002009953

Printed in the United States of America.

10 9 8 7 6 5 4 3 2 1

For the next generation
Caitlin, Alex, and William

Acknowledgments

I want to start by thanking the many couples interviewed for the book: your honesty surprised me and your insights shaped the book. I really appreciate your letting me look in on you, wherever you are in your journey.

This book would not have happened without the unwavering support and guidance of my literary agent Denise Marcil and her team, and the vision of my editor Debra Englander at Wiley. The production team at Wiley and Beehive Production Services polished up the book, and the marketing team has been great at getting the word out—thanks. Very special thanks to John Harrington, photographer and friend, for his good eye and wonderful cover photo.

Thank you to some of my dearest friends: Jodie for keeping me in touch with the real world, Scott, Leah, and Vanessa for offering philosophical distractions, Dominga and Rick for helping my life run smoothly, Wallace for inspiring me to be fabulous, Dr. John for providing a dose of sanity, Ysette, Carina, Adrienne, Donn, and Alok for checking up on the progress, and my many wild women friends who make my life so rich. Thanks to my parents Ed and Donna Young, my brothers Ian and Michael and their wives Jane and Joan—I appreciate the moral support from afar.

Finally, special thanks go to the wonderful team at Tryst, who kept me going with peppermint tea and the best sandwiches on earth. Keeping writers fed and watered is a noble calling.

D.K.

Contents

PART THREE

Seven Skills for Financial Harmony
79

PART FOUR

Four Lifestyle Decisions That Make or Break Your Finances
217

CONSCIOUS SPENDING FOR COUPLES

Introduction

In June 2001, I met with two couples as part of an *Oprah* show on Conscious Spending, the topic of my previous book. As I got to know more about their financial backgrounds and current situations, it became clear that their money issues were not just about money. I was invited on the show as a personal finance expert, but the couples could just as easily have been helped by Oprah's resident relationship expert, Dr. Phil McGraw. Although poor money management was a symptom of the troubles they faced, the cause was much more than numbers on a page. Entangled in their financial issues were emotional issues. I am not a psychologist, yet even I could see that frustration, fear, and control issues were muddying the financial waters. And the effect? The relationships were becoming unbalanced. The marriages were stable and loving, but no relationship can be unaffected by one partner having to step forward and parent the other, taking away credit cards and watching over the spending. Just try saying "You can't spend any more this month" *without* sounding like you are talking to a naughty child. Can't do it. Such actions inevitably erode equality, and possibly respect, within a relationship. It was a lightbulb moment for me. Although I had always known that money is not something that we deal with rationally, I had not seen clearly how often money is used within a relationship as a proxy for power, for control, for you name it. . . .

A couple of months later, I tuned into *Oprah* to see Dr. Phil working with couples about some similar issues. As he put it: "Deal with financial issues financially and emotional issues emotionally."[1] Yet that is *so* difficult for many couples. Money and emotions are intertwined. How can couples manage the emotional issues of their personal finances and the financial issues of their emotional relationship appropriately?

Throughout this book you will see that the answer lies in a blend of psychology, finance, and plain, old-fashioned common sense. Good relationship skills are as important as solid financial know-how, and neither is sufficient alone.

My previous book, *The Ms. Spent Money Guide* (Wiley, 2001), looks at how individuals can manage their personal finances better by becoming Conscious Spenders. This book looks at how my Conscious Spending concept can help couples.

Whether you have a harmonious financial relationship or a rocky one, whether you know a lot about managing money or just a little, *Conscious Spending for Couples* can guide you to build a stronger financial relationship with your other half. It addresses the emotional side of your financial relationship as well as the financial side of it. Of most importance, it gives you practical tools to move toward financial bliss by building a closer relationship and better finances.

Part One gives some background on why a harmonious financial relationship is important for couples, and looks at some of the reasons why our financial lives get entangled in our emotional lives. It looks at how men and women differ in the way they handle money, and how that can keep a couple from financial bliss. Part Two looks at three rules that should underlie a couple's financial life, creating a fair and strong foundation. Part Three teaches you seven skills that are needed for a couple to become

---

[1]Dr. Phil on Money and Marriage. *The Oprah Winfrey Show*, June 2001.

conscious about their money and create an abundant future. And Part Four looks in detail at the four biggest decisions you will make in your financial lives and how you can manage them.

This book is interactive, with many action items that range from creating plans together to simplifying your underlying structures. I recommend that you take the time to work through the action items together. I touch on some concepts, such as investing, fairly lightly—many of you may know much more already—however, I aim to cover a range of concepts in a way that couples who have differing levels of financial understanding can use together. And as far as your finances are concerned, I hope you go on to learn much more. This book will serve as a good starting point for helping you work together to direct more of your money toward the needs, wants, and dreams that you have as a couple.

Some Brief Explanations

- Editors don't allow authors to use "it" when referring to a generic person and "them" is often the wrong pronoun, so we are stuck with he and/or she. Saying "he or she" every few lines gets boring to write and boring to read. So at times I throw a dart and pick a gender. Not all of the He statements are just about men, nor are the She statements necessarily about women. Men can overspend. Women can overspend. Men can be savers. So can women. And men can get off on buying drapes, whereas women can get off on buying power tools (you should see my compound miter saw!). Please don't imagine sexism that is not intended.
- Sometimes I refer to marriage, but this book is written for all adults who share their expenses or money management with another adult: married or not, straight or not, couple or greater multiple, whatever! I spoke to a range of people of all races, creeds, genders (all two of them), and so on in writing this book and believe the advice spans any of those

classifications. Even if you still live at home with an elderly parent, if you share money, this book is for you.

- Stories in the book may use real people with their real names by permission, but some stories are composites and use made-up names. The real people know who they are. I thank them for their time and sharing.

PART ONE

LOVE AND MONEY

The words are lodged in my memory: "I'm not a mind reader, you know." I can't remember whether that clichéd statement came out of my mouth or his in the middle of a disagreement about something silly. However the truism is that none of us is a mind reader, even when it comes to the ones we hold nearest and dearest to us. Part One looks at the various factors that affect our beliefs about, and behavior with, money.

Chapter 1 describes Conscious Spending and how it applies to couples. It looks at what financial harmony is and how couples too often avoid talking about money. Chapter 2 looks at why money is so difficult to deal with. Reviewing psychological studies, we see that money is often a proxy for many emotional games within a relationship. Other research shows how men and women approach money in different ways—it's no wonder that money can be laden with misunderstanding within a relationship.

Chapter 3 looks at spenders and savers and how they interact within a couple: whether your relationship is a case of opposites attracting or of birds of a feather flocking together. Finally, Chapter 4 looks at how you can begin to build a stronger financial relationship by uncovering your assumptions about money and beginning to find common ground and shared rules.

CHAPTER 1

Conscious Couples and Financial Harmony

Her face catches the candlelight and the murmur from other tables envelops them in their plush corner booth. A dark-lashed waiter tops up their champagne, clears the plates, and fades into the background, leaving them alone. The man looks nervous, but happy, as he reaches for her hand. They bump fingers and laugh, then he wraps his strong hand around hers and gazes into her eyes. "There is something I need to ask you," his deep voice resonating under the rising violins. She smiles, not breathing. "Will you commingle your assets with mine?"

Love and money. Romance and the ultimate romance killer. Somewhere between the first date and the first shared utility bill, money nudges into a relationship, creating a threesome that is sometimes harmonious, sometimes hard to deal with. For some couples, its intrusion sounds a warning bell—disagreements about money are said to be the largest cause of divorce. For other couples, it slides in easily, just another aspect of an already strong relationship.

7

Love and money are a complicated mix. Whether money is a source of conflict or cohesion, couples need to work together to create a strong financial relationship, and a comfortable financial future. Creating a harmonious financial relationship involves starting with what you have—two people with perhaps two very different views on money—and learning how to draw on each other's strengths and avoid each other's weaknesses. For some couples, a harmonious financial relationship comes very easily, but for most, it requires work and know-how.

In Perfectville, people live within their means, invest wisely, and leave their money untouched for years and years until it grows into a large and healthy sum. People also eat well, work out three times a week, and drive no faster than the speed limit. Ah—that's why Perfectville is a mythical place. People are human. They don't start saving soon enough, their plans change, they get their hands on their money too soon. They also drive too fast, hamburger in one hand, speeding straight past the gym. Bottom line: They get in the way of their own best intentions.

Conscious Spending and Couples

Conscious Spending is the art of getting more of what you want with what you earn. I created the term to describe the financial behavior required to use money as a tool to realize your dreams. It is the attitude underlying the behavior that is really key. Conscious Spending requires being clear about your goals and values, and being willing to make the short-term trade-offs needed to reach your long-term goals.

I coined the term Conscious Spending after seeing so many people blow through their income with very little of lasting value to show for it. Too many people are unconscious about how they spend their money. The result is that their money "just goes" before they can use it to realize their dreams.

When you are a Conscious Spender, you balance three competing goals: to live within your means, take care of your future, and still have some fun with your money. The first two goals are critical for sound financial management: You cannot have a strong financial relationship if you have a weak financial foundation. The last goal is not frivolous: You work hard for your money and this goal reminds you that it is completely valid to aim to get some of what you want with the money that you have. And having some fun with your money doesn't mean that you need to spend on passing fancies, such as the pair of shoes that caught your eye; it means doing whatever is really aligned with your personal values. For example, it may involve spending money on a very important goal such as educating your children.

Managing money alone can be tough. Managing money as a couple is even tougher, not because there is more money to manage, but because there are two sets of opinions, needs, and beliefs to take into account. A single Conscious Spender simply has to understand his own goals and make the decisions needed to reach those goals on his own. Conscious Couples have a different challenge: They have to work together to balance the "mine, yours, and ours" goals.

Financial Harmony

So what is the end goal a Conscious Couple aims for? Financial harmony exists when a couple work together to reach shared financial goals. Money becomes purely about money, and the appropriate actions to build a strong financial foundation are taken without conflict arising. Each of you lets go of the emotional games that drive some financial behaviors. Financial harmony does not involve having piles of money—and all the luxuries it affords—though it may if that is your goal and you implement a plan to make it a reality. And it's more than just not fighting about money. Financial harmony comes about when you are both being adult about money, letting go of childlike irresponsible behaviors or parentlike controlling of your partner's use of money. Money management happens easily and with little, perhaps no, conflict. Any disagreements about money are dealt with cleanly, not dragging in other emotional issues. And if other issues rear their head, they are acknowledged and managed as emotional, not financial, issues.

Conscious Couples who have reached financial harmony:

- Treat money—and each other—with respect.
- Commit to living within their means and taking care of their future.
- Know what their major individual and shared goals are, what they will cost, and when they hope to reach them.
- Develop a plan and follow it.
- Understand how to meet their goals through smart spending and investing.
- Protect each other, and any dependents they have, by putting together a strong financial safety net.
- Communicate when concerns arise and work together to find solutions that are acceptable to both of them.
- Get outside help as required to keep their finances and financial relationship strong.

In a financially harmonious relationship, financial roles and responsibilities may be distinct, but goals are shared. The result is two people working together to build a solid foundation. In some cases, the road to becoming a Conscious Couple is not long: In choosing your partner, you may have instinctively or deliberately selected a mate with compatible goals and financial behavior that supported those goals. For most couples, however, the journey to becoming a Conscious Couple requires work. It may require negotiating a shared set of goals. It may require changing behaviors and attitudes. It may require learning to communicate better with your partner.

Getting It Right from the Start

If we chose our partners for purely rational reasons, we would all marry spouses whose money styles are compatible. Issues about differing styles would be ironed out before the wedding day, a shared plan would be implemented using each other's best talents, and our investments would grow happily ever after.

We know love is not rational. Too many people fall in love with someone whose financial style is not only incompatible, but perhaps even an assault to their core values. Others do just fine until the world changes when baby makes three at the same time as the dual income goes solo. And sometimes boredom, loneliness, anger, or revenge gets expressed through the seemingly safer language of money.

It is not surprising that money becomes an issue in so many relationships. Talking about money and attitudes regarding money is unromantic, and throughout courting and the honeymoon stage it's easier to avoid potentially touchy topics. A conversation about money is riddled with land mines, raising questions such as:

- Does he think I'm after his money?
- Who is she to question what I spend my hard-earned money on?
- Will she respect me if she realizes she earns more than me?
- Why should he care how much I earn if I am going to stay at home as soon as we have kids?
- Is he going to make me sign a prenuptial?
- Is she going to take me to the cleaners if we get divorced?
- What will he do to my credit rating?
- Will she make me feel guilty for every penny I spend?

Talking to a potential partner about money issues is difficult for both men and women. Men have been socialized to play the role of provider and may be reluctant to start a conversation that could suggest that they are unable to take care of the whole household. Many women fear that they will appear to be gold diggers, more likely to have read *How to Marry Money*[1] than this book. For either person, caring about how much your potential partner makes and how he or she spends seems shallow. Besides, isn't love supposed to conquer all?

So instead of opening up hearts and wallets and bank statements, many couples avoid the awkward, until the awkward finds them.

---

[1]Yes, it exists. No, I won't give the reference. If you want a book like that, you have to find it yourself.

The Elephant in the Room

Most of us are brought up not to talk about money. Often our parents would not discuss their finances in front of us. And we are more likely to know the details of friends' sex lives than we are to know anything about their financial lives. Money is the new sex: a taboo topic that is hard for many people to talk about, even within an intimate relationship.

In addition, the very process of becoming a committed couple changes how money fits into the equation. A silent power struggle often takes place as two individuals attempt to find the balance between independence and interdependence. In our attempts to pretend a relationship is between two exact equals, we avoid admitting that money often represents power within the relationship.

Yet even if we are willing to talk about it, do we really know all the emotional meanings that we link to money, or do most remain hidden, even to ourselves? Psychologists Edward M. Hallowell and William J. Grace Jr. point out, "Most people surround their feelings about money with so much anxiety that they are unable to focus on the topic long enough and calmly enough to discover its various disguised meanings."[2] In Chapter 2, I discuss the many meanings applied to money.

Money and Conflict

Not all relationships have conflict about money, and not all conflict-ridden relationships fail. Yet, if there is conflict about money, it has a cost. Financially, the underlying behavior that triggers the conflict may be costing you a comfortable future. And emotionally, the conflict eats away at the caring and respect in your relationship.

Many marriages start out with other areas of conflict taking center stage; however, psychologists Daniel Sternberg and Ernst

---

[2]Edward M. Hallowell and William J. Grace Jr., "Money Styles." In *Money and Mind*, eds. Sheila Klebanow and Eugene L. Lowenkopf (New York: Plenum Press, 1991), 15.

Beier found that within a year or so of marriage, money is usually the top troublemaker. They interviewed couples shortly after marriage and then a year later to determine if the sources of conflict changed over time. "The three most significant topics of conflict for the newlywed husbands were concerned with politics, religion, and money, while husbands, a year later, rated their most significant conflicts as money first, politics second, and sex third. With wives it used to be friends, politics, and money, but now it is money, friends, and sex." The toll? Husbands were not any unhappier from one study to the next; however, "wives . . . showed a significant increase in unhappiness. Altogether, there was a change for the worse . . . It seems from this data that the first year of marriage sheds illusions and centers on hard-core problems."[3]

The honeymoon is over. Too often relationships suffer over financial issues. Money is fertile soil to grow marital discontent. Poor money management can lead to fights about money. And constant fights about money can deliver a fatal blow to a relationship.

Money problems are only one of the catalysts of divorce. Researchers find that jealousy, infidelity, spending money foolishly, and drinking or using drugs are the most consistent predictors of divorce. "These problems appeared to increase the odds of divorce, regardless of which spouse was perceived as having caused the problem and regardless of whether husbands or wives were the respondents."[4] Yet compared to other causes of conflict, spending money foolishly, along with jealousy, can pull the plug on a relationship fairly quickly.

Sometimes, though, money keeps couples together for all the wrong reasons. Divorce is expensive and leads to a decrease in living standards, and 70 percent of people surveyed say the lack of money has caused them to make some tough life decisions: about

---

[3]Daniel P. Sternberg and Ernst G. Beier, "Changing Patterns of Conflict," *Journal of Communication* 27, no. 3 (1977): 97–100.
[4]Paul R. Amato and Stacy J. Rogers, "A Longitudinal Study of Marital Problems and Subsequent Divorce," *Journal of Marriage and the Family* 59 (August 1997): 612–624.

18 percent saying they had stayed married because of lack of money to divorce.[5]

So what's the cure? More money? No. No one has found that more money is likely to lead to a happier marriage. Stanley Koutstaal, in his doctoral thesis, found "no indication of a significant relationship between income and marital satisfaction."[6] Couples tend to fight over what they *do* with money, not how much they *have*. However, if a couple is financially satisfied, they are more likely to be satisfied in their marriage. And the amount of income is only one factor affecting financial satisfaction. "For husbands, higher levels of financial satisfaction were associated with increased age, longer marriages, fewer children at home, higher family incomes, and a greater proportion of the family income contributed to charitable organizations. For wives, higher levels of financial satisfaction were associated with higher family incomes and a higher proportion of the family income being contributed [by the wife's earnings]."[7]

For couples who argue about money, it is hard to imagine that money cannot only be neutral, but can actually be a source of connection. Money is the intersection between dreams and reality. It is the place where you can choose what is really important to you as a couple: how you want to live, what you want to do, where you want to go. As a Conscious Couple, you can use money as a way of building a life that meets both of your dreams.

Psychologist Marcia Millman sums it up in this way: "In the end, money doesn't corrupt love or families so much as it illuminates them. As the stain on furniture shows the deep grain of the wood, so does money reveal the hidden structures and rules of family life."[8]

---

[5]Money and the American Family telephone survey, quoted in *The Allure of Money*. AARP/*Modern Maturity* Press Release, May 16, 2000.

[6]Stanley W. Koutstaal, "What's Money Got to Do with It: How Financial Issues Relate to Marital Satisfaction" (Ph.D. diss., Texas Tech University, 1998), 100.

[7]Ibid., 94.

[8]Marcia Millman, *Warm Hearts and Cold Cash: The Intimate Dynamics of Families and Money* (New York: The Free Press, 1991), 15.

Does Conflict Matter?

In Seattle, a "love lab" studies what makes and breaks relationships. The head of the lab, psychologist John Gottman, has done probably the most extensive scientific studies of how couples deal with conflict. And his conclusion is surprising: "If there is one lesson I have learned from my years of research it is that a lasting marriage results from a couple's ability to resolve the conflicts that are inevitable in any relationship."[9] Notice that he did not say it is about whether a couple has conflict, but what they do with that conflict. In his book *Why Marriages Succeed or Fail* he discusses three types of stable marriages:

1. Validating: partners who hear each other's side of issues and seek to find common ground.
2. Volatile: partners who don't hear each other's point of view in the heat of the argument and actively defend their own point of view.
3. Avoidant: partners who minimize or avoid conflict, agreeing to disagree.

Although each type of marriage handles (or avoids!) conflict very differently, they can all be stable. "What is far more important than actually solving the issue or problem is feeling good about the interaction itself, and each of these types of couples has its own way to do that."[10] The difference between couples that make it and couples that do not boils down to the balance between negative and positive actions and feelings toward each other. And couples should aim to be Conscious Spenders not only to eliminate one of the most common causes of relationship tension, but also to build the likelihood of positive interactions around money.

---

[9]John Gottman with Nan Silver, *Why Marriages Succeed or Fail, and How You Can Make Yours Last* (New York: Fireside, 1994), 28.
[10]Ibid., 47.

Coulda, Shoulda, Woulda

. . . .

Geetha, a 27-year-old graduate student engaged to Richard, recognizes that her family's culture has influenced her spending style. "My parents came here from India, and for new immigrants, there is a certain status in being a consumer. You know you have finally arrived when you can purchase things." Geetha finds her habits strongly influenced by her family, who are "very very consumer oriented: whenever they have free time, they go shopping." Although Geetha is what Richard, also a graduate student, terms "a responsible spender," Geetha admits, "I find myself shopping when I am bored and it is inevitable that I purchase something. It is really hard to break the habit."

Richard also comes from a family where shopping is considered a hobby, but he has rebelled against his parents' values. "Both my parents are big spenders. They are equating their value with the quality and quantity of toys they have to play with. That's not something I feel comfortable with; I would much rather go walking in the woods than go shopping."

Before they marry, Richard and Geetha are seeking to find a middle ground between Geetha's shopping habits and Richard's tendency to be overly frugal. It was only at Geetha's prompting that he replaced his disintegrating backpack that had seen him through 10 years of daily campus life with a smart one that was not much more expensive than the bargain basement version he would have chosen alone. "Having a joint credit card has helped a lot because every month we go through the bill and divide it out and see what we are spending," Richard says. They applied for a joint credit card to save fees and accumulate frequent flyer miles more quickly. "[Analyzing the bill] gets both of us thinking about how we are spending money. It's a healthy step and I think we are both good influences on each other."

. . . .

Geetha and Richard are a perfect example of a financially mismatched couple who are doing a great job of finding a middle ground. They're doing all the things that couples need to do early in the relationship: talking openly about their differences, recognizing that many of their behaviors stem from their family histories rather than from active choices, and consciously choosing new behaviors that support their shared goals.

If you could restart your financial relationship, what would you do differently? While we cannot turn back time, this book aims to help you think through the decisions that you made in the past so you can make better ones for the future, building on what you already do well.

These are the financial matters you should have talked about before the furniture was moved in, the knot was tied, or the joint account opened. Money: what you earn, what you spend, what you want. What you think is okay, great, or terrible to do with money. What your credit rating is. What you want to earn. Whether you think debt is a convenience, a sign of weakness, or an entry ticket to consumer society.

What if you had had such conversations and found that your views were completely different and you had uncovered a huge well of conflict? Congratulations! You would have: (1) worked out what common ground could be found and compromised on the biggest differences; (2) found a way to get some of what you want while preserving the differences through a prenuptial; or (3) not married each other. Any one of these options is a better outcome than (4) spending a fortune on marriage counselors and divorce lawyers.

If you've never had these conversations, go directly to Part Three: Seven Skills for Financial Harmony. Do not pass Go. Do not collect $200. Or even spend it. Actually, do read through to there, but that is the place where there is a good framework for discussing money, starting at the positive place of where you want to go together, and then working back to how to get there from where you are.

CHAPTER 2

Understanding Each
Other's Point
of View

"ISO TALL, ATTRACTIVE PARTNER WHO ENJOYS WALKING ON THE beach at sunset, watching old movies and balancing the checkbook. Must have warm heart and good credit record. Nonsmoker with no debt and no children preferred. For dating, and possibly much more."

There's a reason why personal ads don't read like this one. Even if it were what someone wanted, he or she would be unlikely to admit it up front. People are conflicted about money. Although most people say they do not have enough money for today or their future, they still don't seek a lot of it. A survey found that most people—80 percent—fear that wealth will "turn them into greedy people who consider themselves superior," and 75 percent fear that wealth promotes insensitivity to others.[1] This love–hate relationship leads to a very deep conflict about money, according to psychologist Elizabeth Atwood: "As a culture, we are both obsessed by the potential for the accumulation of wealth and disgusted by it. We love to read about how to make more money, at

---

[1]Money and the American Family telephone survey, quoted in *The Allure of Money*. AARP/*Modern Maturity* Press Release, May 16, 2000.

the same time as we love to track the downfall of greed-driven people like Ivan Boesky, Michael Milken, and Imelda Marcos."[2]

Our feelings about money are anything but logical.

What Money Means

Why is money such an emotional issue? Money is not just about money. Because it's a limited resource, it brings out our fears about not having enough, not getting our needs met, being undervalued, being weak, feeling obliged, or missing out. Alone, managing money is a challenge. As a couple, the challenge increases exponentially, because suddenly you are in a sandbox and you have to share your toys. Some kids learned how to play well with others. Others never quite got over their favorite toy being handed over to their younger cousin. Even for a couple with equal income, plenty to live on, and similar values, money can be rife with psychological baggage.

The reason money is the center of problems in some relationships is that, as one person put it, money has "psychic currency." A review of psychologists' writings on money shows that money can symbolize a wide range of feelings, a different mix for each of us.

- "Often money is equated with love. The giving to another of money or the goods that money can buy is widely and perhaps universally perceived as being synonymous with loving that person." (Sheila Klebanow)[3]
- "Money weaves its way deeply into the texture of the lives we spin and eventually we can't distinguish ourselves from it. Money represents all things: a measure of our value; a source of power over other people, or a means to be free of them; a

---

[2]Elizabeth Baker Atwood, "Money and Marriage: An Exploration of the Psychological Meanings of Money in the Couples Relationship" (Ph.D. diss., Massachusetts School of Professional Psychology, 1998), 115.

[3]Sheila Klebanow, "Power, Gender and Money." In *Money and Mind*, eds. Sheila Klebanow and Eugene L. Lowenkopf (New York: Plenum Press, 1991), 51.

way to show care to others and to figure out how much they really care about us." (Marcia Millman)[4]

- "Money . . . may symbolize self-esteem and regard for others, power and omnipotence, innocence and worldliness, fear and security, caring and disdain, purity and dirt, acceptance and rejection—any individual meaning. Its emotional connotations stem from family values, cultural background, early experiences, and symbolic needs." (Ann Ruth Turkel)[5]
- "Money is symbolic of many emotional needs—such as for security and power—and goes to the core of our individual value systems. . . . Our feelings about money and value are so personal and often idiosyncratic." (John Gottman)[6]
- "Money in any relationship can symbolize commitment, self-esteem, power, love and acceptance. . . . Money is frequently a cause of marital discord in terms of power, control and autonomy." (Naomi Leiter)[7]

The result of this muddling of emotions and finances is that money is a major cause of stress in many people's lives. A *New York Times* survey found that money is equal to job pressure as the greatest cause of stress in peoples' lives, and beats out all other causes for those with lower earnings.

Gender Trends: How Men and Women Differ

If my circle of girlfriends is a valid indicator, men and women are very different creatures. "I just don't understand him!" "Men!"

---

[4]Marcia Millman, *Warm Hearts and Cold Cash: The Intimate Dynamics of Families and Money* (New York: Free Press, 1991), 125.
[5]Ann Ruth Turkel, "Money as a Mirror of Marriage." In *Money and Mind*, eds. Sheila Klebanow and Eugene L. Lowenkopf (New York: Plenum Press, 1991), 67.
[6]John Gottman and Nan Silver, *The Seven Principles for Making Marriage Work* (New York: Three Rivers Press, 1999), 194–195.
[7]Naomi Leiter, "Money and Divorce." In *Money and Mind*, eds. Sheila Klebanow and Eugene L. Lowenkopf (New York: Plenum Press, 1991), 79.

"What could make anyone think that?" "What was going through his head?" "Can't live with them, can't. . . ." They refer to men as being a different breed, race, or species. They roll their eyes, gnash their teeth, and pull their hair out over issues of love, sex, and communication. My guy friends, more politic due to being in my company, express a similar confusion and bemusement about how the other half operates. The consensus: Neither gender understands how the other ticks.

As kids we learn to focus on the physical differences between men and women. As adults, those may still be intriguing; however, we know that the differences run deeper. Men and women may differ due to nature and nurture. First, we are hardwired differently: Our brains simply work in different ways. And we are brought up differently. These differences flow through to our attitudes and behaviors around money.

Psychologists found that parents' expectations about money differ dramatically for male and female children. A study of college students found: "Sons . . . perceived and evaluated their parents as expecting them to know how to work and to save. Sons were introduced to discussions of family finances at an earlier age than were their sisters, reported that they currently work more than do women, and received less financial support from their families than did women. Daughters are either protected from parental fiscal problems or do not perceive or evaluate them in the same ways as do sons."[8]

How Men and Women Feel About Money

Feelings about money vary from person to person; however, there are interesting gender trends that emerge within our culture. Money often represents power, yet women and men are socialized to have different views about power and that colors their views about money. Men tend to feel confident about money, whereas

---

[8]Michael D. Newcomb and Jerome Rabow, "Gender, Socialization, and Money," *Journal of Applied Social Psychology* 29, no. 4 (1999): 865.

women tend to have mixed feelings. Economic psychologist Melvin Prince found: "Males and females were both likely to see money as closely linked with esteem and power, but males were more prone to feel involved and competent in money handling and take risks to amass wealth. Females had a greater sense of envy and deprivation with respect to money as a means of obtaining things and experiences that they could enjoy."[9] Other studies find women are not just reticent about money; they have negative judgments about the power it represents in relation to themselves and others. "Men felt that those who earn money are rational, responsible, and attractive. Money makes men feel lovable, happy, in control, and provides them with a feeling of self-worth. Men also envy those who earn a great deal of money. Women, on the other hand, were repelled by and considered immoral those who earn good incomes. Women also believed that earning more than their parents would make them feel guilty."[10] The result: 40 percent of women say they do not want to become wealthy, compared with only 27 percent of men.[11]

Can all of these differences be overcome? We cannot expect to unlearn years of training and generations of evolution. We can, however, try to understand the other sex, as well as recognize our own weaknesses, and learn ways to work with each other. I discuss two areas in which men's and women's financial behaviors differ—shopping and investing—and the end result of those differences—wealth.

Sex and Spending

Men and women differ in the way they shop. The individuals of any couple who have spent time in a mall together have probably

---

[9]Melvin Prince, "Women, Men, and Money Styles," *Journal of Economic Psychology* 14, no. 1 (March 1993): 175–182.

[10]Newcomb and Rabow, "Gender, Socialization, and Money," 866.

[11]Money and the American Family telephone survey, quoted in *The Allure of Money*. AARP/*Modern Maturity* Press Release, May 16, 2000.

been frustrated by each other's shopping style. Retailing guru Paco Underhill in his book *Why We Buy*[12] notes that men and women are very different creatures the moment they step into a store.

Some behavior that Underhill uncovered sounds contrary to many stereotypes: walking down the aisle, for example. Although it is supposed to take guys a little longer to walk down the aisle for marriage, at a supermarket, they're ready to sprint. And men who can't keep their eyes to themselves? It's different when they shop. Men don't look at anything that they do not intend to buy, whereas women browse. What about asking directions? This time its the same as in the car: Men don't like to ask where things are—if a male shopper can't find what he is looking for in two circuits of the store, he will leave the store without asking. Is he just a guy who can't say no? Men are more easily upgraded—it's easier to say yes and get out of the place—and also like to say yes to kids' demands. Of course, there are exceptions. At traditionally "guy" stores, men are more likely to behave in the way women behave in other stores. So, as soon as he enters, say, a computer store, he's suddenly a slow-walking, big-time browser.

As shoppers, women are both more deliberate and more experiential, according to Underhill. They are likely to shop with a list and look at price tags. They take the time to compare. Women find shopping a bonding experience, even when alone. They are more likely to ask questions of the sales staff, and if they are shopping with a female friend, they are likely to spend longer in a store than if they go in alone. Some of women's shopping tendencies are very troubling. Another study found women are more likely to buy something without needing it (36 percent versus 18 percent of men), buy because the item is on sale (24 percent versus 5 percent), shop impulsively (36 percent versus 18 percent), and shop to celebrate (31 percent versus 19 percent).[13]

---

[12]Paco Underhill, *Why We Buy: The Science of Shopping* (New York: Simon & Schuster, 1999).

[13]Tahira Hira and Olive Mugenda, "Gender Differences in Financial Perceptions, Behaviors, and Satisfaction," *Journal of Financial Planning* 13, no. 2 (2000): 86–92.

. . . .

Frank and Melissa could have leapt from the pages of a statistical study. They carry $9,000 in credit card debt—about the national average—spread across eight cards. They have little in the way of savings—also typical—yet they keep spending. They know that they need to prepare for their financial future, but never get around to it. "I know I buy things I don't need," Melissa admits. "But I want our home to be comfortable. Frank's parents are coming to stay and our guest room needed a bit of freshening up. I just picked up some new sheets, a pretty yellow, and a few other things for the living room. It wasn't much."

Frank snorts. "It was $250 by the time she got home. It really adds up. And we didn't really need any of it."

"Like we needed another power drill!" Melissa shoots back at him. She turned to me and attempted to spread the blame for their spending. "Frank spends all this money on the house, so he feels it's justified. We'll use the new sheets more than the cordless drill, I bet."

. . . .

Frank and Melissa are typical. It's as if there is a well-defined line between inside and outside the home, with men more likely to shop for everything outside—the grill, the workshop equipment, and garden tools—while women feather the inside of the nest—the soft furnishings, the dinnerware, food, and clothing. "Women have been taught to invest in lifestyle and children. Men have been taught to invest in things that hold value—a house, retirement,"[14] says Ruth Hayden, a financial counselor and author. This difference gets highlighted when you compare couples where the man is primarily in charge of the money with other couples: When he holds the purse strings, "the couple is likely to save a higher proportion of its income and to have a higher proportion of its gross assets in variable dollar form, that is, in the form of real

---

[14]Ruth Hayden, quoted by Jay MacDonald, "Gender Spender: Sex Sets Your Money DNA." Bankrate.com, June 20, 2000.

estate and negotiable securities."[15] In other words, women's spending behaviors often don't build the couple's long-term financial foundation.

Many of the men I interviewed cloaked their purchases in a veil of need. A new power tool that gets a job done faster is, in their eyes, a necessity, even if the project it will be used for is not critical, the time saved uncertain, and future use unlikely. In their eyes, their purchase is easily justified because it *does* something, whereas throw pillows or scented candles don't *do* anything. Perhaps this is why men have to be educated into not giving women household appliances as gifts—their natural inclination would tell them that an iron or toaster is a good gift because it *does* something.

Are these stereotypes always true? No, not for all people. I know plenty of women who hate shopping and get out of the store with as little time spent as possible,[16] and many men who can happily bond with their partner as they try on several dozen sweaters. However, the research shows stereotypes grow out of statistically significant observations.

Sex and Investing

How do gender differences affect the way men and women invest? At first glance, it appears that women are not as good at investing as men. They start later than they should, save less than they need, and tend to invest in more conservative investments—too much in the money market and bonds, and not enough in stocks. But scratch the surface, and the differences are more about education than gender. According to financial writer Jane Bryant Quinn, "Inexperienced investors of either sex tend to be cautious, and with reason. They don't yet know what they're doing, so they take less risk. . . . Women on average are less exposed to investing than

---

[15]Robert Ferber and Lucy Chao-Lee, "Husband–Wife Influence in Family Purchasing Behavior," *Journal of Consumer Research* 1 (June 1974): 50.
[16]Me, for one.

men. So naturally, surveys show that the average woman has less stock market know-how. But that's our average experience, not our sex."[17]

Lack of experience costs many women their financial security. The National Center for Women and Retirement Research found that a little over half of women surveyed owned no stocks or stock funds at all. What do they do with their money? Eighty-six percent put their money into passbook accounts and certificates of deposit (CDs). Some of this conservative investing may be due to the role many women play in their household finances. An Oppenheimer study found that women are likely to be a relationship's bookkeeper: 62 percent balance the checkbook, 58 percent pay the bills, but only 15 percent have the sole responsibility for making investment decisions.

Yet not all women are novices when it comes to investing. Merrill Lynch found that 57 percent of women felt they were knowledgeable about investing compared to 78 percent of the men. Not equal, but at least more than half. Their figures are higher than many other studies, but all of the studies consistently show a gap between men's and women's comfort levels.

When women do invest, they tend to be too conservative. A study of mutual fund owners by the Investment Company Institute showed that about a quarter of women shareholders are unwilling to take any risks with their money compared to just 11 percent of men, and only a quarter of women would take considerable risks to earn above average returns compared to 40 percent of men. Another study is particularly telling. In 1989, bonds were the primary investment vehicle of slightly more than 30 percent of men and women, an approximately equal proportion. By 1998, this statistic shifted dramatically. Only 14 percent of men still invested primarily in bonds, compared to 20 percent of women.[18] Could it be that as interest in the stock market grew, men gained knowledge and confidence more quickly than women? It seems

---

[17]Jane Bryant Quinn, "Gender Isn't About Sex," *Washington Post*, Sunday, 18 February 2001, sec. H02.
[18]Employee Benefit Research Institute survey.

so. What drives women's cautious investment behavior? Perhaps it's because they read less, talk less, and experiment less than men do when it comes to money. Women fear making a mistake 50 to 60 percent more than men do.[19] Most women underinvest and invest too conservatively, but as they gain knowledge, those behaviors seem to fade.

Some aspects of women's conservative tendencies stand them in good stead. Women spend 40 percent more time researching a mutual fund than do men, and are less likely to buy based on word-of-mouth tips.[20] When women invest, they ask more questions of their financial advisors, friends, and other sources, and are more likely to see their adviser as a partner and sounding board.[21] They also hold their stock purchases longer, generally a good thing, whereas men trade 45 percent more than women.[22] Those good behaviors pay off: Several studies show that female-only investment clubs earn higher returns than men-only and mixed-gender clubs, and that women who invest in individual shares tend to outperform men.

Men have plenty of weaknesses too when it comes to investing. As noted previously, they tend to skimp on research, buy based on tips, and hold their investments for a shorter time. More risky still, they are more likely to invest too much in their employers' stock than do women (45 percent compared to 29 percent).[23] The failure of Enron highlighted just how risky it is to hold a large portion of your investments in a single company, particularly when it is also your employer. On the positive side, men start investing younger and are willing to take more risk for a higher reward.

---

[19]Christopher L. Hayes of the National Center for Women and Retirement Research, quoted in Diane Harris, "Why Can't a Man Invest More Like a Woman?" *Individual Investor* (February 2000): 88.
[20]Ibid.
[21]*Women and Investing III: An Index of Investor Optimism Special Report.* UBS/PaineWebber publication, 2001.
[22]University of California, Davis study, quoted in Diane Harris, "Why Can't a Man Invest More Like a Woman?" *Individual Investor* (February 2000): 86.
[23]*Women as Aggressive as Men with 401(k)s.* Watson Wyatt Press Release, May 5, 1998.

The End Result: Uneven Wealth

The way women and men handle money differently has very real ramifications for many people. Divorced and widowed older women are the fastest growing segment of the population living in poverty. In the first year after a divorce, a woman's standard of living typically drops 27 to 45 percent, whereas a man's rises 10 to 15 percent, according to the U.S. Census. Of widows living in poverty, 80 percent weren't poor while their husbands were alive. This problem is of even more concern when you take women's longer life-spans into account: Typically women live 7 years longer than men and the average widow is only 56 years old. That means that there are a large number of older women who are going to be living in little comfort for years.

Women do not have to accept lower levels of wealth. We can see that the more women know about investing, the more likely they are to invest wisely in stocks with long-term growth, and the less likely they are to end up living in poverty. And the good news is that more and more women are taking this advice to heart. UBS/PaineWebber found that almost half of all substantial investors—those with $100,000 or more in assets to invest—are women.

Money, Gender, and Your Relationship

So what do these gender differences mean for you as a couple? They mean that you should not assume that the way you interact with money is shared by your partner. Don't assume that your partner is a mind reader. Even if you feel that it is glaringly obvious that you are having a horrible time trailing your partner around a mall, are desperately worried about your retirement savings, or are concerned about your partner's spending habits, do *not* assume that your partner has any idea of what is going on in your head. Your other half may have a completely different frame of reference—due to gender, culture, or past incidents—and may be oblivious to what is going on in your reality. That does not make your partner bad or unfeeling. It makes her human. Later in the book I discuss how to improve your communication as a couple so you don't fall into the trap of assuming you know what the other is thinking.

The link between money and gender also means that you need to understand each other's inclination toward both good and bad financial habits. As a couple, you can work together consciously to leverage the best of your habits and minimize the damage of the worst. The key is in working together. As relationship expert John Gottman says: "Whatever your disagreement over finances, you'll defuse the tension by working as a team to devise a plan you can both accept, even if it doesn't give you everything you want right now."[24]

Action Item: Understanding Each Other's Point of View

Find a quiet time to discuss the following questions, taking turns at answering each one:

- In your family, what financial beliefs and behavior did your mother and father model? What did they teach you? How has that affected your behavior toward money?
- What assumptions about money have you accepted without question? How do those assumptions affect the way you treat money?
- If you had a lot more money than you have today, how do you think it would affect you and your relationship? Would it be a good or bad thing?
- If you had to face a financial crisis together, how do you think it would affect your relationship?
- What is the one thing that you would most like to change about your financial relationship?

---

[24]Gottman and Silver, *The Seven Principles for Making Marriage Work*, 199.

CHAPTER 3

Managing Your
Money Styles

IN RELATIONSHIP MYTHOLOGY, OPPOSITES ATTRACT. NEAT FALLS for messy. Calm for fiery. Controlled for impulsive. Buttoned up for creative. Perhaps we are attracted to the idea that our other half counterbalances us, provides yin for our yang, sweet for our spicy. Or perhaps we simply are more inclined to notice the few differences than the many similarities.

Yet most couples have more in common than in opposition. And even the differences they have may not cause tension. However, differences in money styles can create significant amounts of conflict. For many couples, love is about attraction, lust, compatibility, enjoying each other's company . . . all manner of intangible things. Considering financial compatibility may appear shallow, scheming, and downright unromantic. Yet it is an important factor in overall compatibility, says psychologist Elizabeth Atwood: "Money is intimate and particularly important in marriage not only in terms of wages and their connection to nurturance, but because money is one of the ways in which we evaluate our fit with another."[1] Compatibility of money styles can be important for the long-term harmony of a relationship—though not necessarily critical for its survival.

---

[1]Elizabeth Baker Atwood, "Money and Marriage: An Exploration of the Psychological Meanings of Money in the Couples Relationship" (Ph.D. diss., Massachusetts School of Professional Psychology, 1998), 109.

Let's look at how individuals relate to their money as spenders or savers, and the combinations that arise when individuals pair up.

Spenders and Savers

There are a number of ways to categorize people's financial habits. All are generalizations and have their uses. Because we are looking at couples, I look at one simple way of dividing people: spenders versus savers. Not only does this categorization keep the number of combinations manageable (spender + saver, spender + spender, saver + saver), but it also provides a simple way of looking at whether you and your partner tend to handle money well or not handle it well, and the impact of your tendencies as they interact.

A spender is someone who enjoys spending money and is not so interested in saving it. A saver is someone whose natural inclination is to put money away for the future, and limit his or her spending today. Of course, this is not a simple demarcation: it is a sliding scale. At one extreme, overspenders burn through money before they earn it, building up debt and feeding an insatiable desire to buy more, more, more. Like an alcoholic, they use spending to numb out, feed a gaping hole in their self-esteem, or provide a quick hit of adrenaline. At the other extreme, the most frugal savers shun shopping and are oblivious to the threads fraying at their collars, even though they know the value of their portfolio down to the dime. Like survivalists, they are constantly stocking their bunker with enough supplies to last through a disaster larger than they are ever likely to face. Fortunately, most of us are somewhere in between, some with a very healthy balance, others with a noticeable tendency toward either spending or saving. The decisions that are made in small, everyday ways are what are most likely to distinguish a spender from a saver.[2]

---

[2]A more detailed discussion of spenders versus savers can be found in my previous book *The Ms. Spent Money Guide: Get More of What You Want with What You Have* (New York: John Wiley & Sons, 2001), 36–38.

Most spenders and savers have an underlying fear: Spenders fear that they will miss out on something nice today; savers fear that they will not have enough tomorrow. Such fears are deep-rooted and often not conscious. Because such fears are so much a part of your view of how the world is, it is hard to realize that your point of view is simply that: *your* point of view.

Action Item: Are You Spenders or Savers?
. . . .

Take turns filling in the questionnaire provided as Figure 3.1. Without looking at your partner's responses, select the answer that best represents your views. Then calculate your score and compare results.

                                                          He says   She says

1. You find something that you think you would
    like, such as a CD, but can do without. Do you:
    A. Automatically say no, the purchase is a friv-
       olous waste of money.
    B. Think twice, but decide against the purchase
       because there's something you'd prefer.
    C. Consider the purchase and then decide to
       buy it.
    D. Buy the CD straight away ... after all
       money is there to be enjoyed.
                                                          _____   _____

2. You think people should:
    A. Be allowed to do whatever they want with
       their money. If they go bankrupt, that's
       their business.
    B. Enjoy their money today as long as they can
       pay the minimum monthly balance on what
       they owe.
    C. Only borrow for big-ticket items such as
       school or a car.
    D. Pay for everything except a house in cash.
                                                          _____   _____

Figure 3.1   Questionnaire for evaluating your money attitude.

He says   She says

3. You know:
   A. The balance of your accounts down to the nearest dollar.
   B. The approximate amount you have in the bank and how much you have put on your credit card this month.
   C. Approximately how many credit cards you have.
   D. The exact starting date of the best sales in town.

4. You regard credit cards as: _____ _____
   A. Free money, a license to spend.
   B. An easy way to get what you need when you want it and pay for it when you can afford it.
   C. A useful tool that should be used in emergencies only or paid off fully monthly.
   D. The devil's spawn.

5. If asked about what you would like to buy, you   _____ _____
   could list:
   A. One or two things at most, and even then, you don't really need them.
   B. A couple of items that you are currently saving toward.
   C. A small catalog worth of stuff.
   D. Enough things to spend the next year's salary on.

6. The longest you have waited to buy something   _____ _____
   you wanted to purchase is:
   A. Waited? Only a minute as your credit card goes through.
   B. A few days, until you're next in a store that sells the item.
   C. A week or month for smaller things, and years for large goals such as a house.
   D. You are still waiting for some things, but now that you have the money, they just don't seem so important.

                                                             _____ _____

Figure 3.1   Continued

Scoring:

	A.	B.	C.	D.	He says	She says
Question 1.	1	2	3	4	_____	_____
Question 2.	4	3	2	1	_____	_____
Question 3.	1	2	3	4	_____	_____
Question 4.	4	3	2	1	_____	_____
Question 5.	1	2	3	4	_____	_____
Question 6.	4	3	2	1	_____	_____
				Total	_____	_____

Results:

- If you scored between 6 and 8, you are an extreme saver. There's careful and there's cheap. You're probably cheap. While it is great to plan for the future, your fear of it is paralyzing you and leaving you with little fun today. Chances are that you are driving your partner and friends away by being too careful with every penny. Unless you move toward more balance with your money, you may end up sacrificing too many of life's pleasures.
- Between 9 and 14 means you are a saver. Your natural tendencies will help you accumulate wealth over your lifetime. Make sure you strike the right balance between having some fun today and having some tomorrow.
- Between 15 and 20 means you are a spender. Your focus on enjoying today means that you are not building the wealth you need to enjoy spending in the future. You need to rethink your priorities and find a way to have some fun today, but not at the expense of a stable financial future
- If your score is above 21, you are an extreme spender. Of all the categories, yours is the most dangerous. While extreme savers may live a pretty cheap and unfun life, at least they are not likely to harm those around them. Your tendency to spend with little control may cost you your credit record, your freedom, and your relationship. Take control before your tendency to overspend costs you more than you can afford.

Figure 3.1   Continued

Opposites Attract: Spender Versus Saver

So what happens when a spender and a saver get together? In the best of cases, they moderate each other's extremes. In the worst of cases, all marital hell breaks loose. Most of the time, however, there is simply ongoing tension.

. . . .

Together 17 years, Dovid, a rabbi and coach, and Ester, who runs a home-based childcare center, are still seeking to find a comfortable balance in their styles. Their budget is very tight: much of their income goes toward the food, clothing, and education for their nine children aged 16 years to 8 months old. They have relied on state-provided health insurance for children and pregnant and nursing mothers for the last three years. The most they can do while Dovid builds his coaching business is hope to get through the month with enough money; planning for the future simply doesn't happen. Yet even the end of the month seems far away when a check arrives.

Dovid spends when there is money at hand, and Ester has learned to jump into the fray before the money is gone. "I now realize that when the money comes in, that's the time to spend, otherwise there is nothing left. The first in gets what they need, so if I know I need $100 for uniforms for the children, I will mark it as gone from the account at the beginning of the month, as if it has already been spent."

Dovid justifies much of his spending as being necessary for the home or his work, yet admits that the joy of having a new tool or computer program leads to a rush. "When I see something that I know will make life so much easier, I want to get it. The right tool for the job makes all the difference in the world. I like tools. It's like when you buy a new car, you want to see how far and fast you can take it. It's the same feeling—I go out and drill everything in site and there's a feeling of power. I excuse [the spending] because it is an investment. Most purchases are under $50 and there is a reckoning that $50 won't make or break our budget, no matter what."

Both admit that the unchecked difference in spending styles is taking an emotional toll on their relationship. Ester says, "As the financial situation changes, tension comes and goes. At the 6-year mark when I took over the budget, that was a major thing." The family accounting is now back in Dovid's hands, as he uses Quicken to track, but not plan, their spending.

Ester admits to "a certain amount of wanting to be more self-sufficient. There's a feeling that when things like tuition or a wedding come along, we will be relying a lot more on community resources than I would want to."

Dovid now recognizes the impact his spending has on Ester. "Ester has quietly swallowed without me having an idea about how she is feeling about it, and so over the years, I have taught her a different philosophy: If you want something and it strikes you, go ahead and get it and enjoy it. I taught her to become an impulsive buyer."

Ester is still, at heart, a saver. "We have very different views of what is needed. I translate a lot: for example, a toy car for $3 equals a sack of potatoes and flour and margarine. I'll see something and want it, but not spend the money. If he sees something he wants, he'll get it."

....

How do a spender and a saver find harmony? Couples with more extreme differences may find themselves with one partner being pulled into the patterns of their other spouse. Savers, such as Ester, start forcing themselves to spend in order to get some of what they need, or spenders find themselves restricted by their saver partner who controls the flow of cash. Others may find their tendencies exaggerated, with a spender racking up debt while their partner gets ever more frugal, in a passive–aggressive attempt to teach their spouse a lesson.

In the case of Dovid and Ester, a shared commitment to becoming conscious about money will be required before harmony is found. They could learn from Geetha and Richard, in Chapter 1, who found a middle ground. Geetha and Richard's chance of financial harmony is high, despite different tendencies, because they are talking about their finances before troubles arise, and are making conscious modifications in their behavior. Their story contrasts with many couples whose differences do not emerge until well into their marriage, usually when they hit a financial tight spot.

Two of a Kind Type One: The Overspending Spiral

. . . .

Debi and Jim waver between embarrassment and defensiveness. "We know we spend a bit much," Jim starts. "But we can make the payment on our cards, and we are young . . . why shouldn't we have fun before we get too old to enjoy it?"

Debi joins in: "We'll change our ways before we have kids. And we would like a house, though we kind of know that it might be hard to get a mortgage, given our credit." Sitting in their sunny living room, I looked around. It was nicely but not extravagantly furnished.

"To be honest," Jim says, "We don't know where it all goes. We eat out a bit, and we have had to buy a lot of things to just set up our home."

Their mantle is crowded with framed photos of their friends and family, and Debi notices me looking at them. "I like to have the photos around. I guess each frame cost about $20, not much really, but when I count the number of frames . . . fifteen frames. That might be $300 just on our mantle," she calculates out loud.

"And if she can spend $300 on frames, I don't see why I shouldn't spend that much on an MP3 player. I want to enjoy our lives now. There's plenty of time to pay it back." I nod, resisting the urge to respond: Sure, Jim, sure. Heaps of time. Your whole future.

. . . .

The most financially fatal combination is two spenders. Some couples I spoke to had started this way and then pulled out of the tailspin once the bills got hard to juggle. Too many others were busy digging an ever deeper hole of debt, figuring it didn't matter as long as they had a ladder. Debi and Jim seem to be headed toward a spiral of overspending, promoted by Jim's sense of needing to get his fair share of the spending fun. Rather than checking each other's spending behavior, they simply leverage it to justify spending more.

Some couples who are both spenders manage fine for a long time, overspending, but always able to manage their debt (do you think they could have learned that from Uncle Sam?). However, they never put enough away for retirement and they are easily thrown off path if one of them loses a job or they are hit with an unexpected expense. They simply don't have the flexibility to deal with it. One other downside: Over a lifetime, they spend a small fortune on interest.

Two of a Kind Type Two: Two Cheap Together

I'm a saver. Big time. If my cash cushion dwindles down to below 3 months' expenses, I become completely stressed out, obsessed with looking at my financial spreadsheets, and deeply fearful. This reaction has been particularly true since I've been self-employed; however, I've always had a strong orientation to saving because in my belief system, money equals freedom and security. And freedom and security are core values for me. I was once sharing my life and home with a man who was as much a saver as I am. We had just graduated from business school and each bought a car, and our spending and savings styles moved from the careful to the slightly crazy, as we spiraled into a competition about who could be debt free first. Fortunately, we both earned enough so that we could save very aggressively while still having some spare money for fun. However, our standard of living was significantly lower than most people in our income bracket, living in a one-bedroom beach apartment in Los Angeles. He won the competition by a couple of days, making an early final payment to finish off his car loan the week I was planning to pay my last payment. In some ways the spiral of frugality served us well—we were both completely debt free less than a year after graduating—but if we had stayed together, we could have fallen into the trap of being too cheap, forgoing fun for frugality.

Two savers are the most likely to build wealth. While they will make trade-offs as they go along, in the long run they will live a lot more comfortably than most couples. The trick is to plan an appropriate balance between having some money to enjoy today and squirreling away money for tomorrow.

Which Couples Last the Distance?

So who do you think will last the distance:

- A mismatched spender–saver couple who argue over money?
- A couple of savers squirreling away for their future?
- Two spenders building up a mound of debt?

The answer: who knows? Maybe all will survive, maybe none will. As we saw in Chapter 1, the way the couples manage conflict is the biggest predictor of success. However, the couple who are both savers have less reason for conflict. By sidestepping a major cause of disagreements, they have less conflict to handle. And they'll have a much more comfortable life too, with money for their life goals available when they need it. Of course, the financial relationship is only one part of the relationship as a whole—there are plenty of other causes of disagreements that may erode the quality of the relationship. However, when partners disagree about how to use money or stretch their finances tighter than tight, they are adding an unnecessary stressor to their relationship. And not every relationship will survive the stress.

Can We Really Change?

Can we really expect to change? Like the old joke about how many psychologists it takes to change a light bulb (none—the light bulb has to want to change), a couple will be unlikely to change their financial relationship until at least one of the pair wants to change.

And unfortunately for some couples, that point only comes when the financial situation becomes untenable. The trigger may be the loss of a job, the realization that poor credit will keep them from buying a home, another argument over the mishandling of money, constant calls from creditors, or one of countless other circumstances that shines a harsh spotlight on to their financial situation. Fortunately for most other couples, the realization that they need to change is less dramatic.

A saver can let spending tendencies emerge, and a spender can educate herself to be a saver. However, often the change also requires dealing with the emotional issues that underlie the old behavior, such as low self-esteem, boredom, resentment, or fear. The bottom line is that if economic circumstances forced you to live on 20 percent less than your current income, you'd find ways to trim your expenses to fit the income. So, yes, you can change.

As a couple, you need to decide how to change. If you are a spender–saver combination, you need to find a way to support the spender's need to moderate his spending without making it feel like he is not allowed to have any fun with money. The saver in a relationship doesn't want to feel like she is always nagging, so she should ask the spender to draw up a list of ways that he would like to be reminded to stay on track. If you are two spenders, you need to support each other in changing in much the same way as if you were on a diet together: celebrating each other's victories and supporting each other through temptation. And if you are two savers, you need to simply check in once in a while to make sure you are not spiraling into severe frugality.

CHAPTER 4

....

Creating Financial Harmony

....

Sara and Steve's shopping list is long: have a wedding, followed by a month-long honeymoon in Europe; move to Colorado; buy a home, a Corvette for him, and a Miata for her; and perhaps have Steve go to law school. It sounds like a lot for a young couple with a $50,000–60,000 income. Yet they are well on their way to making their dreams a reality.

At only 22 and 23 years of age, they are getting it right from the beginning. Together 4 years and only recently out of school, they have been aggressively saving for their wedding and honeymoon and will pay for both without going into debt. They have kept their eye on long-term goals too: saving for the move and down payment on their home, and thinking ahead to retirement by funding their IRAs.

Sara has been in the workforce 18 months longer than Steve, and is better at handling her money. "She knows how to deal with money, how to budget, what she can afford. I feel like we have major expenses coming up, so every time I think about spending, I see it taking away from the wedding and the honeymoon. I know we do have some money to play with, but I still have a really hard time parting with it."

Sara also has more insight into the money because she uses Microsoft Money to track their spending and savings. "Steve is a little disconnected from the cash flow; therefore, more hesitant to spend."

41

Their financial relationship is harmonious. "I don't recall having disagreements, we feel we are both really on the right track," Steve says.

Sara agrees: "The times we've argued are when I feel I have to balance our tendency to both save a lot. Steve can be too nervous about money, and I prod him to enjoy some of his money."

They are both, by nature and nurture, savers. Both Sara and Steve grew up in families where money was treated with care. Steve's father has been a great role model for him: "He tends to spend money on things really important to him. He won't spend money on clothes or eating out much, but he'll go and buy a boat or a two-week fishing trip to Canada. He can always afford the things he really wants because he is very frugal with other things."

So how do two people get their money relationship off on the right footing from the start?

"A lot of it is luck," Sara admits, because they met when they were so young, without an eye to a lifelong commitment. "I'm really blessed to have found someone with similar values." However, she realizes that she would have had trouble getting serious with someone who had very different views about money. "Security is a value that is so ingrained, I'd have a hard time respecting someone who doesn't have an ability to save, have respect for money."

Steve believes communication and clear goals are key to their success. "We are sitting down and talking about our goals, prioritizing what is really important to us, and knowing how much money we are spending, say, on eating out three times a week."

. . . .

Moving forward in your financial relationship can be difficult. It would be great to be able to start young and fresh as Sara and Steve did, but most couples experience years of bad financial habits before they realize that they need to make some major changes. If you have been together a long time, you may have fallen into a destructive rut that wears away at your wallets and even your hearts. We saw in Chapters 2 and 3 how money is closely linked with our sense of self. Because of this, our financial attitudes and habits—good and bad—are deeply ingrained. This situation makes changing your interactions with money and with each other challenging.

Money is only one aspect of a relationship, and couples may find balance in many other areas of their relationship while having an imbalance in their financial relationship or vice versa. Yet financial imbalances are often related to other problems. Many of the couples I interviewed felt that their financial dysfunction reflected a more general dysfunction in their relationship; in some cases, they felt the financial imbalance actually *caused* the general dysfunction. Control issues with money reflected control issues overall. Irresponsibility with money reflected a desire to shrug off responsibility for other things in the relationship. In general, major financial conflict was usually a sign of serious problems in the relationship.

I often meet people who recognize that their financial life needs to change yet their other half either disagrees or resists change. Whether you have to make minor improvements or major changes in your financial lives, working together will help, although it is not essential. Even if just one of you begins changing—setting goals, taking actions, and showing your partner where the money goes—it begins to alter the dynamic of your financial relationship.

Love, Respect, and Apron Strings

The end state that you are aiming for—financial harmony—involves a delicate and flexible balance. It involves creating shared goals but still respecting each other's individuality within the relationship. Too often one or both partners put individual goals aside, and end up feeling invalidated despite reaching shared goals. And financial bliss requires making adjustments as you move ahead. You cannot design the perfect solution today and expect it to work well for the rest of your lives. Life intervenes.

. . . .

Caroline and Scott had their financial life running fairly smoothly. Apart from his tendency to blow a little too much cash, they were doing well. Then came the kids. Caroline and Scott agreed that Caroline would stay at home, taking on some part-time consulting and being their two daughters' primary caregiver. But the change in income contribution has tipped the balance of perceived power in the relationship. "Scott includes me as an equal on all decisions, and I actually manage our money and make the investment decisions because of my financial services background, but I have a hard time with spending decisions now that I'm not earning," Caroline says. Before she left the full-time workforce, she and Scott had similar incomes. Today she struggles with feeling financially equal, though she knows Scott does not expect her to spend less than he does just because she now earns less. "Even if I cost out my taking care of the kids and give that to myself as a phantom income, it is such a small percentage of what I could make in a job outside the home. So, I feel guilty spending on myself and resent that he doesn't feel guilty spending on himself."

. . . .

Caroline's dilemma is highlighted by the fact that she and Scott used to have equal incomes. I have heard a similar lament from women and some men who have never earned as much as their partner. A financial relationship based on respect needs to allow for the fact that you make different contributions to the relationship: emotionally, financially, and physically. True respect means understanding that the complex equation goes beyond numbers on a page. It has more to do with commitment, effort, and willingness to each take responsibility for 51 percent of the relationship, more than your "fair share."

Another issue that often arises with couples is the confusion between controlling the money and controlling the relationship. Often one person in a couple is more committed to digging out from financial troubles or trying to change financial habits. Their insistence on changing their own financial behaviors and those of their partner can feel very controlling to the less money-conscious partner, as if he or she is back in grade school and being given an allowance. Often the language used in conversations about money becomes more like that of a parent talking to a child than two equals interacting. For example, a friend of mine, Susan, handed her paycheck over to her husband, John, initially as a way of managing their expenses in an efficient way. Soon after, she felt that every penny she spent had to be justified to John, even though their finances were not that tight and he felt free to spend on items that he enjoyed. Rather than developing a spending plan together, John created and imposed a budget for the household without her input. Their financial relationship spiraled downhill, and after the divorce, they both recognized that his control over money was a reflection of a bigger lack of trust and respect. Working through the first couple of skills later in the book should help clarify how to control the finances without changing the balance of power in your relationship.

Action Item: Understand Your Contribution

. . . .

Find a quiet time to talk and take turns completing the following statements:

- Aside from my income, I also bring _____ to our relationship.
- I appreciate that you bring _____ to our relationship.
- Having unequal incomes makes me feel _____.
- To feel valued as a fully equal partner, I need _____.
- My level of commitment to improving our financial relationship is _____.
- My perception of your commitment to improving our financial relationship is _____.

. . . .

The Couple Advantage

As a couple, you have an advantage over singles. You have the potential to earn two incomes while living with not much more than one person needs. For example, two people can get by with not much more space than one person lives in. And as two, you will use little more than one in the way of utilities such as phone, electricity, and gas. Health insurance is usually cheaper for two, and your employer may even pick up the full cost of your partner's health insurance. You may find your food costs fall as you cook for two. You may be able to get away with one car or at least decrease the total mileage that both cars are driven. Vacations are nearly always priced for double occupancy. And you are fortunate to eliminate those expensive first dates.

However, many couples increase their costs when they get together, because all of a sudden dreams that have lain dormant for years burst onto the scene. Your lifestyle morphs into a "grown up" lifestyle, with "real" housing, furniture, vacations, and so on. Suddenly the one-bedroom apartment is not replaced by a slightly roomier two-bedroom apartment, but a whole house. The furniture that was fine a year ago starts to look flimsy. The china that worked well gets put aside for married-people's patterns. And if you have kids . . . you can kiss your days of double the love at half the money goodbye. The couple's advantage is easily lost in a rapid rethinking of priorities.

Does Marriage Matter?

In many senses, the technicality of the marriage contract is irrelevant to this book. After all, two people dealing with joint finances are likely to face similar issues regardless of the legal relationship between them. One of my good friends has been with his same-sex partner for 5 years. When we get talking about money, the conversation mirrors very closely that of my heterosexual married friends. Worries about saving for a home, each other's spending habits, the need to get on with retirement savings, the power struggles underlying the differences in their earnings. . . . If you read a transcript of a conversation between them you could not tell whether they were straight or gay, married or living together.

However, researchers have found that there are some differences: "Money in marriage is domestic, personal, private, joint, cooperative, and nebulous. Cohabitation money, like marriage money is domestic, personal, and private, but it differs from marriage money in that it is separate, individual, and calculable."[1] In other words, couples who are living together but not married are likely to mentally separate their money in a way that a married couple may not. Although the study did not look at how finances were organized, it is likely that a couple who are living together are also more likely to structure their finances separately than do a couple who are married. What is consistent, however, is that emotional and financial issues get entangled whenever there are two people dealing with one set of expenses.

Rules, Skills, and Decisions

The remainder of this book offers a detailed action plan to help you become a Conscious Couple when it comes to your financial relationship. Three concepts are important: rules, skills, and decisions.

Rules are the guidelines that underlie your financial life. Often people bring unstated rules with them into a relationship; for example, "It's okay to have debt." Becoming a Conscious Couple requires not only understanding the rules you have operated under in the past, but also developing new, empowering rules that will support your move toward financial bliss. Part Two looks at three rules that can bring you closer to your goals.

Skills fill your financial tool kit. It's one thing to know what you should do, but unless you know how to do it, you're stuck. Part Three takes a look at seven skills you need to develop as a couple to strengthen your financial foundation. And because we have

---

[1]Supriya Singh and Jo Lindsay, "Money in Heterosexual Relationships," *Australian and New Zealand Journal of Sociology* 32, no. 3 (November 1996): 57–69.

seen that many financial issues have emotional roots, one of the most important skills is learning how to communicate in a way that will help you grow together.

The decisions you make every day will affect your ability to achieve your financial goals as a couple. Part Four looks at four major decisions that will make or break your financial life: where you live, what you drive, whether you have children, and when you retire. Each of these decisions is complex and has a long-lasting effect on your financial health.

Adopting shared rules, building good skills, and making some major decisions together will go a long way toward ensuring that your feelings about money don't undermine your actions. If you already have a fairly healthy financial relationship, these rules, skills, and decisions will shore it up, helping you build a very solid financial foundation for going forward. If your financial relationship has been a little shaky, they will help you redraw the plans, reinforce your foundation, and build your ongoing relationship on stronger ground.

PART TWO

THREE RULES FOR FINANCIAL HARMONY

Financial disharmony, which can spill into so many other areas in your relationship, often occurs because each person brings unstated "rules" about the way he or she should behave into a relationship. Your assumed rules may have come from your family, from rebelling against your family, from lessons you learned through life experiences, or from past relationships. Yet when you bring two different people into one relationship, there is a good chance that their rules won't match exactly. If, for example, one believes that credit card debt is fine as long as you can afford the minimum payment, whereas the other believes that any debt is a chain that shackles him to the 9-to-5 grind, there is a good chance that the couple won't reach financial harmony unless the underlying rules are brought out into the open and agreement about a shared rule reached.

Part Two looks at three rules that can iron out most of the disharmony that a couple experiences. If you and your partner can reach agreement on having these three rules underlie your financial decisions and actions, you will have a solid base not only to build your financial future, but also to create financial harmony. In my previous book, *The Ms. Spent Money Guide* (Wiley, 2001), the rules, as stated for an individual, were: live within your means, take care of your future, and maximize your pleasure. In this book, the rules are reworked to address the areas of conflict that can arise in a household: staying out of debt, maintaining financial flexibility, and meeting both of your needs.

The three rules speak to the areas where most conflict arises between partners. The first rule—If You Don't Have It, You Can't Spend It—addresses the issue of debt. If a couple has differing views about whether it is acceptable to get into debt to cover wishes, wants, and random expenses, conflict will arise. And if a couple both embrace debt, there is a good chance that they will face conflict the day the first one realizes that they have mortgaged their future.

The second rule—The 80:20 Rule—speaks to the issue of managing to live well within your means so that you retain the flexibility to live the life you choose. It recommends that you keep your everyday expenses at only 80 percent of your earnings. This ensures that you are saving enough for retirement, and that your household can survive a decrease in earnings in the case that one wants to stay at home with children or loses his job. Couples who live on the edge of their income have many more chances for conflict.

The final rule—Even Big Kids Get to Play—speaks to two issues: mutual respect of each other's needs and the need to manage your financial lives in a way that allows for each of you to retain some independence.

The rules aren't carved in stone; couples break them every day. However, if you choose to adopt these three rules, you will have a much greater chance of having a harmonious financial relationship.

CHAPTER 5

Rule 1: If You Don't Have It, You Can't Spend It

"I was horrified when I realized how much debt Cecile had," Mike confessed. "I very nearly called the whole wedding off. I couldn't understand how she could be so irresponsible. It's not like she had had a financial disaster to deal with. I didn't get how she could consider going into debt just to go out with friends, buy clothes, and take vacations." Instead of running screaming, Mike sat down with Cecile. "I tried hard not to sound preachy, but I probably failed. I laid out the costs of being in debt—not only the interest, but also the damage to her credit record—and let her know that I could not feel comfortable with her debt levels. I really wanted us to be able to buy a home together one day." Fortunately Cecile already knew she was out of control and felt Mike's concerns were reasonable. "I think I had been waiting for someone to shake me up a bit. It was as if I resisted growing up." They worked out a plan for her to pay down half of her debt before they married and he agreed to help pay off the rest after they married as long as she eliminated all but one of her credit cards. "It's hard," Cecile says. "I still sometimes slip up because it seems like such a little thing to spend $50 on a pair of shoes on sale. But I try to keep a picture of the home we want to buy in my mind. I've managed

to stay debt free for 2 years, except for 2 months when I went over my planned amount."

. . . .

Couples in debt have more reason to be couples in conflict. As debt grows, available income shrinks, with interest payments and bank fees taking a larger slice of your spending money, which creates a spiral of overspending as it becomes harder and harder to live within your means without changing your underlying living standard. At the same time, the challenge of managing your finances grows as you juggle debt from one credit card to the next low-interest offer, and pay funds from one account to another. If debt is out of control, the challenge mounts exponentially as you struggle to keep the whole house of cards from collapsing.

Without debt, there is no juggling of credit card balances, no calls from overdue creditors, no sinking feeling of being increasingly over your head. Being debt free is not necessarily financial nirvana, but the chances of harmony are greater.

Standing near a couple of kids who were about 6 years old in a store one day, I listened in as they debated which toy they would buy. It was a long and fanciful conversation about what they could get if they had $5, $10, and $20, ending with one noting in a resigned tone: "But if you don't got it, you can't spend it." Without the luxury of debt, they walked away empty-handed.

Rule 1 is a basic statement of living within your means: if you don't have it, you can't spend it! You should only spend money if you have it. In most areas of life, such logic is immutable: You can't eat food you don't have and you can't spend 25 hours in a day. Yet money is a different creature. Thanks to this thing called debt, you *can* spend money you don't have. Unfortunately, however, you can't earn money you are not paid, so getting into debt means committing to use future earnings for today's spending decisions. In addition, you are losing the opportunity to grow the sort of wealth that will bring ease later in life.

If you are both savers by nature, this rule is a no brainer. Spending only what you have seems as logical as eating only when you're hungry. The couples who have trouble with this rule are those where one or both of the partners feel that debt allows them to live the way they would like to live today when they simply don't earn enough. It's the equivalent of sneaking an extra chocolate chip cookie when you're not hungry. And just as overeating damages your health in the long run, overspending damages your financial health.

Perhaps the greatest conflict comes with couples where a debt-happy person is married to a person who would never consider being in debt. A person who has an ingrained belief that debt is bad finds it almost impossible to put herself in the shoes of someone who sees debt merely as a convenience, a warping of time between when one earns and when one pays. To someone who finds debt an uncomfortable shackle, interest is the most wasteful of expenditures, money for nothing but money. To a debtor, it's the cost of convenience, of keeping up, or of having it now.

If you are in debt, you are not alone. Household debt is at record levels in the United States, and the Federal Reserve says about a fifth of low-income households are heavily in debt, meaning that debt payments are more than 40 percent of their income.

And what is all this debt costing? The Federal Reserve estimates that the average household spends about 14 percent of its disposable personal income on debt service: 7.7 percent on consumer debt and 6.1 percent on mortgage debt. As far as interest goes, the average household spends 3.2 percent of its income on interest, up from 2.2 percent in 1995, even though interest rates have been falling.[1] That's a large proportion of your money going for something you can't eat, drink, or sleep under.

What Is Debt Free?

Can you live your life without any debt? Possibly, but it is not the wisest thing to do. There will be times throughout life when you will want to borrow money. Mortgages are good debt, not only

---

[1]Anna Bernasek, "Honey, Can We Afford It?" *Fortune* (September 3, 2001): 129–132.

because you are unlikely to be able to afford to buy a house with cash, but also because you are able to deduct the interest for a home loan on your tax return, lowering its effective cost. However, a huge mortgage on a huge home that is much more than you need to live in is not so good—it is good only inasmuch as the home it buys is needed. Student loans that help you buy an education can be a good investment if they raise your earnings in the long run, though it makes sense to do what you can to keep the loans small. Short-term loans to get you in a car that you need to get to school or work make sense, too, as long as you are not going overboard and getting something well beyond your means.

So what debt is bad? Debt incurred for everyday living expenses. Debt incurred because you were bored and went to the mall. Debt incurred because you saw this cute little top. Debt incurred because the power painter might save you an hour of work when you repaint your living room. Debt incurred because it's the holidays and you want to give generous gifts to friends. Debt incurred because you're too sexy for an old car. Any debt incurred because you live beyond your means in small, everyday ways is considered bad debt. And living beyond your means in large, grandiose ways is simply stupid. Debt can be a useful tool; however, it should not be used to live a life you cannot afford.

The most common response to my diatribe on debt is: "But I will earn more tomorrow." True, perhaps. But you will want more tomorrow too. So if you go into debt today to get the latest wide-screen, high-definition TV, you will probably go further into debt tomorrow to get the latest satellite radio system for your car. There's always something more on the shopping list.

Credit cards have made getting into debt a lot easier. If you had to pay for an extra whatnot by check, you would not write the check unless you knew you had enough to cover it (I hope!). However, a credit card allows you to skip that simple mental check of "do I have enough money to pay for this?" at the time of purchase. The question is traded in for convenience and it may be weeks later when you get your credit card statement that you notice you don't have enough money to cover all of your spending.

If you have trouble resisting debt, you should limit the amount of debt you have available to you by keeping the limits on your credit cards low. Why? Having an available credit line is likely to tempt you to carry more debt. Financial researchers at Wharton business school found "that increases in credit limits generate an immediate and significant rise in debt. This response is sharpest for people starting near their limit."[2]

If, as a couple, you can commit to getting and staying debt free, you are also committing to putting off purchases until you can afford them. This commitment will mean that you will need to talk about what you want and make trade-offs. The advantage of making a list of things to save for is that often when you get close to having enough money, you find either that the newfangled technothingy is cheaper than it was when you put it on your list, or that you really are not as enamored of it as you were a few months ago.

The irony is that by not overspending, you will actually have *more* to spend. A debt-free family has an extra 3.2 percent of their income to spend on something more fun than interest . . . perhaps the wide-screen TV that the typical family went into debt to get last year.

Action Item: Talk About Debt

"The time has come," the Walrus said, *"to speak of many things. Of household debt and revolving lines, of interest rates and things."* Apologies to Lewis Carroll, however the time has come for you and your partner to sit down and create some clear guidelines about debt in your household. Unless you are both good savers by nature, you may find that you have different views about what is acceptable to borrow money for

---

[2]David B. Gross and Nicholas S. Souleles, "Consumer Response to Changes in Credit Supply: Evidence from Credit Card Data," The Wharton Financial Institutions Center, University of Pennsylvania (February 2000).

and what is not. And you may choose to disagree with my definition of good and bad debt (though you'd be wrong!).

Take 10 minutes each to look at the list below, adding any other items that you feel are necessary, and determine how you would categorize each one:

A. Okay to borrow as much as we need to purchase it.
B. Okay to borrow, but try to minimize the amount borrowed.
C. Borrow if necessary, but pay off as soon as possible.
D. Borrow only in an absolute emergency.
E. Wait until we can pay for it without debt.

House	Furniture	Groceries
Vacation	Electronics	Eating out
Car	Clothes	Renovations
Second car	Gifts	Lunches

Compare notes with your partner and discuss the areas where you have differing views. How much debt is acceptable for a mortgage? If you believe that debt other than a mortgage, student loan, or car loan is acceptable, how much is acceptable? Under what circumstances?

. . . .

Digging Out of Debt

If you're starting off debt free, you're at a great advantage. Many couples reading this book will find themselves already in debt. The challenge for those of you in debt is to not only get out of debt, but also to stay out.

It is not unusual for people juggling a lot of smaller debts to significantly underestimate their total debt. Many people I have worked with found their debt was almost double what they estimated once they summoned up the courage to add it all up. If you have reached a place where you are so deep in debt that you feel that making anything more than the minimum payment is a struggle, you are probably a candidate for debt counseling.[3]

Action Item: See Where You Stand

Over next month, develop a detailed list of all the debt you have. Start with any accounts that you can find statements for, and, as new statements come in, check your list to ensure that you include every debt. On either a spreadsheet or a piece of paper, create a list that includes: amount of debt, minimum payment, interest rate, average monthly interest, company money is owed to, and type of debt (student, mortgage, store card). Mark each debt "Good" (mortgage, can't-live-without home improvements), "Okay" (student loan, car loan), or "Eliminate" and subtotal each category. What is the total of the debt that you want to eliminate? What is the total of the minimum monthly payments? How much are you spending on interest each month? How many different accounts is the debt spread across? Are any overdue?

Recognizing that you are standing in quicksand is the first step. Working out how to get out is the next. Start by seeing if there is a way to lower your interest and simplify your debt either by getting one loan to consolidate all the debts or by transferring balances to the lowest interest rate account.[4] If you own a home, see

---

[3]See Chapter 14 for information on whether you need a debt counselor and how to choose one.

[4]First make sure that the rate charged for balance transfers is attractive and the credit limit is high enough. Many credit cards charge a different rate for purchases than for balance transfers. It is worth calling the company to see if they will lower the balance transfer rate.

if you can take out a home equity loan or line of credit to consolidate the loans. The advantage is that a home equity loan may be at a much lower interest rate than regular consumer loans and also may be tax deductible.[5] However, be warned that if you fail to pay the loan, you are putting your house at risk because it secures a home equity loan.

The next step is to work out how much extra you can afford to pay each month toward the loans. Paying the minimum amount due on credit cards will keep you in debt for decades. Even if you consolidate your debt using a home equity loan, you should pay it down faster, even though you are getting a tax break. Why? Because this is debt that you incurred for all the wrong reasons. Aim to free yourself of the debt created by living beyond your means.

Finally, begin to consistently pay down your debt. If you are unable to consolidate the debt, pay off the ones with the highest interest rates first, keeping the minimum payments on the others.

Action Item: Plan to Pay It Down
. . . .

Call your bank and tell them that you are planning to consolidate your debt. Ask them what loans they offer and what the interest rates will be. If you have a home, ask about a home equity loan or line of credit. Then call the company providing your lowest interest rate credit card and ask about transferring balances of other cards at the low interest rate and possibly raising your limit to accommodate your other debts (so long as you close accounts to keep your total limit the same or smaller). Once armed with this information, decide which is the best way to simplify your debt structure and lower your interest payment. Ask the bank or credit card company to calculate how long it will take you to pay off the debt if you make the extra payment you can afford each month.

Then set up an automatic payment for at least the minimum payment, preferably much more. Also add extra payments

---

[5]See Chapter 15 for more information about home equity loans and lines of credit.

with any leftover money that you have as often as you can afford to.

. . . .

Staying Out of Debt

Once you are out of debt, how do you stay that way? Never go near a mall again? Melt all of your credit cards in the oven? Swear off consumerism and live like a monk? I hope you won't have to go to any of those extremes. Making a clear commitment as a couple to follow Rule 1 and holding each other accountable to the rule will go a long way toward succeeding. Eliminating the source of temptation by closing unnecessary credit cards and leaving your remaining ones at home helps too, as does simply staying away from the source of temptation: the mall, home improvement store, and other places where you are most likely to spend. Part Four outlines a series of skills that will help you stick to your commitment of staying debt free. The first and most important skill is to plan your spending, which is described in Chapter 8. Chapter 9 looks at how to keep your financial infrastructure simple, and Chapter 10 discusses how to get into the good habits that can keep you debt free. Yet sometimes bad debt happens to good people. Having the right health, disability, and income insurance is also important, and that is discussed in Chapter 13.

And if you slip up, stop and try to recover quickly—too many diets collapse with the first unplanned cookie. Your financial diet should not fall apart with the first unplanned indulgence.

CHAPTER 6

Rule 2: Follow the 80:20 Rule

Betsy and Chuck were proud of being debt free. "We just assumed that we were doing all the right things: keeping out of debt and contributing to our retirement plans. It amazes me how quickly the house of cards came tumbling down." Chuck lost his software development job when his company went broke. "Not only did my income stop, but all the wealth I thought we had built in stock options vanished, and so did half of my retirement portfolio." Even though Betsy had strong earnings, the next 6 months were extremely tough. "All of my income went on the mortgage and car leases," she explains. "Each month we racked up thousands in debt to cover our other bills and Chuck's job search. We resisted cashing in what was left of Chuck's retirement portfolio, but it was a very scary time for two people who are financially conservative."

Fortunately, Chuck found a new job despite a tough economy. With $23,000 in credit card debt, he also found a new commitment to financial security. "I will never cut my financial life that close again. We simply can't afford the emotional stress of letting our cost of living eat all of our income."

Many households live from paycheck to paycheck, spending everything they earn. They leave themselves vulnerable, inflexible, and unable to afford their major life goals.

The concept of the 80:20 Rule comes from the management consulting field where consultants in the 1950s found that, for many companies, 80 percent of revenues came from only 20 percent of customers. This statistic was revealing, because it means that if a company takes care of the most important 20 percent of its customers, it will succeed.

I am adapting the rule to spending management. The term "80:20" represents the ratio between what you spend and what you save. For every $100 you take home, plan to spend $80 and save $20. If you take care of 20 percent of your income for major financial goals—the most important 20 percent—you will succeed financially. The rest will take care of itself . . . provided you also follow Rule 1 and stay out of debt!

Many households live on a spend:save ratio of 100:0, that is, for every $100 that they earn, they spend $100 and save $0. That means all of their money goes toward everyday expenses, leaving nothing for their long-term goals and financial security. Other households live at a ratio that is more like 110:–10, they spend $110 but only earn $100, resulting in –$10, or $10 debt. Their everyday expenses are greater than their earnings. They are slowly digging a deeper and deeper hole of debt, growing it not only by the amount they overspend, but also by the interest that accumulates on the debt. It is difficult to break the habit of overspending, and even more of a struggle to climb out of the hole. Why? Because they have to move from living at, say, 10 percent above their means to living well below their means. Why do they have to live below their means? Because they have debt to pay off in addition to having to start saving for their future and their big goals. The great news is that when they finally get out of debt, they find living within their means much easier because they are no longer spending a significant slice of their income on interest payments.

So why is 20 percent such a magical number? First, because you need to live at least 10 percent below your means to afford the retirement of your dreams. It is a great, and simple, rule of thumb to aim to put at least 10 percent of your income toward saving for your retirement. When you think about it, every dollar you earn today has to go toward three things: yesterday's excesses (debt repayment), today's needs, and tomorrow's wants. Let's say that you study until age 22, work until age 55 and live until age 77. In the 33 years that you work, you have to pay for any debts you accumulated when you were a student, and you also have to save enough to fund 22 years of retirement. In this example, it means that for every 3 years that you work, you need to be able to fund at least 5 years of life (3 years of work plus 2 years of retirement). More if you start with student debt. Thanks to the joy of compounding returns, you don't have to put away $2 out of every $5, or 40 percent, of your income. From that perspective, putting away only 10 percent of your earnings for retirement is getting off lightly. Of course, you need to run the numbers to see if 10 percent is enough for the retirement you dream of: If you didn't start saving from day one or want to retire very young, it may not be.[1]

The second reason 20 percent is a magical number is that throughout life there always seems to be a big goal that requires extra resources. There's an expensive dream for every step of the way. The progression may look like this: pay off student debt, get married and have a honeymoon, buy your first home, have children, buy a larger home, renovate the kitchen, upgrade to a larger car, save for the kids' college, have a midlife crisis, buy a vacation home, go on a second honeymoon, help pay for a child's wedding . . . the list never seems to end. By putting away the balance of your 20 percent on a consistent basis, you will always be moving toward making those dreams a reality. If you are currently in debt, the balance of your 20 percent can be used to pay off the debt and then to save for the big goals once the debt is paid off.

---

[1]See Chapter 18, When You Retire, to determine your retirement savings needs.

The Flexibility Advantage

The 80:20 Rule allows you both to take care of your future and to save for big life goals. However, it has another great advantage, one that Chuck and Betsy learned the hard way. By living 20 percent below your earnings, you can afford a great degree of flexibility. If you live completely within your means, you will not have the flexibility to handle challenges and take opportunities that you would have if you lived below your means. The challenges you may need to handle include losing a job, being laid off temporarily, or being forced to take a pay cut, or facing a large, unexpected expense such as fertility treatments to conceive a child. The opportunities that may present themselves may include taking the job of your dreams at a little lower salary, working part time, staying at home while your children are young, taking an unpaid sabbatical, studying part-time to improve your qualifications, or going on a second honeymoon.

By living on 80 percent of your salary and using the other 20 percent for retirement savings and for major life goals, you can more easily adapt to the challenges and accept the opportunities. For example, if you are a two-income family living on 80 percent of your earnings and one of you loses your job, you can probably get by on one income for a while until you are both employed again. How? First, stop all unnecessary spending, such as clothes, hobbies, and so on. This cutback strips your cost of living back to the basics such as housing, food, and transportation. Second, stop saving for retirement and the major life goals. For the period that you are unexpectedly on one income, you will need to use 100 percent of the remaining income for your everyday expenses, so it's fine to break the 80:20 Rule during a financial crisis. Then if, and only if, you need to, dip into the savings that you have accumulated toward one of your major goals. Not retirement savings—usually they are in tax-advantaged accounts that make them expensive to access—but your other savings that the balance of your 20 percent had been going toward. Chances are you will get through the crisis without having to rack up much debt or damage your credit record.

Compare that scenario to a couple who are living on 100 percent of their earnings. The day that one paycheck stops, they are scrambling. Yes, they can also cut back on unnecessary spending, but that alone is unlikely to be enough. Chances are the remaining paycheck barely covers the mortgage or rent and utilities. Suddenly, they are juggling credit cards to cover their basic living costs, and a month later having to find enough money to cover the minimum payments on those credit cards. They have little or no savings to draw on and are forced to make drastic decisions if the situation doesn't change quickly: build up a lot of debt, dip into retirement savings and face a tax penalty as well as harm long-term goals, or make a substantial change in their lifestyle.

Save 20 Percent? You Can't Be Serious!

Twenty percent sounds like a very ambitious goal, perhaps too ambitious. After all, the average U.S. household barely saves a penny. The personal savings rate—measured different ways by different government bodies—declined from around 8 percent in the 1950s to 1 percent today.[2] That means that as a nation, we spend virtually everything we earn. Or rather, for every household that is taking care of its future needs, there is another digging a deep hole of debt. And we expect to fund our retirement *how*?

The key here is whether you can reach your financial goals without saving 20 percent of your earnings. First, it is not as if the entire 20 percent will be sitting in an investment account somewhere. Half of the saving is for retirement and will be in accounts that are held separately and are away from temptation. The other half is for goals that you will continually reach, such as buying a home, funding your kids' college, or paying for a second honey-

---

[2]Bureau of Economic Analysis. Its calculation looks at total income less the total spending on goods and services. The Federal Reserve measures the savings rate differently, but shows similar trends.

moon. Therefore, that is money that accumulates and then gets used, then accumulates again. Yet, by thinking of it as savings, you are able to put it to one side to move toward goals that are important to you. Without the discipline of putting money away as you earn it, chances are that you will need to go into debt every time you reach one of those life events, and will end up paying much more for it. And there may be some goals you simply never reach. So the reality is that you have a choice: whether to save now and spend when you can afford it, or to spend now and *save* retrospectively (that is, go into debt!), paying a boatload of interest in the meantime.

Twenty percent is a goal. If you are currently spending every cent that passes through your hands, it may take you some time to reach this goal; however, it is achievable.

Live on 80 Percent? How on Earth?

How is it possible to live on only 80 percent of your earnings? If you are currently living on every penny you earn, this will take a lifestyle adjustment.

When I work with people, I first ask them to estimate where their money is currently going. Generally they can guess where about 70–80 percent of it is going. Most people honestly don't know where the rest of their money goes. As they begin to track their spending and understand where it actually is going, they usually find some areas that they are shocked by. Some find it is the big-ticket items, such as their house and car, that most surprise them. Most find it is the little bits of convenience spending, such as take-out meals and random snacks, that really add up. And many people forget about whole categories of spending, such as personal care and gifts. The areas of spending that surprise you provide a good place to start adjusting your lifestyle so that you can move toward following the 80:20 Rule.

Chances are, even if you know exactly where your money goes, you may not be able to find enough places to cut back in order to live on 80 percent and save 20 percent. We look at a couple of ways to get your cost of living down so you can follow the 80:20 Rule. Even if you cannot make the changes overnight (and I'd be surprised if you could), the important thing is to commit to the goal and to begin managing your cost of living.

Tackle the Big Items

The first areas to look at to cut spending are those where you spend most of your money. The average couple spends about half of their income on their house and its related costs and their car and its related costs. Trim those costs by 10 percent and you free up a full 5 percent of your total income. Some of the savings may be painless: refinancing your mortgage at a lower rate, adjusting your thermostat a couple of degrees to cut utility bills, cutting back on the minor decorating expenses that add up over time, choosing to buy rather than lease a car, and keeping the car for a few extra years. However, you may also have to make some tough decisions, especially if you are currently living beyond your means. It may be that you simply cannot afford the lifestyle you have and you may need to downscale your car or even move to a lower-cost house to avoid having your major expenses eat all of your money. Although you may not be able to make the savings overnight, in time you should be able to lower your housing and transportation costs. Chapter 15 on Where You Live and Chapter 16 on What You Drive have other suggestions on how to manage these two major lifestyle costs.

Scrimp on Small Stuff

....

As I write this, I am at my usual table in a coffee shop. I bought my usual bagel and peppermint tea for breakfast and I will sit here for most of the morning, because I am more productive when I can't get up and wander away from my computer every 2 minutes as I do at home. It only took a week of being here to learn the other cast of reg-

ular characters. There are some who, like me, use the coffee shop as an office, some focused on their own work and others meeting with a stream of business contacts. There are a number of men who stop by for a hot breakfast and newspaper. Single, I guess, and welcoming the warmth of someone else getting breakfast for them. There's an artist who seems to have taken up permanent residence on a couch at the back, doing detailed, abstract pen and ink drawings. And there are plenty of people who stop in while walking the dog, taking the kids to school, or heading to work. Each of us spends $2 or $3 on a drink, many spend more for a bagel or muffin or a sandwich at lunch to go with their drink. When I first started writing here, I decided that if I was going to camp out for at least 5 hours a day, I needed to spend at least $15, including tip, to stay guilt free. After all, one expects to pay rent on an office. I quickly did the math. My decision to write in the coffee shop is costing me over $300 a month, $3 at a time.

. . . .

The second place to look for substantial spending cuts is in your everyday spending on very small things. It is so easy for a whole lot of nothing to add up to a big something.

There are many ways that you probably spend a lot a little at a time. If you tend to buy lunch, you are probably easily spending $25 a week. If you stop by fast-food restaurants while you are running around, you are probably spending $4 a person for a meal on the run. If you throw a new video into your shopping basket at the supermarket rather than rent it, you are probably spending $15. If you enjoy browsing at bookstores and inevitably pick up a book that you want to read, despite the pile of books by your bed that you haven't gotten around to reading, you are probably spending $25. It's very, very easy to blow several hundred dollars a month on little nothings.

Unless you enjoy being a penny pincher, you don't want to have to watch where every penny goes. So how can you control the spending on little items that add up? First, assess your habits and notice where you are most likely to spend. Then, look at where you are willing to cut back, and find ways to substitute for the item. For example, you may be able to spend a little up front to buy a coffeemaker, good coffee beans, and an insulated cup and brew your coffee at work or home, or buy plain tea or coffee instead of the expensive lattes. You may choose to stock your car with snack bars to avoid drive-through meals. You may watch movies playing on TV and read the books you already own.

Find ways of making your change in spending habits easy. I use cash for the little random spending that I do and I only take a certain amount out of the ATM each month. The cash covers all small spending, including parking, newspapers, and take-out and convenience food. It's easy to see how I am doing on the random spending because I can just look at how much cash is left. When the cash is gone, it is gone.

Flatline the Basics

An easy way to cut costs is simply to be content with the status quo and let inflation do its job. By committing to keeping your spending on the big-ticket items constant until you are following the 80:20 Rule will help you reach the goal sooner. This strategy is particularly effective with your car and your home.

Take, for example, your home: If you choose to stay put for a while when you could afford to move to a bigger, better place, you can save a lot of money in the long run. This fact is especially true if you own rather than rent your home. It takes only a few years of inflation for your mortgage payment to seem less painful than it was when you first borrowed for your home. Similarly, if you own and keep your car for a number of years, your expenses will be dramatically lower than if you lease or upgrade your car regularly.

It can be tough to put off spending increases when you feel you can afford them. If you have never saved a lot of money before, you may find it difficult to look at a bank account and see a large balance without starting to fantasize about how to spend it. For example, as a writer I have an uncertain income. To manage that uncertainty, I keep at least 6 months of living expenses aside. Yet the temptation to touch that money is always there. Currently, I have to buy a new refrigerator because the old one is dying a loud and slow death. It took only one visit to the appliance store to trigger a full kitchen renovation fantasy. It started with the white versus stainless steel argument, and then escalated into the illogic of spending frenzy thinking: "It's silly to spend good money on an appliance I would like to upgrade soon, so I should get stainless steel. If I get a stainless steel fridge, it will make the other appliances look old, so perhaps I can upgrade all the appliances . . . after all, the dishwasher is pretty old too. And there are these great cabinets that would let me use the space better, and I could fit so much more in. It would be neater and more efficient, and I would cook more and entertain more. . . ." Suddenly I am assuming my whole life will change if only I have an updated kitchen. Now, my kitchen is not too old, probably 15 years or so, but it was renovated as a rental apartment, so it has the cheapest cabinets in that boring apartment oak and very basic appliances in late-eighties beige. It is perfectly functional as it is. I know that if I did not have a cash cushion sitting around, I simply wouldn't waste the time (and potentially the money) thinking about unnecessary lifestyle upgrades.

It can be hard to resist upgrading your lifestyle when your income rises. Choosing to stay put where you live or keep your old faithful car when you can afford something nicer requires resolve. Yet, if you can keep your major expenses level, time will do its magic and soon you will be a lot closer to following the 80:20 Rule. Flatlining—or choosing to hold expenses steady—helps you reach the 80:20 goal in the long run.

Cut the Trend Spending

Just as flatlining holds some costs steady, fighting the rising tide involves willingly choosing to lag trends. If you are inclined to get the latest and greatest gadget, you pay dearly for it. At the moment, flat-screen TVs that are only 4 inches deep and are scaled to show movies in their theater proportions are the new thing, and the price tag reflects it. Give them a couple of years, though, and they will probably be affordable.

You can also fight the rising tide when it comes to fashions. If you are a fashion plate wearing the latest style, there is a good chance you spend a lot on clothes and have closets full of things you would no longer be caught dead in. I'm not suggesting you wear last year's fashion, but that you choose a couple of key pieces that define the season instead of a closet full of items that will be out of date well before they are worn out.

Action Item: Plan for 80:20
. . . .

This exercise should be done in conjunction with creating a spending plan, which you will do in Chapter 8, Skill 1: Planning Together. Determine your after-tax income, adding back in any retirement savings that you save through your employer. Take 20 percent of that amount and determine how you need to split it between retirement savings, debt repayment, and saving for major goals. Also work out if you can live on 80 percent for the rest of your expenses without pinching every penny. If not, work out what short-term and long-term changes you will need to make to follow the 80:20 Rule in the future.

. . . .

Beyond 80:20—The Crisis-Proof Plan

Keeping your cost of living below 80 percent of your take-home pay is a great goal. An even better one for two-income families is to also keep your fixed costs lower than the lowest income. Let's say you have two incomes, with one of you taking home $2,500 a month and the other taking home $2,000 a month after taxes. Under the 80:20 Rule, you will commit to keeping your spending below 80 percent of $4,500, that is, $3,600. You can make your life even more crisis proof by ensuring that your basic food, housing, and transportation costs (including insurance, utility bills, and so on), do not rise above $2,000. This means that even if the highest earning person in the household loses her job, you will be able to survive without accruing any debt.

CHAPTER 7

Rule 3: Even Big Kids Get to Play

"I was so mad at him," Monique said, blood rushing back to her face as she remembered. "Not only were things pretty tight that month, but I had planned to buy him a DVD player for Christmas. But he just went out and bought it without even asking me." Damien rolls his eyes and smirks at me while she talks. "Aren't couples supposed to consult each other about stuff like that?" she asks, looking to me to agree. I wear the half smile of someone determined not to take sides.

Married for 3 years, Monique and Damien came from very different backgrounds. "I grew up with a mother who made decisions by herself," Damien explained. "She had to. My Dad wasn't in the picture. And I had survived pretty well until age 34 without having to get someone else's opinion about everything I buy. I work hard for my money, I should be able to enjoy it."

"Our money."

"I'm fine with you spending some of your earnings any way you like to. It's not like you ask me every time you buy clothes. And I don't want you to either."

"Clothes are different. That's not something we will both share. It's just that I feel pushed away when you make decisions like that

alone when we could have enjoyed shopping for the DVD player to-gether." Still struggling with their boundaries within the marriage, they agree to develop guidelines that will make them both comfort-able, letting Monique feel like she is part of a couple who make deci-sions together without making Damien feel like he is checking in for every decision.

. . . .

The transition from being two independent singles to two halves of a couple can be very tough. Although there can be great joy in sharing even the little things—shopping in a supermarket to-gether, picking out a holiday card—there can also be tension as you find the balance between independence and interdependence. Where one of you may find cooperating leaves you feeling con-nected, the other may find sharing everything feels stifling.

Rule 3 is designed to ensure that joint finances don't become a shared prison cell. No matter how much you enjoy togetherness, Rule 3 ensures a little space as well. The rule is: Even big kids get to play. The reason we work so hard is so we can have the life we want. And that means that even two big, responsible grownups need some of their own fun money. After all, even as little kids, our allowances were our own money to make our own decisions about. There was a thrill in deciding if you wanted to spend your allowance on baseball cards or marbles, a new lip-gloss or candy. The joy, the power, of choice! Why do we think that we want to surrender all of that independence once we get involved as a couple? And why do we think grownups no longer have a need for fun?

A pattern I observed in some of the spender–saver couples that I interviewed is that the saver would actively withhold from buy-ing anything considered fun so that he would highlight his part-ner's financially frivolous ways. This emotionally destructive behavior turned a saver's spendthrift ways into a sabre, his with-holding into a weapon.

Consciously Creating Assumptions

Each of us brings assumptions to a relationship. Many of the assumptions about how a couple should interact with money come from what we observed as children. Did your mother handle all the daily finances? Did your father handle all the investments? Did one parent live on an allowance handed out by the other? Did your parents talk about every little decision? Did one parent make big-ticket decisions without consulting the other? Did you grow up with one parent who managed all the financial issues by his- or herself? The chances are the financial interactions you observe growing up become the starting point for how you assume you will interact with your partner. If, however, you react against the financial relationship your parents modeled, it may become the counterpoint for developing a largely opposite relationship with your partner.

During the last holiday season, Lexus had a television ad where a husband surprised his wife, a mother and her children surprised a father, and parents surprised their daughter with a new Lexus. Of course, the recipients of the very generous gifts looked thrilled. Now, I'd never look a gift car in the mouth, but, frankly, I'd be rather peeved if such a huge decision were made without my consultation.[1] Unless I had been wandering around dropping blatant hints about exactly which model, color, and options I wanted, I'd feel as though an important part of the process had been stolen from me. At the same time, if it were my car being bought with my money, I would not expect my partner to be involved in the purchase process unless he wanted to be, and I would not give him veto power over my choice of car unless it affected my ability to contribute my share of living costs. What are your assumptions about how your financial interactions should take place?

---

[1]Though if you send me a Lexus out of sheer appreciation for the wisdom of this book, I will be unequivocally thrilled. Even more so if it happens to be the hardtop convertible in deep green with a cream leather interior.

As with all areas of compromise within a couple, finding the balance between working together and making independent decisions requires communication. However, the bottom line rule needs to be: Even big kids get to play!

You are, when it comes down to it, two separate people who choose to be together. As a couple, there are some areas of your life that may remain separate. Even the closest couple don't share every interest, every value, and every friend. Your financial life needs to reflect the balance between togetherness and separateness. It needs to give both of you the space to make some independent decisions, without feeling obliged to check in. Yet it also needs to involve you both in joint decisions.

Monique and Damien's fundamental argument lies in whether the entertainment system was his hobby or their shared item. Damien sees electronics as being as much his realm as Monique's wardrobe is hers. Monique feels that because they both will use the system and watch movies together, it is a shared item in the same way that furniture is shared. Price is a factor too. Monique feels that either of them can buy a $20 CD without asking the other, but any decision of $100 or more should be shared (though she often spends that much on a jacket without consulting Damien, as he is quick to point out). Damien had assumed that as long as they were both contributing equally to shared costs and both taking care of their retirement savings as they had agreed, all of the rest of each person's money was his or her own to play with. Both of their perspectives are understandable, and neither is *right*; however, agreed guidelines are needed to avoid future disputes.

One of the challenges in finding the right balance of mine, yours, and ours is that many things we spend money on as a couple are primarily driven by one-half of the couple yet have a joint benefit. If one person cooks more than the other, is his desire to have top quality knives or new kitchen gadgets a joint cost or should it come from his play money? Chances are that meals could still be prepared without the expenditure, so it is in some ways completely optional; however, both benefit from the end result: homemade pasta with finely julienned spring vegetables for dinner. Is a throw pillow that one person feels adds to the look of the living room a shared cost if the other sees throw pillows as one of life's more bemusing annoyances? And who really gets most value out of the black lace lingerie? If you wanted to get nitpicky about it, most spending is driven by one of you more than the other . . . and being a couple means sharing.

The key is not to break down all costs by who benefits from the expenditure, but rather to allow for some separate money—some fun money—that doesn't need to be accounted for or reported on, and to agree on an overall plan for the rest. Once you have agreed on how much play money each of you gets, that money becomes off limits for arguments. You can splash it on lots of little indulgences, or hoard it until you have enough for one big splurge. Who cares whether your, say, $1,200 of fun money a year goes toward having your toenails painted with sunset designs or on gold-plated stereo cables. That's your decision alone. Sure, you can tell you partner, but you don't have to ask his permission. The exception to this spending rule is if your decision has a direct effect on your partner; for example, you may want to talk about it first if you want to spend your fun money on bungee jumping. Your partner might have an opinion about the value of your having an intact skull.

R-E-S-P-E-C-T, and Not Just a Little Bit

For your relationship to succeed— emotionally as well as financially—it is essential that you maintain respect for each other. It is easy after 5 years of seeing each other cleaning teeth, wearing baggy flannel pajamas, and taking out the trash to forget all the little things that were enticing about your honey when you first met her. However, although the wonder may fade over time, the respect shouldn't.

There is an underlying respect for each other's needs inherent in Rule 3. It requires seeing your partner's hobbies, interests, and indulgences as a valid expression of who your partner is. Even if you simply don't understand why your partner would want to spend his spare money on a collection of rare flowers or her money on handwoven baskets, by allowing each partner to have some play money, you are giving each one room for self-expression. If you ask why your partner enjoys spending that money, you may be surprised by the answer. Men who assume that pedicures are about vanity will be surprised to learn that they are about feeling indulged, nurtured, and special. Women who assume that power tools are about getting tasks done well will be surprised to learn that they are about feeling competent and smart and in charge.

The other need you are respecting is the need for freedom. Picture relationships as being like a dance. At times you move toward each other, at other times you spin away, still holding hands. There is an oscillation between close and distant, attached and apart. As close as you may be as a couple, having some money that is purely your own allows for that dance to go on.[2]

How exact do you need to be? It's up to the two of you to decide. Some couples may prefer to put aside a set amount for each person every month, others may just want to check in every so often so that they both feel comfortable with the amount of fun money being spent. Generally, the larger the gap between your general cost of living and your income, the less tension there is likely to be about this. The key is to notice if either of you starts to feel that there is not enough for his or her interests or that the split is not fair.

The other key is to make sure that money is available. You need to plan for the play money so there is not tension every time a tight month comes by. Earmark the fun money at the beginning of each pay period, before everyday expenses soak it up. Consider putting it into a separate place; however, don't incur extra costs by

---

[2]This analogy is used in Eileen McCann, *The Two Step: The Dance Towards Intimacy* (New York: Grove Press, 1985). It's a funny, insightful cartoon-illustrated book that does a better job of explaining the complications of togetherness than almost any other I have read.

opening an account with fees. If you know you will spend the money in lots of little amounts, simply take the money out each month along with your everyday expense money.

Action Item: Picking Your Play Money

Spend 5 minutes each writing a list of spending that you perceive as specifically your own fun spending. Then, next to each item, write the approximate amount you expect to spend on it in a year. Add up the amounts. Here are sample lists to get you started:

DAMIEN		MONIQUE	
Electronics	$ 300	Manicures and pedicures	$ 600
Baseball tickets	450	Collectible china	300
Home brewing supplies	250	Decorating classes	200
Fly fishing trip with the guys	600	Spa trip with the girls	1,000
Total	$1,600	Total	$2,100

Once each of you has a complete list, compare notes. Are the total amounts comparable? Are there items on each other's list that you feel should be shared instead? Do you notice anything your partner has skipped?

Then, discuss what you feel is fair. Should the amount of play money that you each have be approximately equal, proportional to your incomes, or simply based on your wants? Should there be a cap on the amount that either of you can spend on one item before agreeing to consult with the other?

Finally, determine whether you can afford to put that much of your total spending plan aside for each other's play money.

PART THREE

SEVEN SKILLS FOR FINANCIAL HARMONY

Love and money are such a complicated mix. We have seen that a few fundamental rules can take some of the tension out of your financial life. However, there are also a lot of day-to-day actions that will impact how you interact with your money and your spouse. Part Three gets down to the nitty-gritty of seven skills that can make a difference in your financial relationship both in little everyday ways, and in lifelong, life-changing ways.

This section looks at seven skills that are vital to your financial harmony:

1. Planning together.
2. Creating a simple structure.
3. Getting into good habits.
4. Communicating through conflict.
5. Investing for strong returns.
6. Creating a safety net for two.
7. Getting help when you need it.

Will you need all seven? All seven are important; though there may be some skills that you and your partner are already using. If you picked up this book, there are probably some skills that you are missing, whether they are technical skills such as knowing how to invest well, or relationship skills such as communicating well in times of conflict.

Skill 1 is creating a plan together. More than simply filling in a spreadsheet, planning involves getting clear about each other's values and how those values impact the way you interact with money. At the end, you will have a spending plan that ensures that you both have money for some of what you each value.

Skill 2 is a liberating one for many couples whose daily finances involve a tangle of accounts and a juggling of funds between them. This skill involves streamlining and simplifying, to take much of the work out of money management. In addition, creating a simple structure involves building on each other's strengths and side-stepping each other's weaknesses.

Skill 3 is adopting financially healthy habits. Like a simple structure, good habits make your everyday financial management much easier and remove the opportunities for conflict.

Skill 4 underlies the implementation of many of the other skills. Although not financial, good communication skills are critical in the implementation of the other skills. Even if your financial life is in order, communication skills are great to have for all other parts of your relationship.

Skill 5—investing for strong returns—is vital if you are going to turn savings today into enough wealth to live comfortably tomorrow. Basic investment skills can help your money make money for you, a particularly important skill for long-term success. Even with good savings, moderate spending, and a good financial structure, you may be shortchanging your chances of a great future by investing in the wrong way. Working out what investments pay off for your long-term plan is important. And don't forget that investing in career skills may be as critical as growing the returns in your portfolio.

Skill 6 sounds a little pessimistic. By creating a safety net, are you inviting disaster? Not at all. Preparing today for what could go wrong in the future simply means that if you face a disaster, you only have to deal with the disaster itself. The last thing you need in times of trouble is the stress of a financial disaster added to the mix. Some of the action steps will involve assessing your estate plan, building a cash cushion, and ensuring that you have appropriate insurance.

Skill 7 involves tapping other people's skills. Great managers surround themselves with experts. You can do the same for your relationship by getting the specific help you need. Don't go it alone. There is a myriad of specialists who can help you finesse your financial life. This skill involves understanding the array of specialists that you may draw on, when you need their expertise, and how to choose the right person. And it's not just about financial planners, investment advisors, tax advisors, and estate planners: Sometimes, when it is not just about money, marriage counselors and therapists are the specialists to turn to.

CHAPTER 8

....

Skill 1: Planning Together

....

A couple have been driving for 6 hours and finally pull into a small hotel by a mountain stream. The husband announces, "We're here," and starts unpacking his waders and fishing rods. His wife sits there looking mystified, with a bag in the trunk packed for a beach vacation.

....

You would never go on vacation without planning what sort of vacation you wanted. Yet many couples head toward their future without planning what they want their future to be. The most financially harmonious couples that I interviewed are very clear on what their long-term goals are and what that means for their financial plan.

If you create a plan, you are streets ahead of most couples. Households with a financial plan accumulate twice as much wealth as households that do not have a plan.[1] A full financial

_____

[1] A 1996 CFA/NationsBank study, quoted in *New Study: More Than Half of Americans Behind in Saving for Retirement*. Consumer Federation of America Press Release, April 26, 2000.

plan involves much more than planning your spending—it includes planning for college savings and retirement, ensuring that you have adequate insurance, and managing your investments—yet it starts with controlling your spending, which this chapter discusses. From a relationship perspective, however, the process of coming to an agreement on the plan is almost as important as the plan itself. In developing a plan, you are creating a shared-life vision and working out how you will make that vision a reality. You are prioritizing your dreams, clarifying your goals, and putting down a timeline for making them happen. A financial plan is not about money, it's about *what money will be used for*. Planning, therefore, doesn't start with a numeric target, but with a vision of a lifestyle.

During the early days of courtship, most couples talk about their plans, but often in vague, romantic ways. Prior to marriage, few couples sit down and get more specific about those goals. Dreaming of living on a boat for a year may have been sweet conversational nothings while wandering home after a date; however, if you are serious about a goal like that, it is going to take some planning to turn the romantic notion into a real possibility.

Starting with the Big Picture

The first step in planning together is to look at your major life goals. Then, those big goals need to be broken down into small steps that translate into an annual and monthly spending plan. The amount of money you need to put away for your large dreams determines the amount left to spend today.

Setting goals is more than just wishful thinking. It is great to dream, and dream big, but if you want those dreams to become reality, it helps to get very specific. The most frequent mistake people make when approaching the financial-planning process is to fail to set measurable financial goals. Almost 70 percent of people make this financially fatal error.[2] A poor goal is like rice pud-

---

[2]CFP Board Certificant Survey, March 1997.

ding: sweet, but mushy and not clear. A good goal is specific, measurable, and positive. For example, a poorly defined goal might be to retire in style. A well-structured goal might be to retire in 2015 and live in Florida in a fully paid-off $300,000 house with $75,000 a year income. The poorly defined goal doesn't tell you how much to save by when, which doesn't mean that you will miss the goal, but the chances of reaching it are a lot lower, unless you have easily affordable goals compared to your income, or tend to squirrel away every spare penny without thinking. For most people, it is a lot more powerful to know how much you need to save each year to make your goal a reality. Also, many people find a clear vision much more motivating: You are a lot more likely to be able to forgo today's little splurge in favor of tomorrow's desired lifestyle if you can picture the house and imagine the lifestyle.

You may need to revisit these goals over time, and reaching agreement on shared goals may not be easy if you have never discussed the details of your future together. If you find there is conflict between your and your partner's goals, try to focus on the underlying values that those goals represent. Does her desire for a large home represent her love of family or her need for nesting? Does his desire for a lot of travel represent his love of adventure or his yearning for learning?

A small aside: Inflation erodes the value of money. It is important to account for inflation when determining how much needs to be saved and what returns you need to earn; however, it is easier to discuss goals in terms of what they would cost this year and then factor in the inflation into later calculations because you have a clearer picture of what a $75,000 lifestyle in today's terms is like compared to, say, a $180,000 lifestyle in 2015 terms.

Action Item: Define Your Life Goals

Answer the following questions separately, skipping any questions that are not relevant to you. Some people like to be creative as they do this, for example, making a collage of pictures

to represent their goals. However, it is important to be as specific as possible where you can be, listing the year that you would like to achieve each goal.

- What sort of house do you want to live in?
- Do you want to own a second home?
- Do you want to take time off work at any stage?
- Do you want to have children? If so, when and how many?
- Do you want to pay for your children's college? If so, what sort of college?
- Do you want to go back to school at any time?
- Do you have any expensive hobbies that you would like to pursue?
- At what age do you want to retire?
- Do you expect to work at all once retired?
- Where do you want to live during retirement?
- What sort of lifestyle do you expect to have in retirement?
- Do you want to leave money to your children?
- Are you likely to receive an inheritance?
- Are there other major expenses that you expect to face, such as caring for an aging parent or a disabled child?

Once you have compared your views, work together to create a shared list of goals that embrace the most important elements of each of your answers. Where you can, put a dollar figure on the item (e.g., you want to live in a $300,000 home during retirement). In Chapter 14, Skill 7: Getting Help When You Need It, I recommend that all couples, except those struggling to meet their current debts, use a financial planner to fully develop a financial plan. The output of this action item is a key input into the financial-planning process.

....

Discussing specific goals helps to create a shared plan. Even simple questions, such as retirement age, may not be so straightforward. One couple I interviewed both said they want to retire at age 50 and they are well on the way to being able to afford to do

so. There is only one problem: He is 7 years older than she is and his picture of retirement involves them doing things together. They had never thought through what will happen in the time after he reaches 50 but before she does.

Once you have a clear picture of shared-life goals, prioritize those that are most important or will require the most commitment to achieve. At the same time, take a look at the goals on a timeline (Figure 8.1) to understand the potential sequence of achieving them. A timeline looks at when you want to reach the goal, as well as the period prior to the goal that you will need to save for it and the time during/after it that you may be paying debt. For example, if you have a goal of buying your first home in 5 years, your timeline would start at today and go through to your retirement years. Five years from today it would indicate when you aim to buy a house. In the 5 years between now and then you would show that you planned to save for the deposit and in the 30 years afterward you would show the mortgage being paid. The timeline should include all foreseeable major goals so you can get a sense of the current and future demands on your income. Remember the 80:20 Rule? When you see all your big goals laid out in a timeline, suddenly it is not surprising that you need to put a full 20 percent of your income toward making those goals a reality.

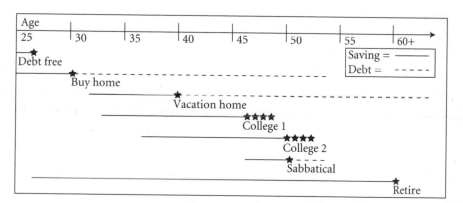

Figure 8.1   Timeline for achieving goals.

. . . .

Peter and Tran shared a vision of a their life in the future and were excited about creating a plan to get there. They wanted to build a home that Peter had designed, travel to Europe, and put their two children through college at state schools. When they talked about their short-term goals, they mentioned Tran's cousin's wedding that they wanted to attend in Australia, the new car that they planned to buy, as well as the savings they needed for their children's college, and a deposit on the land in the foothills nearby where Peter wants to build their dream home. When they started putting numbers down on paper, they simply did not have enough coming in to reach all their goals. It quickly became clear that the trip to Australia was at the top of the list for Tran, while getting a start on their kids' college savings while their kids were young was more important to Peter. Eventually, they prioritized their goals and decided that the new car could wait 3 years and the trip to Europe would have to wait for some time if they were going to get to Australia for the wedding.

. . . .

In drawing out your timeline, you may realize that your goals could eat up much more of your earnings than you can afford—the smorgasbord effect where your eyes are bigger than your stomach—and you may have to make some tough decisions. You have several levers you can pull: delay or eliminate goals, aim to increase your earnings, or decrease your cost of living. Don't take any action until you have a sense of what each dream will cost. Goals are just goals. They may change over time or life may get in the way. For example, you may plan to have children in 3 years, but find once you start trying that you need fertility treatment, which may delay your goal by years and cost thousands of dollars for which you did not plan.

Action Item: Create a Timeline
. . . .

Take a piece of paper and a pencil and eraser. I like using graph paper or turning lined paper sideways so each line can represent a year. Draw a line that starts at this year on the left and is long enough to extend at least 5 years into your retirement. Start with retirement—your most costly goal—and mark the year that you hope to retire and draw a solid line to the left of it extending across all the years that you expect to be saving for your retirement. Draw two lines if you expect to retire at different times. Below it, mark your other goals, with solid lines to the left for the period that you will save for each and dotted lines to the right if you expect to get into debt to achieve the goal. Don't forget to include a goal of becoming debt free. I prefer to exclude cars from this process as that is a lifelong cost that will be included in your standard of living. This process is for the goals above and beyond your normal living expenses. (For the same reason, I exclude the cost of a mortgage in the next step of pricing out your dreams, because once you buy a home, your mortgage replaces your rent as the cost of having a roof over your head. However, I mark when the mortgage will be paid off on the timeline simply as a sobering milestone).

I suggested using a pencil and eraser because you may find this process opens up further discussions about priorities and timelines—I have seen several couples rethink when they want to have kids after realizing that their first years of retirement would coincide with their kids' first years at college.

. . . .

The next step is to put dollar figures on the amount you need to save today to reach those goals in the future. You will not reach your goals unless you know how much you need to put away today for your goals. There is a good chance that the plan you create today is beyond your reach, and you may need to focus on some interim goals, such as getting debt free before starting to save for a deposit on a house. However, do not delay starting toward your long-term goals, such as retirement, because you will probably need every year of compounding investment returns to reach your retirement goals.

Working out exactly what your retirement goal translates to in terms of dollars and cents to be saved today is complicated and there are a lot of variables, such as what percentage return you expect to get. For the sake of this discussion, assume that you need to put away 10 percent of your income. A more detailed discussion on saving for retirement is included in Chapter 18 on when you retire. I strongly recommend that you sit down with a financial planner[3] to run the numbers and make sure that you know exactly how to get from here to there. Goals that are years away, such as paying for a child's college education, can benefit from compounding interest and tax advantages. Do not put them off, however, because they are far away; you will need every year of compounding you can get. A financial planner can help you determine exactly what those goals translate into today, or you can use a planning tool on the web.[4] However, at this stage, put a rough price tag on all the goals that you want to save for this year. These figures will feed into your spending plan so if you find you have goals that add up to more than 20 percent of your income (10 percent for retirement and 10 percent for all others), you may have to rethink your dreams.

Action Item: Put a Price Tag on Your Coming Year's Goals

Take the timeline you created and identify the goals that you want to take action on in the coming year to make the long-term vision a reality. Make note of any hurdles you need to overcome before beginning to move forward on the plans, such as getting out of debt or cleaning up your credit rating.

Fill out the work sheet provided as Figure 8.2 with your goals that require immediate action. To simplify, we will ex-

---

[3]See Chapter 14, Skill 7: Getting Help When You Need It, to read about choosing a financial planner.

[4]There is a wide range of tools on the web. The *Money* magazine/CNN site, www.money.com, has a good variety of interactive calculators, as does www.quicken.com and www.usnews.com. All of them are good; my favorite is Quicken.com, which allows you to slide each variable up and down to see the impact it has on your goal.

Goal	Target Time	Total Cost	Months until Goal	Monthly Goal
Example: Buy second car	*3 years*	*18,000*	*36*	*18,000 ÷ 36 = 500*
Total savings required per month				

Figure 8.2   Cost of goals work sheet.

clude interest in this approximation of how much you need to save, as the earnings on most short-term goals will be minimal. If you want to include the interest effect, use one of the on-line calculators mentioned to determine your monthly savings required for each goal.

If you are unable to manage the monthly savings you determined you needed, prioritize the goals and determine which are less important. Remember, however, that putting off large goals such as saving for college can cost a lot more in the long run.

Developing Your Spending Plan

A spending plan is a critical tool in managing your money. You'll notice that I don't use the term budget. The trouble with the b-word is that spenders assume that a budget is restrictive and will stop them from having fun. It is a word that is as demotivating as "diet." The aim here is to *plan* your spending, not to *stop* it. You don't need to plan and track every penny of spending, but you need to understand enough about where you want your money to go so that you can manage your spending and avoid letting a significant slice of your money slip through your fingers. By being very conscious about what you spend on, you can get more of what you want.

A spending plan helps you clarify how you want your money to be spent, and can be compared against a record of how it is actually spent. This comparison not only helps you see if you are spending too much, but also where your greatest areas of temptation or poor planning are. As a couple, such a comparison can help you work out what habits you each need to change so you can reach your joint goals. A spending plan takes account of how much you want to save to spend at a future date.

Are there couples that should not bother with a spending plan? A spending plan can be a very useful tool in the early years of a relationship as you get to know each other's spending styles, areas of weakness, and financial values. It is also a critical tool at times when you have major changes going on, say, if you have children, buy a home, or drop down to one income for a time. However, some financially competent couples skip the plan altogether. A financial planner who studied his client base found that 79 percent had never developed a budget of any kind.[5] I'd argue that his sample is probably not a good role model for most couples who buy this book. For one thing, the fact that the couples he studied see a financial planner regularly indicates that they are probably more financially responsible than the average couple. And most are well on their way to building wealth, so they have some leeway if a sudden, unexpected expense hits them. Don't skip creating the plan unless you are already well on your way to reaching all your goals.

. . . .

Greg, an editor, and Tina, a technology writer, living in the Pacific Northwest, have never planned their day-to-day spending in their 12

---

[5]Though they nearly all track their expenses, according to Ric Edelman, *Ordinary People, Extraordinary Wealth* (New York: HarperCollins, 2000), 177.

years of marriage. "We don't have a budget," Tina says. However, she does use Quicken to track where their household money goes. "I'm the family bookkeeper, and manage my personal and our joint account, and Greg handles his own investments." Tina and Greg are both strong savers, and it is their tendency not to spend that makes it easier to get by without a written budget, Greg says. "We talk about what our joint expenses are; however, I feel that we don't really worry too much about it because we are really of one mind when it comes to spending. We save a lot and think about purchases before we make them." Two savers who are happily building a very comfortable nest, they only plan for larger projects, such as vacations and remodeling. "A big part of our financial harmony is that we have the same habits in terms of spending and saving. We spend modestly, do not have expensive taste, and both save as much as we can," Greg says.

. . . .

Notice that Greg and Tina do track where their money goes even though they do not have a plan for where it will be spent. Their ongoing discussion of where the money is actually going gives them a quick way of seeing if too much is being drained by expenses that are not aligned with their shared goals. Only use this approach if you are both savers by habit, live well within your means so that there is wiggle room in case something goes wrong, and have been together long enough to know and trust that you and your partner's spending will be well within what you can afford.

Most couples need to be more specific in their planning until they get into good financial habits. For probably everyone who buys this book, a spending plan is a vital tool. There are a number of ways that you can create a spending plan. I go into detail about my recommended approach in my previous book,[6] and give a shortened version here.

---

[6]Deborah Knuckey, *The Ms. Spent Money Guide: Get More of What You Want with What You Earn* (New York: John Wiley & Sons, 2001).

The Conscious Spending Model

The Conscious Spending Model (Figure 8.3) is a tool that I use to plan spending. It groups spending into seven categories. Like the food pyramid, the basics are at the base of the model and the really fun stuff, which is included in a category called Soul, is at the top. Unlike the food pyramid, however, you can aim to get as much of the good stuff as you want, as long as you follow the three rules discussed in Part Two: stay out of debt, use the 80:20 Rule to plan for your big goals, and make sure you both get some play money.

    The last rule is to make sure that you still have fun with your money, whatever that looks like for you. For some people it may be traditional fun stuff, such as vacations or jewelry, for others it may be less obvious fun that is still strongly aligned with their values, such as creating a home that is a nurturing retreat. The key is

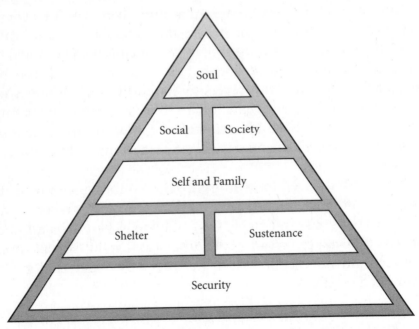

Figure 8.3   The seven categories of the Conscious Spending Model.

to ensure that you are building a strong base of security while still having some of the nice things that you work so hard for.

To summarize, the categories are:

- *Security*. Savings, investments, and insurance that ensure that you can weather financial storms and be financially independent in your later years. It includes life and disability insurance, retirement savings, and a cash cushion to protect you from unexpected events.
- *Shelter*. Everything to do with putting a roof over your head, including your rent or mortgage, home and contents insurance, utilities, and maintenance.
- *Sustenance*. All costs associated with feeding and taking care of your body, including groceries and convenience take-out and restaurant meals (as opposed to social meals), health insurance, health care, and fitness costs.
- *Self and Family*. Other everyday expenses for your household, such as transportation, clothing, haircuts, kids' allowances, and so on.
- *Social*. Money spent in social interactions with people outside your immediate family.
- *Society*. Contributions to charity and other ways of giving back to the community.
- *Soul*. All the added extras in life that fall outside the other categories and are consumed to add to the quality of your life. It may include spending on cable, books, magazines, vacation, massages, hobbies, jewelry, or electronic equipment.

It is important that you create a plan that you both agree on. After all, if you disagree about where you want to spend your money on paper, you will really disagree about it when the money is actually spent. Remember, there is really no such thing as a fixed cost: *all* of your current spending can change based on decisions you make. Change may take time (waiting until a lease is up) or even money (paying a penalty fee to end a contract early), but you can change your spending. So, if you find your spending is greater than your income, or that you do not have enough to pay down your debt as quickly as you would like, take a look at *all* of your current expenses and ask whether you would be willing to make the lifestyle changes that would result from cutting back each expense. Sometimes these are very difficult decisions and ones that may be hard to agree on. For example, you may realize that your spacious home is great, but not worth feeling over your head financially for, yet it may be at the top of your partner's list of favorite things. Downshifting your lifestyle is a major decision, and probably one that will create a lot of friction, but it may be the right decision if you cannot decrease your expenses enough any other way. Of course, the other lever you can pull is that of income: Perhaps instead of cutting spending, you will choose to focus on increasing your income so that you can comfortably afford your planned spending.

Keep your spending plan as a living document and revise it every time you have a significant change; for example, when you pay off your credit card debt, move house, or change jobs.

Action Item: Create Your Conscious Spending Plan

Create your spending plan using the work sheet provided as Figure 8.4 or, better yet, use a spreadsheet[7] or financial software[8] where you can easily define the categories to meet your needs and quickly see how much of your income you have accounted for. Start with the amounts that you need to save for your 5-year and lifetime goals. Then fill in major categories and predictable bills such as your housing and utilities, and then work your way to smaller items. The total of the amounts you plan to spend should not exceed your after-tax income. I also like to include a fudge factor of between $500 and

---

[7]Available on my Web site, www.deborahknuckey.com.
[8]Both *Microsoft Money* and *Quicken* have good planning tools. You can customize the category names to reflect the categories in the Conscious Spending Model.

Category	Spending Current	Planned	Gap
Soul			
Travel and vacation home			
Cable, books, periodicals, and music			
Hobbies, classes, sports, and toys			
Electronic equipment			
All the rest			
Body indulgences (e.g., massages, manicures, a personal trainer)			
Jewelry			
Art and collectibles			
Other			
Soul subtotal			
Society			
Charitable contributions			
Helping gifts			
Donated goods and services			
Society subtotal			
Social			
Outings, events, and restaurants			
Group and team activities			
Communication			
Gifts			
Social subtotal			
Self and Family			
Transportation			
Vehicle			
Auto insurance			
Gasoline			
Maintenance			
Taxis and public transport			
Clothing			
Personal care			
Haircuts			
Personal care products			
Dry cleaning			
Education and work-related costs			
Allowances			

Figure 8.4   Conscious Spending Plan work sheet.

Category	Spending		
	Current	Planned	Gap
Other household costs	_____	_____	_____
Tax preparer	_____	_____	_____
Bank charges	_____	_____	_____
Other	_____	_____	_____
Self and Family subtotal	_____	_____	_____
Sustenance			
Groceries and household supplies	_____	_____	_____
Takeout and nonsocial meals out	_____	_____	_____
Health care	_____	_____	_____
Health insurance	_____	_____	_____
Unreimbursed health expenses	_____	_____	_____
Dietary supplements	_____	_____	_____
Fitness	_____	_____	_____
Gym membership	_____	_____	_____
Fitness equipment	_____	_____	_____
Pet food and pet health care	_____	_____	_____
Sustenance subtotal	_____	_____	_____
Shelter			
Mortgage or rent payments	_____	_____	_____
Property tax and home-owner fees	_____	_____	_____
Home and mortgage insurance	_____	_____	_____
Household running costs	_____	_____	_____
Utilities	_____	_____	_____
House maintenance	_____	_____	_____
Mowing/gardening services	_____	_____	_____
Cleaning services	_____	_____	_____
Shelter subtotal	_____	_____	_____
Security			
Cash cushion	_____	_____	_____
Retirement savings	_____	_____	_____
Life insurance	_____	_____	_____
Disability insurance	_____	_____	_____
Umbrella liability insurance	_____	_____	_____
Savings/debt repayment	_____	_____	_____
Security subtotal	_____	_____	_____
Unrecorded	_____	_____	_____
TOTAL	_____	_____	_____

Figure 8.4   Continued

$2,000 a year for expenses that I cannot plan, such as having to pay an insurance deductible, having unexpected medical bills, or needing to fix my car.

Adjust your plan until your planned spending equals your take-home income plus the value of any nontax items that are taken out of your paycheck before you receive it, such as retirement savings. For example, if you take home $4,000 a month plus contribute $5,000 a year to your employer's retirement plan, the total of your plan should equal $4,000 × 12 + $5,000 = $53,000. The $5,000 retirement savings should be included in the Security section.

Additional columns are provided for your current spending and the gap between your current and planned spending. Many couples find that the plan they aim for is quite different from their current spending patterns, and using these columns can help you highlight where you need to make the greatest changes to your spending.

. . . .

Taking Another Look

What happens if, on this very first step, you hit an impasse? This can be a very difficult process for couples who have never talked specifically about their financial goals, sometimes because of the realization that their goals are not as aligned as they had assumed they were, or other times because the tensions and concerns about each other's financial habits tend to rear their ugly heads. In addition, planning throws a spotlight on your current spending habits, which may be a source of conflict if one or both of you spends more than you can afford. Skill 4, Communicating Through Conflict, may help you come to an agreement about your plan in a way that respects each other's goals and dreams.

Over time, you will finesse the numbers. It is easy, for example, to plan to spend only $100 a month on snacks and lunches, and then find at the end of the month that you have spent more than double the amount. When that happens, either adjust your plan to more realistic figures, or ask your partner to help you find ways to stick to the plan.

This planning tool can also be used as you look forward. How will it change if you have children? How will it change if one of you stops working or decreases your hours? How will it look after you retire? Before you make major financial or life decisions, such as having children or buying a second car, play with the numbers to see whether you can afford it while still following Rule 1 of staying out of debt.

CHAPTER 9

Skill 2: Creating a Simple Structure

Each week, Debbie and Rav perform financial twists and turns worthy of Olympic gymnasts. They believe they have their financial life running like a well-oiled machine, because each Thursday evening they sit down with bills received that week, checkbooks, and a calculator. As each bill is opened, they choose which account to pay it from, often using a credit card that gets them air miles. Stamps are put on and each envelope marked with the date it should be mailed, 5 days before the due date. Then they calculate the balance of each account, and write checks between the various accounts to ensure that no checks bounce.

Once a month they sort through the statements that have arrived and calculate how much money is left over and write a check from each account, leaving a $50 cushion above the expected expenses in the coming 2 weeks. The extra money is split between paying down their credit card debt and an investment account. Each time they shop, they consciously choose between the various credit and store cards they each carry, with a list of interest rates and available credit floating in their heads. They're proud of their system, yet Rav concedes, "It takes hours every month and lots of mental energy to be in this much control."

Despite their organization, mistakes happen. A check may arrive late, or a miscalculation in an account triggers a late fee. And each month they write more checks than their banks provide for free, triggering further charges.

. . . .

Debbie and Rav's system does run like a well-oiled machine, but it's a complicated machine requiring an excessive amount of oil and maintenance. In an attempt to be financially fit, they have created a time-consuming nightmare that gives them a sense of control simply because they are juggling furiously all the time—juggling running chainsaws at that.

Your Financial Structure

Have you had arguments that started because someone forgot to pay a bill on time? Have you been charged fees or bounced checks because one of you wrote a check on an account without telling the other? Does one of you seem to spend a large amount of time every month managing money while the other simply spends? Managing your household's finances *should* be a simple task. Too many households invite friction by creating complex financial systems and adopting poor financial habits, which are discussed in Chapter 10. The more complex your financial structure, the more time and energy you waste managing that structure. In addition, your chance of making errors increases. Simplifying your financial life can increase the harmony in your relationship and having good financial habits can sustain that harmony.

Your financial structure is the underlying organization of your financial life. It consists of all the accounts, loans, and credit cards you have, as well as the tools such as financial software that you use. The simpler your financial structure, the less time you will have to spend managing it and the less chance you will have of making slipups.

Simplifying Your Financial Structure

How much time should it take to manage your money? Not much at all . . . and probably a whole lot less than you currently spend. In financial advisor Ric Edelman's study of his firm's clients, he found that his clients spent only 2.4 hours a month on average managing their money.[1] This figure includes time spent paying bills. How do they spend so little time? Many have simplified their financial life by consolidating the number of accounts, and letting their investments grow without lots of fuss and trading. In addition, many of them appear to be savers and are old enough (with an average age 57) that they have fallen into a rhythm with their spending, though they do track it.

The key to simplifying your financial structure is to streamline your accounts and to automate the system. These actions limit the number of bills you receive and accounts that you have.

Couples tend to manage their finances in one of two ways: combining their finances completely (the All-in-One-Pot structure), or keeping separate accounts and opening a combined account for the shared expenses (the Mine-Yours-Ours structure). Both structures have their advantages, and couples usually have a very clear rationale for the structure they choose.

How people arrange their financial systems seems to be related to the relativity of earnings. Social psychologist Rosanna Hertz found that All-in-One-Pot structures are more common when the wife earns less than the husband, and separate accounting structures are more frequently used when the wife earns as much or more.[2]

Other experts have found that the way a couple manage their money changes over time. Researchers Robert Ferber and Lucy

---

[1]Ric Edelman, *Ordinary People, Extraordinary Wealth* (New York: HarperCollins, 2000), 170.

[2]Rosanna Hertz, *More Equal Than Others: Women and Men in Dual Career Marriages* (Berkeley, CA: University of California Press, 1986), 74.

Chao-Lee call the person managing the financial details the "family financial officer." That role includes "both decision-making and execution with reference to: a) Looking after the payment of bills; b) Keeping track of expenditures in relation to budgets; and, c) Use of money left over at the end of the pay period."[3] By the second year of marriage, only a third of couples shared the role, with the responsibility going more often to the wife rather than the husband. When one person took charge, the couple usually still shared decision making about how to use the money remaining at the end of the month. Ferber and Chao-Lee also found that the person in charge of the money influences how the money is ultimately used.

Decision making within relationships varies by gender, another study found, with women more likely to check in with their partner before buying a product. Couples married longer seem to have less need to get each other's consent, most likely because they have learned what is and what is not okay with their partner over the years.

Regardless of whether you choose to use the All-in-One-Pot or the Mine-Your-Ours money management structure, consolidating accounts within that structure and keeping all of your accounts at one financial institution simplifies things as it enables you to more easily transfer money between accounts and may cut the fees you pay. The day of needing separate savings, checking, and investment accounts are over and financial institutions that insist that you have three separate accounts are fast becoming dinosaurs. More and more financial service companies offer accounts that act as an umbrella, combining checking, saving, and investing in one account. The money in the account earns a return in a money market fund, can be invested in stocks or mutual funds, and can be easily accessed using checks, ATM machines, or debit cards. I am a big fan of these accounts because they not only take the management out of money management, they decrease

---

[3]Robert Ferber and Lucy Chao-Lee, "Husband–Wife Influence in Family Purchasing Behavior," *Journal of Consumer Research* 1 (June 1974): 43–50.

the chance of bouncing checks. Many also offer overdraft protection of some sort, using the balance of your investments as a "float" if you accidentally withdraw more than the amount of cash or money market funds in your account. These accounts are often offered by major national banks as well as large brokerage firms, and some will have a minimum balance requirement, but it is bound to be lower than the cash cushion you need to have. I don't actually have a bank account. Not one. I simply have an umbrella account through a brokerage firm that offers me a great deal of flexibility and operates like a bank account, only better.[4] The account I have allows my balance to be invested in a large number of assets including stocks, bonds, and mutual funds. I can also keep my retirement funds with the same broker, so I can easily see my total financial picture. And I still follow the "if I don't see it, I won't spend it" rule because I have learned to look only at how much I have in the money market fund, and treat the rest as inaccessible.

The All-in-One-Pot Structure

. . . .

Susan, a freelance writer, and her husband Steve, a dentist, have a highly streamlined financial structure. "We have one joint account, and everything is joined except for our retirement accounts, which cannot be combined, and my business account, which is separate for record-keeping purposes." Susan manages most of the day-to-day transactions; however, nearly all of their bills are on automatic payment. "Even our Citibank credit card is linked to our bank account and paid in full every month. There are just some business-related expenses that I write checks for," she says. Although their retirement accounts are separate, Steve researches investments and they make

---

[4]Note that the cash portion of an account held at a brokerage firm is not necessarily FDIC insured, so choose wisely if you have an umbrella account with a brokerage firm.

their investment decisions together. "I've read the Wall Street Journal *every day for years," Steve says. "I recommend stocks, but usually Susan has already heard of the companies or her father, who is an accountant, has recommended them to her."*

Steve feels that part of their success comes from their shared goal of buying a house and part from their shared tendency to be savers. "Our financial relationship works well because our expectation of how much money should be spent on various things is the same. No one ever comes home and says: 'You spent $500 on what?' "

. . . .

The All-in-One-Pot structure involves a minimum of four items:

1. One joint checking/investment account with a debit/ATM card.
2. One credit card with two cards issued for the account.
3. His retirement account.[5]
4. Her retirement account.

The structure probably also includes a mortgage and perhaps other loans such as a home equity loan or student loans.

The advantage of this structure is that it minimizes fees, eliminates the need to transfer money between accounts, and makes it easy to see a single snapshot of your financial situation. The disadvantage is that many couples feel it is *too* much togetherness! A couple I met used a variation on this theme: They paid for all shared expenses by check or with their account's debit card, but kept separate credit cards in order to track their discretionary spending. The details of each person's credit card spending was his or her own business, but they both knew how much they could spend on average in a month.

It is important if you use the All-in-One-Pot structure to make sure that each of you builds a strong credit record. All accounts

---

[5]In the United States, a couple cannot mingle their retirement accounts.

that are in both of your names get reported to both of your credit reports. Therefore, any late payments or other credit no-nos on joint accounts will be reported to both of your credit records.

The Mine–Yours–Ours Structure

. . . .

Tina, an editor, was in her thirties when she married Greg, a technical writer 7 years her senior. In the 12 years that they have been married, they have kept their finances separate, except for one account to cover their joint expenses. Tina says, "We were always independent before our marriage, and keeping our finances separate seemed the only way we could do it. It is very important to me that we be equitable. We make similar incomes and put the same amount into a joint checking account for shared expenses." The joint expenses—including groceries, utilities and "things we know we share"—are managed together, and each has free rein with his or her own money. "I really don't care how he spends his money; it's none of my business. We have different interests; for example, he has a motorcycle that he pays for completely out of his discretionary account. It has saved us from having a lot of arguments about money." Tina manages her own account as well as the joint account. "I'm kind of the family bookkeeper, and manage the personal and joint account. Greg handles his own investments."

. . . .

At a minimum, the Mine-Yours-Ours structure includes eight items:

1. One joint checking/investment account with a debit/ATM card.
2. His checking/investment account.
3. Her checking/investment account.
4. One joint credit card (unless all joint purchases are put on the debit card).

5. His credit card.
6. Her credit card.
7. His retirement account.
8. Her retirement account.

The structure probably also includes a jointly held mortgage and perhaps other loans such as a home equity loan or student loans.

The main advantage of this structure is that it affords a level of financial autonomy that many couples prefer. Couples who are living together or have been through divorces in the past, as well as many couples who simply prefer more independence in their finances, often choose this structure. However, it clearly involves more complexity (and usually more fees) than the All-in-One-Pot structure. With that complexity, there is more chance for errors resulting in late fees, bounced checks, and so on. Also, adopting the Mine-Yours-Ours structure involves a lot more discussion and negotiation up front. Some of the decisions that need to be made include:

- What expenses are considered to be joint expenses?
- What proportion of the joint expenses is each person responsible for?
- How will those proportions change as each person's earnings change?
- How will those proportions change if one partner works part time or starts full-time parenting?
- How do disagreements about potential joint expenses get resolved?

These questions are not easy. Take friends of mine who recently divorced. As a couple, they had used the Mine-Yours-Ours structure. They split the cable cost even though she had never subscribed to cable before they met and he chose a package with many of the premium sports channels. He reasoned that they often watched together, so it was a joint expense. When they were in the honeymoon period, she was fine with the arrangement. When arguments about money began to arise a few years into their marriage, however, the cable bill became her favorite weapon as it represented the inequality she felt was rampant in their marriage. Another couple did well with this structure while they were both working in well-paid careers; however, once the wife dropped back to part-time work with her husband's encouragement, she found herself with no personal spending money because she was expected to keep paying "her half" of the bills and also to pick up the cost of the children's clothing.

Ideally, a couple should discuss such issues prior to intermingling their finances; however, too many couples have an aversion to getting their financial discussions out on the table before marriage because it seems so unromantic. If you are yet to intermingle your finances or make the leap into a long-term commitment, get over the resistance and talk about it. After all, having a sound financial structure can help ensure that your long-term commitment actually lasts a long time.

Note that if you run a business, you will require a set of accounts in addition to those discussed in either of these structures. Good record keeping requires that personal and business expenses be separated.

Action Item: Consolidate Your Accounts

First decide which of the two structures you would like to adopt: All-in-One-Pot or Mine-Yours-Ours. Discuss any variations that you feel you have to have, such as extra accounts for special purposes such as an Education Savings Account to save for your child's college education.

Take a large sheet of paper and divide it into three columns, labeled His, Hers, and Ours. In each column, write down every account, loan, credit card, store card, investment account, and other financial account that you receive a statement for each month. How complicated does your financial structure look? Do you have any other dormant or rarely used accounts that you have never closed that also should be included?

Take a highlighting pen and mark those accounts that you would like to have as your core accounts in your redesigned structure. Look at how many different financial service companies you are dealing with. If they are not all with one institution, or if your bank does not offer integrated accounts, consider shopping around to find a financial institution that offers the range of accounts that will most simplify your financial lives. Call the financial institutions of every account that you want to close that has a positive balance, and close it over the phone, asking them to send you a check for the proceeds (simply taking out or paying off the balance will not close an account and may lead to fees for having a low balance or leave you overdrawn for monthly or account closing fees that have not yet been assessed).

....

Consolidating Debt

The average household that has credit cards, has $8,562 debt spread across 6 bank credit cards and 8.3 retail credit cards![6] I checked that figure three times because I could not believe it. Hello? What do you think they are—baseball cards? More is not merrier. Every extra card is an extra chance of incurring late fees or over-balance fees, requires extra work to pay, and creates extra clutter on your credit report. But that's not all. Merely having credit cards means you are likely to spend more. A recent study found that people paying by credit card are likely to pay *more* for the *same* item than people paying with cash, and by quite a large

---

[6]Cardweb.com Inc. On a per person basis, people who have at least one credit card have on average 2.7 bank credit cards and 3.7 retail credit cards.

amount.[7] Too many credit cards makes it too easy to overspend. A simplified structure has few credit cards—no more than one joint and one individual each—however, you may not be able to consolidate your accounts until you can afford to pay off outstanding debts. Resist the temptation to keep special-purpose cards, such as gas or store cards. In Chapter 10 I discuss tracking systems that will eliminate the need to use different cards for different purposes.

To prevent the flood of offers that may tempt you into applying for more credit cards, call 1-888-5 OPT OUT to request that you be permanently removed from the marketing lists generated by the credit reporting agencies for credit card marketers. It takes only a moment, and can remove a lifetime of offers.[8]

What if one of you brought a significant amount of personal debt into the relationship? First, you may want to stick to the Mine-Yours-Ours structure until you get through the problem. Second, keep that debt in the debtor's name only—that way the person with least debt maintains his or her clean credit record. Finally, discuss how you can work together to clean up the debt as soon as possible in a way that you both feel is fair.

Action Item: Consolidate Your Debt
. . . .

If in the previous exercise you were left with more than one or two credit or store cards or loans that cannot easily be paid off in full within a couple of months, consolidate the debt. Do the exercises in Chapter 5 on Rule 1 to consolidate your debt. If your debt is significant, consider finding a credit counselor, as discussed in Chapter 14.

. . . .

---

[7]Sloan School study, quoted in Richard Morin, "Don't Leave Home With It," *Washington Post*, Sunday, 17 February 2002, sec. B5.
[8]Make sure you wait long enough in the automated system for the option of permanent removal—it is at the end of the message.

Consolidating Retirement Accounts

Another area of your financial life that may need simplifying is your retirement savings. Although you cannot mingle your accounts—his is his and hers is hers for life—you may still have unnecessary financial complexity. When you leave an employer, you can usually choose to roll over your retirement savings into an IRA. If you currently have accounts still open through past employers, see if you can roll them all into one account. Not only will that simplify your financial system, it will also give you more control over how your money is invested.

Different types of retirement tools have different rules. The various retirement tools are explained in Chapter 18 on Decision 4: When You Retire. You may not be able to consolidate all of your retirement accounts into a single account; however, it makes sense to consolidate them at one financial institution for easy record keeping. Thus, you may end up with a series of accounts—an IRA, a Roth IRA, and so on—in one financial institution. The key in consolidating your accounts is to find one financial institution that offers the range of products and the level of service you want. You may find that the same institution also has the range of non-retirement accounts that you want, simplifying your financial structure further. Many large investment firms offer a range of investment products not only from their own portfolios, but also from those of their competitors; therefore, you can roll your money into, say, Charles Schwab, and still invest in Fidelity, Vanguard, and Janus mutual funds, as well as individual stocks.

Action Item: Consolidate Your Retirement Accounts

Take a sheet of paper and list all of your known retirement accounts. Then go back through a list of past employers and make sure that you have accounted for all of the retirement savings that may be floating around. Call the benefits coordinator of any previous employers that you are not sure about, especially if you have moved house and they may have lost track of you. Then select a company to roll all of your accounts into. Once you contact the firm and let them know what you hope to do, it will be a simple matter of filling in a few forms and letting them handle the rest. Once all of your retirement savings are in one place, then you will need to structure a diversified portfolio of investments. See Skill 5, Investing for Strong Returns, for information on investment strategies.

Roles and Responsibilities

Recently a friend moved house and I helped him settle into the new place. A trip to a housewares store and a pile of square glass bottles and plastic storage items later, and I was happily reforming this disorganized bachelor. Farewell ziplock bags, hello order! I labeled and filled the jars, sorted the piles of vitamins and cleaning gear into well-categorized caddies, and encouraged him to surrender the mishmash of unmatched silverware. He wisely kept his distance, realizing that this was my idea of having fun. Organizing is as relaxing and energizing for me as hiking is for him. We are very different creatures, and those differences can complement, not conflict. He appreciates a more streamlined kitchen after I have been through it, and I appreciate that he gets me out hiking more often than if I were left to my own devices.

Within every couple there are two individuals. And for everything that you have in common, you have plenty of differences in terms of skills, abilities, and inclinations. In assigning roles and responsibilities in your financial life, you need to tap into the natural strengths and interests of each of you to find an allocation of duties that is fair. So, just because you think that tracking spending is the most painful chore on earth, don't assume that your partner feels the same way.

Most couples I interviewed chose to have one partner in charge of their day-to-day financial management (paying bills, balancing accounts) and the other in charge of managing investments. A few chose to have one person in charge of all aspects of their financial life, and yet others chose to have an investment advisor completely run their investments and update them periodically. There is no right way to divide the tasks; however, it helps to have clear responsibilities so you avoid the "I thought you had paid it" arguments—and the high charges incurred every time such a slip is made.

In addition to your interests, take account of your weaknesses. For example, if you like investing, but tend to be very risk averse and therefore likely to get returns well below those that you need for the long-term goal of retirement, then you may not be the best person to manage your retirement investments.

Assigning tasks does not mean handing over control. Even if one person is responsible for the household bookkeeping, you are both responsible for managing the spending and keeping to your plan. As we saw in Chapter 2, men and women, in general, have different inclinations when it comes to spending and investing. Men and women both have tendencies that may impact personal finances in a positive way and a negative way. Therefore, although you may benefit from dividing and conquering the tasks of managing day-to-day finances and managing investments, neither of you can afford to lose touch of your finances. After all, if your partner makes a series of bad decisions, you will both suffer. You both need to take responsibility for oversight of the process, making sure that you are comfortable with the way decisions are made in the areas that you are not directly responsible for. You each have a responsibility to look out for your own best interests.

Action Item: Roles and Responsibilities Quiz

Take a couple of minutes each to answer the statements in Figure 9.1 as true or false.

	He says	She says
I enjoy keeping my personal files neat and organized.	T/F	T/F
I am accurate and detail-oriented.	T/F	T/F
I am not intimidated by numbers or simple math.	T/F	T/F
I like playing around on the computer and Internet.	T/F	T/F
I like to plan my future.	T/F	T/F
I find business interesting and read about companies.	T/F	T/F
I tune in when the financial reports come onto the news.	T/F	T/F
I enjoy keeping an eye on the big picture.	T/F	T/F
I understand how to choose investments.	T/F	T/F
I have some specific financial knowledge and skills.	T/F	T/F

Figure 9.1　　Roles and responsibilities quiz.

In general, the one of you who is most detail oriented and organized is the best person to manage the day-to-day finances, and the person who has a natural interest in the financial markets is the best one to learn how to manage investments. Note any items where you both answered "true" or both answered "false." Where you both answered "true," you can choose whoever has the most time or interest in a task, or find a way to share it. Where only one of you answered "true," you will find areas where one of you brings a natural skill that will complement your partner's skills. Where you both answered "false," you have a challenge. One of you will need to volunteer to manage some tasks you find unpleasant, or learn additional skills, such as using your computer to manage your money. In the balance of your partnership, there are bound to be tasks that each of you do that aren't that much fun, but have to be done anyway. Even when you "outsource" a task, such as hiring an investment advisor to help you assess your investments, at least one of you will need to be committed to overseeing the advisor and ensuring that she is keeping your best interests in mind.

. . . .

The goal of creating a simple structure is to allow you to have more time and less stress in the long run. The side benefit is that you will also have more money if you currently spend a lot on fees or bounce a lot of checks. Once you have simplified your structure, check it every couple of years to make sure you are not slipping back into complexity.

CHAPTER 10

Skill 3: Getting into Good Habits

Before they were married, John's disorganization seemed charming to Mary-Jo. "He had this rumpled professor style and was such a nice contrast from all of the buttoned-up lawyer types I had dated before him," Mary-Jo explained. "But now, we're on the brink of divorce." Although they and their three young kids can get by on one income, it's a tight juggle. "One slip, and we're bouncing checks like there's no tomorrow. But John seems to actively undermine me. He loses receipts, so I have no idea how much he has spent, and last week we had a huge fight because he went to the ATM without letting me know—again—and I bounced two checks. His failure to tell me about $40 will cost us more than $80 in fees and put another bad mark on our credit record. I could strangle him. It's such a small thing that I am asking."

John and Mary-Jo are quickly learning that bad financial habits have a real cost. Habits are the myriad of small actions that shape your overall situation. In the case of financial habits, they are every little action that adds up to shape your overall financial health. Sometimes habits are conscious decisions, but too often they are simply patterns we have fallen into over time. Deliberately choosing the habits that will support your financial goals is key to reaching those financial goals. Choosing good habits is particularly important if you and your partner started with or have fallen into ways of managing money that are not compatible or are even directly conflicting.

Healthy Financial Habits

Just as simple personal hygiene habits such as regular tooth brushing can prevent major health problems in the future, simple financial hygiene habits prevent major financial problems. Your financial habits should be simple, positive, and effective. Simple habits mean that there is little effort on your part, thus, less danger of slipping up. Also, habits must be positive in that they need to be actions that are motivating, not onerous. Remember, if you find them too difficult, you will not follow through. Finally, effective habits are those that really work, helping you move toward your goals.

Bad habits are those that ultimately move you away from your financial goals. They may be small bad habits such as unconsciously frittering away cash on little indulgences that add up over time. Or they may be big, consistent errors such as failing to manage incoming bills well, and having a lousy credit record to show for it. The cost of bad habits can range from simply not having enough money for the things that are really important to you to good old-fashioned financial ruin.

The Cost of Bad Financial Habits

Some people seem to thrive on making their financial lives difficult. In Chapter 9 on structure, we saw how having multiple accounts can cause confusion and errors. Similarly, poor financial habits can take their toll. For example, a couple who gather all credit card receipts and record them regularly or use software that interacts with their credit card company's Internet site has much less chance of going over their spending limit than a couple who lose their credit card receipts and forget to record their purchases. The more difficult you make your day-to-day money management, the more chances you have to slip up. The easier it is to manage your money on a day-to-day basis, the more likely you are to reach your long-term goals. Having good financial habits involves both simplifying your money management so there is less latitude for error, and avoiding destructive financial behavior.

Bad habits come at a cost. If you are consistently overspending, your bad habits are costing you your financial future and your dreams. Even little bad habits have a way of adding up. Take the ATM. Your bank charges no fees for using its ATM, but other banks charge $2. There is another bank's ATM in the foyer of your office building. Do you fall into the bad habit of using the other bank's machine? It's easy to let small amounts of money like that drift away. But let's look at how something that small can add up. Let's say that currently you use another bank's ATM once a week. That's only $2 a week, $104 a year. The kids won't go hungry over a little thing like that! However, that $2 a week adds up over a lifetime. Thirty years of that habit is costing you more than $12,000 if it is invested at 8 percent, more than $18,000 if it is invested at 10 percent. Now, that's not small change. And if your alternative is to invest the pretax equivalent of $104 a year in your retirement account and your employer matches some of it, you could be talking about double those amounts.

If merely $2 a week adds up to that much, think of all the other financial habits that are costing you your financial future and only providing a little comfort. It takes a little over $67 a month to save $100,000 in 30 years, assuming an 8 percent return. Don't have $67 to spare? Let's get creative with a typical person's habits and find that money.

- Used another bank's ATM four times = $8.
- Returned two videos late = $5.

- Bought $3 gourmet coffees instead of $1.25 regulars every workday = $33.
- Had $16 pizza delivered twice instead of using $5 store bought = $22.

Voila! We just "found" $68 without involving any major sacrifices. You're still stopping by the coffee shop for a coffee, but you're skipping the froth and froufrou names. You're still eating convenience foods, but taking 2 minutes to throw them in your own oven. Tiny habits that are worth $100,000 to you. And again, you can double that figure if you use the money for pretax retirement savings that your employer matches at least 30 cents on the dollar. Do you really value those mindless habits *that much*?

This chapter looks at a few simple habits that can help you manage your money with a minimum of fuss. First, eliminate financial tasks by automating your financial life, or at least using on-line bill payment to take the paperwork out of bill processing. Then, look at how to handle your cash, checks, and credit well. Finally, track your financial life with as little effort as possible.

Action Item: Identify Your Bad Financial Habits

Sit down with your partner and make an honest inventory of the bad habits that are hurting you financially. Some of the habits may be: treating plastic like it is not really cash; keeping a low balance in your main bank accounts; visiting other bank's ATM machines; losing credit card receipts; not tracking account balances; bouncing checks; wandering aimlessly around malls; spending more than you earn; and failing to save. The list could go on and on. Once you have your list, mark the three worst habits you each have and think up creative ways you can combat each one (without getting into a scrimping mindset) and help each other stay on track.

Eliminate Financial Tasks

· ·

Touring a credit card company's enormous facility in Virginia, I watched paper and plastic being produced and processed with frightening efficiency. Mail solicitations, credit cards, and bills zipped through machines, each individualized with other marketing offers before being stuffed in envelopes and sorted for bulk mail. The machines whir at the rate of hundreds of letters per minute. In another part of the building, thousands of incoming payments whiz through a machine that slices the edges off the envelopes, sucks out the contents, and scans the checks. Checks are rapidly deciphered by handwriting recognition software and a scan of the magnetic numbers along the base of the checks. Human interaction is minimal; a small number of employees check the accuracy of numbers automatically input and deal with the few unreadable checks and improperly stuffed envelopes. The investment is considerable. Millions of dollars of machines, software, and staff are devoted to simply sending out bills and receiving payments.

· ·

It's no wonder that credit card companies, along with many of the other institutions that you send monthly payments to, are eager for customers to embrace receiving bills on line and paying them automatically. You should be too.

One of the simplest ways to remove money stress from your marriage is to eliminate as many of the day-to-day money tasks as possible. You cannot fight about whose responsibility it is to pay the gas bill if *neither* of you needs to do it. Technology is making our financial lives simpler by automating mundane tasks. Automating your financial life saves you time and money both directly, by cutting the cost of stamps and eliminating the likelihood of late fees, and indirectly, by improving your credit rating as you build a perfect payment record. It also saves money for the companies that provide you with services every day, eventually enabling them to be more competitive and (it is hoped) lower priced.

Eliminating manual payments can be done two ways: through setting up automatic payments with each company or through using an on-line payment system.

Automatic Payments

Automatic payments are completely hands off. Every month, your bills are paid directly from your checking or savings account or charged to your credit card. What you get: assurance that the bill is paid on time, every time, with no check to write, no stamp to find, and no letter to post. What you risk: If you do not have enough money in the account that the payment comes from, your payment will bounce, late fees will be charged, and your credit rating will be at risk. The key to success, therefore, is to ensure that your account carries enough of a balance to manage the month-to-month fluctuations in your bills. Having a decent cash cushion is one of the most important habits you can get into.

Setting up automatic payments is a simple, one-time process. Contact every company you pay on a regular basis—utility companies, creditors, even your gym—and ask if they offer automatic payments. You will find that most do. Even my water company has renovated its Jurassic-period processes and offers automatic and on-line payments. Most companies require a voided check or savings or credit card account number and your signature to set up the automatic payments. Once the payment has been set up and tested, your bills will begin to be paid automatically, usually on the due date. In the case of bills such as your credit card payment, you can arrange to either pay the bill in full each month or to pay a set amount of the bill. A simple phone call enables you to change the default payment if you need to. Use the checklist in Figure 10.1 (on page 124) to track your progress as you set up automatic payments.

A small aside: If you have a credit card that earns you frequent flyer miles or other rewards *and* you pay the balance in full each month, ask for automatic payments to be made using your credit card if possible. A phone bill of $50 a month adds up to an extra 600 miles toward a free trip each year. It also allows you to "play the float," that is, take advantage of the period between when the amount is billed to your credit card and when your credit card payment is due. Many companies don't offer automatic payments charged to your credit card as an option, because the credit card companies charge them a transaction fee.

The advantage of automatic payments over on-line payments is that they really involve *no* work on your behalf once you sign up. You don't need to do a thing, though it makes sense to check your bill to ensure there are no charges that seem out of line. Additionally, the service is generally free. In the case of loans, some lenders offer a slightly lower interest rate if you have automatic payments because the lenders cut costs and gain confidence in your ability and likelihood of paying on time, every time.

On-Line Payments

On-line payment systems are an alternative way to automate much of your bill paying. Such systems involve having your bills go to a service that then notifies you each time a bill is due and allows you to authorize the payment on line. Alternatively, the company may simply ask you to log onto its site each month and pay on line. The downside is that the service may come at a cost and be less reliable. Some of the services generate a printed check that is then snail-mailed to your creditor, leaving the chance of a late payment and the associated fees; therefore, you need to schedule your payments to go out a little earlier just to be sure they arrive in time. Even if you have to log on to the company's site and the payment is handled electronically from there, you run the risk of forgetting. On-line payments require your hands-on involvement, resulting in the chance of late payments if you are on vacation or fail to log on and manage your bills. The other big downside: fees for such services can add up. For example,

Quicken charges $9.95 a month, Microsoft Money charges $5.95 a month, and Yahoo's bill payment service is $4.95 a month, free if the companies you are paying are part of Yahoo's bill payment network.

If you decide to try on-line bill payment, see if your bank offers it. If not, some places to try are www.yahoo.com, www.quicken

	COMPANY	INFORMATION REQUESTED	FORMS SENT	ACTIVATED
Mortgage/rent				
Second mortgage				
Home equity loan				
Car loan/lease 1				
Car loan/lease 2				
Electricity				
Gas				
Water				
Phone				
Cell phone 1				
Cell phone 2				
Internet provider				
Cable/satellite TV				
Student loan 1				
Student loan 2				
Credit card 1				
Credit card 2				
Store card 1				
Store card 2				
Other				
Other				
Other				

Figure 10.1   Automatic payment checklist.

.com, and www.microsoft.com/money/. The last two require that you use their software, which I discuss later in this chapter.

Action Item: Eliminate Financial Tasks
. . . .

Use the checklist shown as Figure 10.1 as you set up automatic payments or on-line bill payments.

. . . .

Automatic Investments

Another way to eliminate financial effort is to put your investments on automatic pilot as well. Most financial institutions that offer mutual funds allow you to invest a set amount automatically every month, and if your primary bank does not offer a wide range of investment instruments, your employer may be able to automatically deposit part of your paycheck each month into a separate investment account. In addition, your employer-sponsored retirement savings can be put on autopilot if your employer can deduct a set contribution from each paycheck.

Dollar Cost Averaging

Investing on a regular basis takes advantage of something called dollar cost averaging. Imagine that you are investing $200 a month in a mutual fund and the market drops. Is that bad news? Not unless you have to sell your holdings. For example, let's say that the mutual fund had been trading at $40 for some time, meaning that each month, you bought five shares (200 ÷ 40) in the mutual fund. As the market turned sour, the fund fell to $30 and then to only $20. You were able to buy more shares in the fund in the months that the price of the fund was down, because $200 would buy 6 2/3 shares at $30 or 10 shares at $20 in those months. If the market does what markets usually do in the long run—rises—you are in luck because you have more shares in the fund to take advantage of the rising market.

The main benefit of dollar cost averaging is that none of us, not even professional investors, can accurately predict the movements in the price of a particular share or the stock market as a whole. By investing on a regular basis, you invest at an average cost, rather than risking getting in on the worst day of the year (when the price is at its highest). Dollar cost averaging is particularly useful for investments that have no transaction costs. So, for example, dollar cost averaging may not make sense if you are buying shares in an individual company and have to pay a $15 commission every time you make a purchase, because you'll end up paying a lot in commissions. However, it may make sense if you are buying a mutual fund that has no sales load.[1]

If you are investing in the market through a retirement account that receives money every time you are paid, you are already dollar cost averaging.

Action Item: Automate Your Investments

Look at the spending plan you created in Chapter 8 on Skill 1: Planning Together, and see how much you can put away each month for both pretax retirement savings and after-tax investments or savings. Call your employer's benefits office and find out if you are eligible for an employer-sponsored retirement savings plan, such as a 401(k) and, if so, start having a percentage of your paycheck deducted automatically. If your employer does not offer a retirement savings plan, visit an investment company or your bank and ask about plans that are open to you and arrange to have the funds for it deducted shortly after each paycheck arrives. For your nonretirement

---

[1]Sales loads are fees or commissions charged at the time you invest in a mutual fund and are usually a percentage of the amount invested. See Chapter 12 for more information about investing in mutual funds.

savings and investments, determine the time frame you are saving for, the appropriate investment tool,[2] and again talk to your financial institution about having automatic deposits into the money market fund, mutual fund, or other savings or investment instrument.

....

Handle Cash, Checks, and Credit Well

For many people, the toughest challenge they face in learning to manage their money well as an individual as well as a couple is in breaking the spending habit. If you or your partner are a natural spender, it is particularly important to get into good habits with regard to how you manage your cash and credit. Even if you are a saver, good cash, check, and credit habits can help you save more and better track where your money goes.

Be Careful with Cash

Start by looking at how you treat cash. It is easy to have cash simply disappear. A New York couple I worked with were great at tracking their spending, except for the $750 a month that went in cash. It simply seemed to evaporate, with nothing to show for it. By watching exactly where it went for a couple of weeks, and then cutting down on the amount of cash carried, they started to break the habit and halve the amount of cash they spent monthly. Carry less cash. You are less likely to make little spontaneous purchases such as magazines and snacks if you only have $20 in your wallet. The more you use debit cards or credit cards that are paid off in full each month, the more valuable insights you will get into where your money goes. Few stores have a minimum charge to use credit cards anymore.

---

[2]See Chapter 12, Skill 5: Investing for Strong Returns, to learn more about selecting investments.

Another area to look at is how you treat your coins. The U.S. Mint and Coinstar estimated that $7.7 billion of coinage is sitting around people's homes, unused and slowly eroding in value thanks to inflation. The average adult handles $30 in coins every month, Coinstar found, and underestimates the value of coins in a jar by more than half. Instead of having coins sitting in jars not working for you, try to get into one of two habits: Put every coin you handle aside and cash them in every month or two, adding the total to your savings or investments. That is money for nothing—$720 a year between the two of you—that you will never miss because such a small amount is put aside daily. Alternatively, minimize the number of coins you handle by using debit or credit cards where possible and using the coins that you have when you can.

Consider Using Checks

Generally people seem less inclined to abuse their checking accounts the way they abuse credit cards. There is something about writing the amount out in full that makes the money spent by check seem so much more tangible. Make sure, however, that you keep a good running total of your checking account balance if you either keep your account balance low or don't have any sort of overdraft protection: Bounced checks are expensive for all concerned, and you may find yourself facing $50 in fees from your bank *and* the organization you presented the bad check to. Bounced checks also wreak havoc on your credit rating.

Ensure that your checking account has a good cash cushion, easily enough to cover a typical month's bills plus an unexpected extra expense. Aim for a cash cushion of 3 to 6 months of your basic living costs, with a little extra for unexpected expenses.

Control Your Credit Cards

Finally, watch how you handle credit cards. Many people see them as better than a blank check, an invitation to spend. If you know you get silly with credit, consider scaling back to just a debit card, keeping your credit card locked away for emergencies. Also, set up an automatic payment so your card is paid off in full each month; it will force you to think of it as cash. When you do use credit cards, make sure that you keep the receipts so you have an idea of how much you have spent, not leaving it until the you receive a statement to find out you went overboard. Finally, if you do insist on wandering aimlessly around malls inviting temptation to visit, leave the plastic at home. You can always go back for the great stuff.

One of the biggest challenges with handling cash, checks, or credit cards well is managing spontaneity. You don't want to tie your money down so tightly that you can't take up a friend's invitation to meet for lunch, and you need to be able to handle life's bigger surprises, such as an unexpected repair bill or insurance deductible. Therefore, plan to have some flexibility and make sure that you are not riding so close to your limits on your credit card or so close to a zero balance on your checking account that you cannot manage the minor bumps in life.

Measure Your Progress

A local restaurant is for sale and you are thinking of buying it. The first thing you would do is try to find out what it is worth. Businesses use two basic financial statements: a profit and loss statement and a balance sheet.

A profit and loss statement looks at how money flows through a business; the income, less the expenses gives the profit. In the case of a restaurant, the income would be mainly from customers eating there, and the expenses would include wages, taxes, ingredients, equipment leasing, and so on. The statement shows a flow of money over a period of time, usually a year. The equivalent financial statement for your personal finances is a spending plan or budget. It shows how much money comes in and out during a year and what the outgoing money is spent on.

A balance sheet is a snapshot in time. It shows the value of what a company owns—its assets—less the amount it owes—its liabilities. In the case of the restaurant, its assets may include kitchen equipment, furniture, cash in the bank, and even its reputation (accountants will estimate the "goodwill" or value of a company's reputation, but it is an intangible asset, that is, you can't pick it up and feel it). Its liabilities may include a small business loan and the amount it owes its vendors (the butcher, baker, and candlestick maker) on the day that the balance sheet is prepared. The equivalent financial statement for your personal finances is a net worth statement. It shows how much wealth (or debt) you have built.

The final financial statement you might check is the business's credit rating. If a company is not known for paying on time, it may have to pay more money to get future funding. The equivalent for your personal finances is your credit record.

Your financial life is your business. To know how well your life business is running, you need to have a similar set of financial statements. We look at three ways you can track your progress:

1. Tracking spending against your plan.
2. Measuring your wealth.
3. Checking your credit record.

Track Spending Against Your Plan

Emily and Claude were curious about how much money they were spending on everyday meals. They decided to track their spending over a couple of weeks by paying for all snacks, take-out, and casual meals out with cash, drawing from a separate pile of money. They were flabbergasted when they added up the total and found that they were averaging over a $150 a week between them. "No wonder we don't have enough for the vacation we want to take," Emily explains. "We have decided that we are simply going to find a way to cut the $150 to $50 a week total, not each, and not including the times we go to a restaurant with friends. And as of this week, we are putting $100 *a week into a money market fund so we can go on that vacation we keep talking about next year."*

Claude is still in shock from the figures, "I knew we let money slip through our hands, but I had no idea it was that much. I'm not sure I wanted to know!"

. . . .

The first and more important financial habit to measure your progress is to see where your money goes on an ongoing basis. The more insight you have into your spending habits, the more you can see where you need to change. If you have a home computer, take advantage of the great financial software programs that are designed not only to track your spending, but also to compare it to your planned spending, manage your investments, track information you need for tax purposes, and much more. The two main programs on the market are *Quicken* and *Microsoft Money*. They are both great, though some people find *Microsoft Money* a little more intuitive to use at first, and *Quicken* is preferable if you use its sister package, *TurboTax*, for your tax return. Neither program is hard to learn and both take advantage of the power of the Internet, letting you download your financial statements directly from many banks and investment companies, automatically updating the value of your investments, and so on. All you have to do is categorize what the transactions are. If you are technology averse, it would be worth having someone set you up on the program, because once everything is set up, it is easy to use.

If you do not have a home computer, use a paper-based system. These take a lot more time and effort, though you can cut corners by not tracking set expenses such as your rent or mortgage. Check your local bookstore for a budgeting workbook that has pages and pages of tables that you can fill in to track where your money is going.

There is, however, a line to draw with regard to what gets tracked. I do not advocate jotting down every penny that slips through your fingers. Who wants to feel that the Budget Police are sitting on your shoulder every time you have a soda? Simply choose how much you think is a reasonable amount for the little stuff and take that much out of your account once a month, keeping a fraction of it in your wallet at any one time. I prefer to have no more than $40 dollars on me at any time, usually less, because having cash tempts me to spend. Also put everything you can on a debit card attached to your account or a credit card that is paid off in full monthly—that way each bit of spending will be downloaded into your software and tracked for you.

Action Item: Select a Tracking System

If you have a home computer, buy a software package, making sure that it will work with your system. If you are not familiar with the software, take an evening to set it up, creating the different accounts that you have and setting up the links with your financial institutions (sometimes you will need to call the institution to set up the links). If you don't have a home computer, go to a bookstore and browse the personal finance section to see what planning systems are offered. Resist the temptation to wait until a new calendar year to begin tracking your finances . . . the sooner you get into the habit, the sooner you will know where your money is going.

Measure Your Wealth

Do you know what you are worth? Are you a millionaire yet? If you were even close to being a millionaire, chances are that you would already have worked out your net worth and would recalculate it every so often. Most likely, you have not sat down in a while to work out what you have and what you owe, often because the "what you owe" part of the equation is pretty scary for many households.

A net worth statement is important because it measures how you are doing against your big goals. You may not aspire to be a millionaire, but by knowing what you are worth, you can make other decisions, such as what type of will or estate plan you need.

Your net worth does not show you how much you have to spend. If, for example, your net worth is $250,000 of which $125,000 is in retirement accounts, $100,000 is equity in your home, and $25,000 is in savings and investments, the only amount quickly accessible to you is the $25,000. The assets that are cash or can easily be converted to cash are called liquid assets. The money tied up in your home can only be accessed through refinancing and taking some additional money out (which would result in more debt) or selling your home, so it is relatively illiquid. And the money in your retirement accounts may require paying a large tax penalty if you want to access the money before you are retired, so it is illiquid and expensive.

So, what are your assets and liabilities? Assets are items that you own that have a positive value. Liabilities are amounts that you owe. Do not include items that are leased. If you bought a car, the value of the car (if you sold it today[3]) is included as an asset, and the balance of the auto loan is included as a liability. If you lease your car, you do not have an asset or a liability (though, if you were to break the lease, you would likely owe the leasing company some money). Many things you own have little or no value; for example, if you had to sell all your clothes at a yard sale or consignment store today, they would probably get much less than they cost you. Leave items such as clothes, books, electronics, and furniture out of the equation, because you would not be likely to sell them in a financial emergency, and even if you did, you would receive a low, unpredictable amount for them. Focus on the big-ticket items and your financial assets. If you are not sure of a value, remember that it is better to underestimate the value of assets and overestimate debts. For example, if the property market has been hot in your area and you guess that your house is now worth $350,000 even though the most a house has sold for on

---

[3]Find your car's market value at www.kbb.com or www.edmunds.com.

your street is $325,000, then use the lower number, and knock off an extra 6 percent for the cost that you would incur if you sold your house today.

The best way to create a net worth statement is to use a personal finance program such as those discussed earlier. These programs update the value of your financial investments, allow you to adjust the numbers over time, and let you add more categories if you own unusual assets such as a collection of antique bowling balls. Alternatively, you can use a spreadsheet program such as *Excel*, which also allows you to update the numbers as you need to and can do the math for you.[4] If you are not yet using a computer for your personal finances, use the exercise below and round everything to the nearest ten or hundred dollars to simplify the math.

Action Item: Determine Your Net Worth

Fill in the work sheet shown as Figure 10.2 with the current value of your assets and liabilities. If you combine all your finances within your relationship, then just use the right-hand column. If, however, you have a Mine-Yours-Ours financial system, separate the numbers, filling in the amount of each asset or liability into only one column.

Check Your Credit Record

I'm not sure if this Santa fellow knows if you've been bad or good, but credit reporting agencies certainly do. And you better be good for goodness sake! Having a good credit record is more important than most people think. Having a bad credit record not only decreases your chance of getting loans in the future, it can also affect

---

[4]You can download a spreadsheet like the one provided as Figure 10.2 at www.deborahknuckey.com.

	His	Hers	Yours
Assets			
House	⎯⎯	⎯⎯	⎯⎯
Cars	⎯⎯	⎯⎯	⎯⎯
Savings/checking accounts	⎯⎯	⎯⎯	⎯⎯
Investment accounts	⎯⎯	⎯⎯	⎯⎯
Retirement accounts	⎯⎯	⎯⎯	⎯⎯
Other financial assets	⎯⎯	⎯⎯	⎯⎯
Other nonfinancial assets	⎯⎯	⎯⎯	⎯⎯
SUBTOTAL OF ASSETS	⎯⎯	⎯⎯	⎯⎯
Liabilities			
Mortgage	⎯⎯	⎯⎯	⎯⎯
Home equity loans	⎯⎯	⎯⎯	⎯⎯
Student loans	⎯⎯	⎯⎯	⎯⎯
Car loans	⎯⎯	⎯⎯	⎯⎯
Credit cards	⎯⎯	⎯⎯	⎯⎯
Store cards	⎯⎯	⎯⎯	⎯⎯
Other debts	⎯⎯	⎯⎯	⎯⎯
SUBTOTAL OF LIABILITIES	⎯⎯	⎯⎯	⎯⎯
Net worth (assets − liabilities)	⎯⎯	⎯⎯	⎯⎯

Figure 10.2   Net worth work sheet.

your ability to rent an apartment you want, get a low rate on the loans you take out, and even get a job that you want. More and more employers check credit records as part of the hiring process. Many car insurers use it in calculating your premiums. And as I wrote this book, many American auto manufacturers were advertising zero percent loans for new cars, in the hope of boosting flagging sales. A spokesperson for a major car company admitted, however, that fewer than a quarter of the applicants received the zero interest loans because they were offered only to customers with excellent credit records.

Your credit report reflects your recent financial history, showing all forms of credit and the credit line, current amount owed, and payment history. It also includes public records, bankruptcies, liens, judgments, garnishments, secured loans, financial counseling, foreclosures, and any accounts in collections. The good, the bad, and the awful are summarized into a credit score, known as a FICO score. It is based on five factors: payment history, amount owed, length of credit history, types of credit used, and whether you have taken on more credit recently. The first two factors make up about two-thirds of your credit score. At www.myfico.com, you can learn more about the factors affecting your credit score and how to improve your score.

One other big factor affecting your credit rating could be the one that you love. Yes, it is true: bad credit can be contagious. You can have the cleanest credit record around, yet if you open a joint account with someone who fails to pay your joint account on time, goes over the limit, or commits other acts of financial infidelity, your good name will be sullied as well. Any credit in both of your names will be reported to both of your credit reports, even if one person is the primary user of the account. If you have a substantial difference in your credit records, think twice before you cosign loans.

Even if you think you are ready for the Good Personal Finance Hall of Fame, it is important to check your credit rating once in a while. As research for this book, I bought a credit report and my FICO score from myfico.com, and was surprised with what I found. I have always had a very high score because I take care of my finances well; however, I found my score had slipped a whole 50 points in the last 18 months. Why? First, because a number of loan accounts were still considered open even though they had been closed for a long time. These included store cards, one of which I had asked to be closed a couple of times, a recently paid-off car loan, and two mortgages that had been paid off when I refinanced. Because the credit score looks at the available revolving credit as well as the current balance, the inaccuracy hurt my score.

In addition, in refinancing my mortgage, a number of queries had been made to my account, again raising the flags and lowering my credit score.

Your credit report will cost $9 per company for basic reports; however, you may qualify for a free report if you have recently been denied credit, insurance, or employment because of your credit; are on welfare, are unemployed and seeking work in the next 60 days; are a victim of fraud; or live in Colorado, Georgia, Maryland, Massachusetts, New Jersey, or Vermont. Most agencies offer enhanced reports for $12.95, which includes your credit score and an analysis of ways you can improve your score.

Action Item: Request a Copy of Your Credit Report

The three major companies collecting and reporting credit information are Experian, TransUnion, and Equifax. The easiest way to get your credit reports is to buy them and receive them on line. It's quick and easy. If, however, you don't have access to the Internet and a credit card, you can usually order reports by mail or phone. If you apply by mail, include your full name (including Jr., Sr., II), Social Security number, current and previous addresses within the last 5 years, home phone number, date of birth, current employer, signature, and the applicable fee. You need to have the confirmation code from buying your credit report to initiate an investigation of data you feel is incorrect.

- Equifax: www.equifax.com, 800-997-2493, P.O. Box 740241, Atlanta, GA 30374
- Experian: www.experian.com, 888-397-3742, P.O. Box 2002, Allen, TX 75013
- TransUnion: www.transunion.com, 800-888-4213 (only if you qualify for a free report), Consumer Disclosure Center, P.O. Box 1000, Chester, PA 19022

You may not be able to change history, but you can clean up any messes you have made to some degree. It is possible to improve your credit score fairly quickly if there are any errors in your report, and begin to improve it over time.

Fixing errors is a straightforward process that you can do on your own. Do not be tempted to pay a company to repair your credit, because there is nothing they do that you cannot quickly and easily do yourself with no specialized knowledge. All you have to do to fix an error is order your credit report, note errors, and request that each credit reporting agency opens an investigation into the errors that you noted. You cannot have correct information removed, even if extenuating circumstances led to the error. The credit scoring company Fair, Isaac advises: "Report any errors to both the lender who reported the information as well as to the credit reporting agency that produced the credit report with the error. It's important to involve both the lender and the agency to avoid the frustration of fixing an error one month, only to see it reappear again the next month when the lender sends the next batch of credit updates to the agency."

Managing your credit history is a good habit to get into, and once you have cleaned up your current record, don't slip back into bad habits. Some financial glitches live on your credit record for 7 years, so slipups should be avoided at all costs.

Action Item: Clean Up Your Credit Report
. . . .

Building a good credit record takes time; however, there are some actions you can take today that will improve your credit rating.

- Close down any unused credit or store cards and have the issuer report the closure to the credit agencies. Check up on them because many stores will merely suspend your account, hoping you will reopen it later.

- Set up automatic payments so you avoid late payments in the future.
- Avoid applying for new loans or credit cards unless you have to—each inquiry potentially lowers your score.
- If your credit report contains erroneous information, ask the credit agencies to launch an investigation. You can do this on line if you have a confirmation number from buying your credit report.
- If there are extenuating circumstances behind any of your credit glitches, write a brief note of explanation and ask to have it attached to your file.
- Ensure that both you and your spouse regularly pay any debts and credit cards you have so you can both build a good track record. Sometimes joint accounts are only reported to one Social Security number; however, it may be important later for both to have a good record so ask your bank to report joint accounts to both Social Security numbers.
- If you are a sucker for marketing offers you receive through the mail, call 1-888-5 OPT OUT to prevent your information from being included on marketing lists that credit reporting agencies sell.

CHAPTER 11

·····················

Skill 4: Communicating Through Conflict

·····················

In the Hollywood version of love, a couple falls for each other, has one big disagreement that seems to tear them apart, then background music rises as they realize that their love is more important than their disagreement, and they live happily ever after. If only it were so easy for Maria and John. Over time, a series of little niggling concerns and doubts pile up. Then one day, someone slips. John forgets to mention a purchase, and it results in a bounced check. Instead of a simple discussion about a minor infraction, the unsuspecting perpetrator feels the underlying anger in Maria's complaint. Blindsided, John wonders why his one small slipup causes such a vehement reaction and defends himself. Maria gets frustrated that her concerns are being minimized, and the discussion snowballs. John is buried under an avalanche of past complaints, often lobs back a few snowballs from his own stockpile of little-complaints-never-made, and both are left breathless and battered.

The next time, it escalates. Knowing he may be ambushed, John has built up an arsenal of complaints to better fight back with, and

Maria recycles everything that she felt was not really heard the first time. Hollywood would not approve.

. . . .

A couple with a great financial relationship may simply be lucky, just two people who happened to stumble on a mate with shared goals and no annoying behaviors. Possibly, but probably not. Chances are they have developed one of the three types of stable relationships we saw in Chapter 2: validating, volatile, or avoidant. All of those marriage types depend on being able to keep conflict in perspective in order to maintain the "magic ratio" of positive interactions to negative ones, which is five to one.[1]

When you enter a relationship, you may or may not come equipped with good communication skills. Whatever your underlying relationship style, good communication skills can enhance it. They can help you resolve, rather than continuously rehash or sidestep, long-standing gripes. And resolving conflicts—financial or other—can strengthen a relationship. Communication skills will serve you well in all your relationships, not only with your partner, but also with colleagues, friends, and others. Yet, these skills are not intuitive, somehow never make it to high school curriculum, and are not necessarily handed on by parents who may not know or practice them.

Talking About Communication

I take a chapter in this book to talk about communication skills because they can improve your financial relationship with your partner. At times, most couples have differing views about how money should be spent, saved, or invested. Studies show that when conflicts about money arise, they are more likely to be about how the money is to be spent than about how much the couple

---

[1] John Gottman with Nan Silver, *Why Marriages Succeed or Fail, and How You Can Make Yours Last* (New York: Fireside, 1994), 57.

has. And many have disagreements about other issues that play out as financial disagreements. Yet, when a conflict arises—about money or anything else—it doesn't have to devolve into a fight. The skills in this chapter help to separate the financial and emotional issues, and move financial discussions onto less treacherous ground.

All is not fair in love and war. Unconditional love is charming rhetoric when conditions are minor. But real love is conditional. It is conditional on respect and fairness. Good communication skills are one way of keeping respect alive, ensuring that fairness is maintained. Can a marriage survive without good communication skills? Possibly, even if it is volatile or avoidant. However, a relationship will be richer, both emotionally and financially with good communication—emotionally because the connection will be stronger, financially because harmful financial behaviors will be discussed and it is hoped changed.

Communication is a two-way process. It requires being able to say what you mean as well as to hear what your partner is saying. It also requires being able to negotiate until you find common ground or agree to disagree. Understanding communication between partners involves not only understanding what is actually said—the message that is actually said—but also the "metamessage," communication expert and author Deborah Tannen explains. "Two people in a conversation usually agree on what the message is. The metamessage is meaning that is not said at least not in so many words but that we glean from every aspect of context: the way something is said, who is saying it, or the fact that it is said at all. . . . And when family members react to each other's comments, it's metamessages they are usually responding to."[2]

Let's look at some building blocks of good communication: listening, acknowledging, stating your view, making and responding to requests.

---

[2]Deborah Tannen, *I Only Say This Because I Love You: How the Way We Talk Can Make or Break Family Relationships Throughout Our Lives* (New York: Random House, 2001), 7–8.

Each of these skills works with the others to improve communication and take the heat out of disagreements. And, although it takes two to tango, one great dancer can lead the other without them knowing. Even if your partner does not read this chapter and start using these skills with you, you can begin to influence the quality of your communications by sharing your views, acknowledging your partner's views, and making requests in the way that is outlined below. The quality of your communication will influence the reaction to it.

Listening

The first skill in communicating with your partner is listening. As author and relationship counselor Harville Hendrix puts it: "Most of us rarely listen to what other people are saying. When we should be listening, we are responding to the impact of what we are hearing. In other words, we are listening to ourselves react."[3]

Listening is not just about hearing what your partner is saying, but also really getting it and letting him know that you get it. So often the circular nature of arguments arise from one party feeling that his point of view is not heard by the person he is talking to. And the reaction? Generally, the person will continue attempting to be heard. He may repeat what he is saying, adding color and emphasis in the hope that it penetrates the consciousness of his partner. She may escalate the argument by bringing in other examples that support her underlying message (which is why that dishwasher incident in 1994 keeps surfacing). He may give up on attempting to be heard and simply go on the offensive, figuring that if he was not heard the first time, he might be heard if he attacks. She may even walk out of the room, feeling as though a brick wall has been built and dismantling it would be too difficult. He may withdraw into silence, giving up on being heard.

---

[3]Harville Hendrix, *Getting the Love You Want: A Guide for Couples* (New York: Henry Holt, 1988), 143.

How often do you assume that you know what your partner is saying before he or she has finished the sentence? I am really bad at this. My mind leaps ahead and starts saying "Yeah, uh huh, so perhaps if we . . ." and too often my mouth goes along for the ride. The person I am speaking with feels cut off, unheard, and, guess what: they *are!* There is a great arrogance in assuming that you understand your partner so well as to know what is eating her. Even if you do, recognize that your partner gets value from expressing it. It may be that your partner has trouble raising her concerns and has spent a week brewing ideas on how exactly to say what it is she needs to say. And if the response is that she gets cut off, chances are she will either shy away from raising concerns in the future (that is, until the day she surprises you with divorce papers) or will turn up in the future with a quiver full of arrows to throw in case she feels attacked.

So how do you actually listen?

Slow down and prepare to be surprised. You may *not* be surprised, but by approaching a conversation with an assumption that there is always more to discover about your partner's perspective is a great way to get into a listening mind-set. By really being curious about what she is saying or asking, you will keep your mind away from preforming a response. And chances are the first thing out of your mouth won't be a response, but a question to more fully explore her perspective.

Part of listening is pure body language. If you are physically closed off with arms crossed or body turned away, not only do you look like you have already formed an opinion, you probably have. If you are so laid back that you are almost reclining, you will let the words wash over. If you have your back to your partner and are busy unloading the dishwasher, you will miss the communication that involves the eyes, hands, and heart. Even if you are talking on the phone, your partner can hear if you are not fully present and focused on what she is saying. It is so easy to fall into the habit of multitasking while you are talking on the phone: straightening up papers, folding laundry, reconciling bank accounts, all while a conversation is supposed to be occurring (another big sin of mine). Perhaps the reason we stay on the phone so long is that the people we talk to feel they have to say what they mean several times before they are heard. Listen by being truly present. That means turning off the television, putting the laundry down, and, where possible sitting up or standing with your partner, and making eye contact.

Acknowledging

If you are cutting your partner off and offering half-baked solutions before he has finished expressing hid views or concerns, he will know you are definitely not listening. But how does your partner know if you *are* listening? Sitting there in silence doesn't necessarily signal that you *are* listening, even if your body language passes the "I have a pulse" test. You may just be waiting to pounce on what he is saying as soon as he takes a breath, or you may be thinking about something unrelated, or simply gritting your teeth and letting the words bounce off you like tennis balls. Acknowledging what your partner says—proving that you have heard him and that you are trying to put yourself in his shoes—is what makes the speaker feel truly heard.

Acknowledging communicates that you are indeed listening, hearing what is meant, and taking the time to understand his perspective. It is not necessarily agreeing; however, it does involve summarizing and playing back what you were just told. "So you are saying that when I shop for household items without you, you feel dismissed by me." "You are telling me that you have accumulated $10,000 debt and have been too scared to tell me?" "Am I right in hearing that you feel I am spending more than we can afford and therefore you are missing out on what you want?"

Acknowledging is not only saying, "this is what I heard you say," but also asking, "did I hear you correctly?" It signals to your partner that you are truly listening to the content of what he is saying and that you are checking that you have heard him correctly. For those of us used to saying "Yes, but . . ." or simply "that's not the way it is," such acknowledgments can feel stilted and even silly at first. However just wait until your partner acknowledges you. It feels good. The tension of "did they really get what I am saying" begins to vanish and the chance of the discussion escalating into an all-out argument diminishes.

You may get it wrong in your acknowledgment, but that is part of the reason why it is effective. It gives your partner a chance to clarify. "Well, that's not exactly what I meant. It's more that . . ."

Tone of voice is critical when it comes to acknowledging. The slightest touch of sarcasm can turn an acknowledgment from "I hear you" into "I disagree with you." The aim of acknowledgment is to show that you hear *and respect* the other person's point of view, even if you don't agree with it.

What if you feel that what your partner is saying is completely off base? You can still acknowledge him. He is, after all, simply sharing his perspective, how he feels. His perspective cannot be wrong—that *is* how he is seeing things. Let me repeat that: his *perspective* cannot be wrong. However, you may have a very different perspective. Acknowledge first, then compare perspectives. "So you are saying that when I shop for household items without you, you feel dismissed by me?" Stop to check that you heard correctly, then, "I'm sorry that's how it feels to you because I certainly don't intend to dismiss you. I must have misread your reaction last time we went shopping together. I felt that you were bored, and so I felt rushed and unable to enjoy the shopping. I assumed we would both prefer if I went alone."

Sharing Your Views

A friend of mine who is a lieutenant on the narcotics squad in D.C. says that eyewitnesses, as cherished as they may be by juries, are notoriously unreliable. Take 10 people seeing one crime or accident in broad daylight and you get 10 different versions of what happened. The variation in stories can be stunning. When it comes to talking about your personal finances, recognize that while numbers may be purely objective, almost everything else is subjective. The implication of the numbers, the emotional reaction to the numbers, the gap between the actual numbers and the desired numbers . . . there's a lot of room for the emotional to enter the financial conversation.

So when you share your view, note that the key is the word "your." Your perception is simply *your* perception, your reaction simply *your* reaction. It is not a universal truth, as much as it may seem very true to you.

The way to do this is to use "I-centered" language. Don't accuse and don't imply that your perception is a fact. Instead, share how you feel about the issue or action. Therefore, when you share your views, simply share how it is for you. So instead of "You are overspending," try "I feel worried when I see you spending a lot of money on things that are not on our plan." Instead of "You make decisions without me," try "I feel you do not care about my opinion when you make large purchases without consulting me."

By sharing views from this "I-centered" perspective, you decrease the potential for conflict. It is much harder for your partner to disagree with how you feel about something than with a bald accusation. It is important to differentiate between a complaint and a criticism.[4] Complaints are a statement about your feelings about a specific situation. "I am angry that you forgot to pay the cable bill." Criticism turns a complaint into a global attack, making it general and loading it with blame. "You always bounce checks. You will ruin our credit rating." Complaints are okay, criticism is not, and criticism sprinkled with contempt can be a relationship's death knell.

Making and Responding to Requests

All the talking in the world won't result in changes in your financial relationship if you fail to state what it is you would actually like. As much as we would love our partners to be mind readers,

---

[4]John Gottman and Nan Silver, *The Seven Principles for Making Marriage Work* (New York: Three Rivers Press, 1999), 27–28.

they're not. And if they were, there would be nothing to communicate in the first place. So we need the final communication skill of making requests.

Making a request is simply asking for what it is that you want. It's not a pouty, foot-stamping demand. And unless it really is a make or break issue, it is not an ultimatum. It is simply a statement of the solution you think might work. "In the future, I would like you to include me when you are shopping for household items that we both will use." The key is to make the request clear, positive, and actionable. Positive requests involve asking for what you would like your partner to do, not what you would like them not to do. So instead of requesting: "Stop overspending," try "I would like you to cut back on your spending by $300 a month."

Too often, requests are made as demands. The requester may have been brooding on the issue for some time, formulating solutions that would make her happy. By the time the request is made, the requester assumes that her solution is the one solution that will make her happy. A much better approach is to be open to possibilities, to let your partner know what you think may resolve the situation. The more you are married to your solution as the right solution, the less likely you are to find a workable solution that meets both of your needs. At the other end of the spectrum, too often discussions end with no request being made. Without making a request, you are not giving your partner guidance about how you would prefer things to happen in the future.

Does asking for what you want mean that you will get it? Not necessarily. There are three potential responses to a request: accept, reject, or negotiate. Accept means saying yes, I'm happy to try that. You may fail or it may take awhile to remember the request on a regular basis, but by accepting you are agreeing to give it your best effort and be open to reminders.

Rejecting outright means saying no, I don't feel I can do that or I don't feel it is a reasonable request. A blanket rejection leaves the question hanging: well, what now? It invites the dispute to raise its ugly head again.

The third option is negotiation so you can find a common ground where you can both feel that your needs are recognized and validated. Rather than reject a request outright, counter with a way that you feel you can take your partners needs into account while still validating your needs or accounting for your behavior. For example, you may counter that: "I'm sorry but I don't feel I am spending too much given our earnings. Perhaps we can work together on creating a spending plan where you also feel you have enough spending money. If we can't make the numbers work, then I will consider cutting back."

Sometimes a blanket acceptance is also the wrong approach. Saying yes can feel like an easy way to diffuse a tense situation, yet, if you know you really won't follow through completely on the request, you are better off to negotiate something you can follow through on than to let the same old argument raise its ugly head each time you fail to follow through. For example, you may counter that "I would enjoy including you in my plans when it is possible; however, I want you to accept that there are times I simply shop on the spur of the moment and it may be hard to include you at those times." Of course, your partner can then accept, reject, or negotiate your counteroffer.

Dealing with an Impasse

What if, even with the best communication skills and a respectful conversation, you find you reach an impasse? In a business deal, you can walk away—perhaps losing money, but not breaking your heart. However, as a couple, you have a lot invested in finding a way to make things work. It may take many conversations to find shared goals and agree on ways to reach those goals. And those goals will change over time. Also, it may be an ongoing effort to support each other in following through on agreements.

If you reach a complete logjam, or if every discussion about money results in arguments, consider asking a marriage counselor to help you discuss your finances and clean up the emotional junk left from past financial fights.

Can money be a make-or-break issue? Certainly many couples with lousy communication skills have fought about money along with numerous other issues until the relationship ended with a whimper or a bang. However, even couples with good communication skills may still reach a time when they realize that their goals are not shared or their commitment to follow through on joint plans is not strong enough.

There is only so much in life that is in your control. Ultimately, you cannot control another person's behavior, but you can control your reaction to it. If you reach an impasse, look to your side of the equation and see whether you are willing to change your behavior or your reaction to your partner's behavior. If you are not willing to change a behavior that is upsetting your partner, are you willing to accept the consequence that your partner may choose not to be with you because of that behavior? If your partner is not willing to change behavior that is upsetting to you, are you willing to change your reaction to that behavior? It is possible simply to choose to stop being hurt, angry, or annoyed by your partner's behavior. For example, if you have been taking your partner's overspending as a personal attack and as a dismissal of your shared dreams, can you reposition your perception of his behavior? Perhaps you can see it as an expression of his spontaneous nature or his fear of restriction. Maybe you can see it as a counter to your tendency to be too careful. Or perhaps you can see it as simply overspending. At the very least, your new perspective may result in your spending less energy fretting about the issue. You may even find that the heat evaporates from the argument and you discover new ways of working together on the issue.

Couples who practice avoidance are great at sweeping issues under the carpet when they are not easily resolved. They end up walking on bumpy carpet, but find it more comfortable than dealing with the mess directly.

Timing Is Everything

There is a time and a place to talk about money. *Cosmopolitan*, *Glamour*, and their ilk are always advising women that bed is the last place to talk about sexual problems. While it's a fine place to throw in an "oh, that's gooood," it's not the greatest place to give negative feedback or advice. I'm not sure about the consequences of that pop psychology advice. How many car accidents have been caused by a woman telling her partner: "You know what I would really like you to try? Perhaps if you [insert detailed description here]" while he is trying to keep his eyes on the road?

Less dangerous, but more humiliating, are public discussions of financial issues. I have cringed more than once when hearing couples bicker in public over money issues. I distinctly remember one woman haranguing her poor husband in the middle of the pots and pans at a department store. She came out with a continuous stream of criticism about his dumb choices, the debt that he already had, and the small amount he earned. Everyone in earshot (and she was loud) was squirming. There was clearly so little respect left in their relationship, it was sad. Yet the woman trumpeted her complaints and looked around as if she would find a group of women cheering her on. Rather than thinking little of him and all his flaws, I was probably not alone in wondering why he would stay with such a witch.

Conversations about money are private matters, and potentially charged with emotion. Time them accordingly. A passing jab 2 minutes before you head out the door is not fighting fair. Neither is squelching your partner's joy in a new toy by starting in on his overspending the minute you see it. And no one likes to get into tough issues when it is late, they are tired, or they have a pile of work to get through. Hmm, that pretty much rules out most waking hours, especially if you have kids in the house too. Find a neutral time to sit down together. If you have a monthly or weekly routine for paying bills, that can be a good time to raise concerns or revisit financial plans, especially if it helps to have access to numbers. Don't, however, paint your partner into a corner with a pile of financial evidence that will make him feel that you have appointed yourself judge, jury, and executioner.

Action Item: Speaking of Speaking
. . . .

Find a time for both of you to sit down and practice the communication skills. Each select a minor, noncontroversial financial concern you have had in the past year. Start by one of you expressing your perception of or reaction to the issue you choose. Then have the other partner acknowledge what he or she has heard and check that he or she has heard correctly. Then the person who raises the issue should make a request and the partner should negotiate until you come to an agreement that satisfies you both. Repeat, swapping roles.

. . . .

Integrating the Skills

There's a good chance that exercises such as the one above will feel stilted and silly, yet like all skills, it will take time for you to start integrating new communication skills into everyday behavior. Agree to help each other remember to use the communication skills with gentle reminders. Ask questions such as: "What is your reaction to that?" "How do you feel about it?" "What are you requesting?" If you find past events are being dragged into the conversation, ask: "I know that was a while ago and we can't change it now, but what is the common feeling between that event and what is going on now?" If you find yourself well into an argument before you remember, simply stop and comment that you have fallen off the good communication wagon (just like the Good Humor truck, but without ice cream), and agree to take a break until you cool off and can find a good time and place to start over again, this time consciously trying to keep using the skills.

CHAPTER 12

··

Skill 5: Investing for Strong Returns

AH, MONEY. LIFE IS DIFFICULT WHEN YOU DON'T HAVE IT, AND complicated when you do. Assuming you have created a good plan that allows for a strong base of financial security, you will need to start investing those savings. It's tempting to just stick your money in a savings account until it is good and big and *then* do something with it. However, if you can see your money, you may be tempted to spend it. Also, the sooner you start investing, the more your money will grow.

Some couples invest together. Others designate one person in charge of investments. Others simply outsource to an investment adviser, while still others have nothing to invest. Regardless of your structure, it is critical that you both understand enough about investing in order to be able to talk about your investments with each other. This understanding is not so you can second-guess the person designated the investment decision maker. It's so you can build on each other's strengths and insights, and ensure that the bad habits that some men and women tend toward—women investing too conservatively, men overinvesting in their employer's stock and so on[1]—don't harm your long-term returns. You cannot afford to be ignorant about investing in case one day you have to do it alone.

---

[1]See Chapter 2, Understanding Each Other's Point of View.

153

I could write a whole book on how to invest, so this chapter is intended as a basic primer to introduce you to the range of investments and some easy ways to get started.

Investing Concepts 101

The goal of investing is to grow your money. Your money is an asset. If it sits somewhere earning a minimal return, it is not working for you. In fact, if your money earns less interest than the inflation rate, it is shrinking before your eyes. If you invest your money, it is hoped it will grow, though, if you've watched the markets in the past few years, you will also be aware that there are times that investments go down.

Risk and Return

When you invest, you are balancing two things: risk and return. Risk looks at your chances of getting a positive outcome. Return looks at how much the investment might earn. If high-risk investments pay off, they pay off well, but there is a significant chance that they will never pay off at all. For example, companies involved in speculative ventures such as biotech firms trying to cure cancer are a high risk. Low-risk investments have a very good chance of paying off, but, not surprisingly, generate a much lower return. You simply do not need to pay someone as much to put his money somewhere safe as you do to put his money somewhere risky. Government bonds are an example of a very low-risk investment, because they are guaranteed to have value as long as the government is in business. In between, there are many other sorts of investments with various levels of risk. Risky investments are not necessarily stupid investments. There's a big difference between putting money in a small company with a potentially great product and buying a lottery ticket.

So should you invest in high- or low-risk investments? A balance of both. The balance depends on your time frame and your tolerance for risk. Time frame is important because if you know that you need to use your money in, say, 1 year for a deposit for a house, you will not want to risk losing part of your investment between now and then. However, if you are retiring in 30 years, you can afford to ride out short-term fluctuations of riskier investments in the hope of getting higher returns in the long run.

The other thing to take into consideration is your personality. If you are likely to worry yourself silly every time your investment slips in value just a bit, then you will feel more comfortable with lower-risk investments. But there is a *huge* cost to being too cautious. A lower return over a year or two may not make much of a difference; however, over a longer period, it can make a huge difference. For example, $10,000 invested for 30 years at a 6 percent return gives you $57,453. Not bad. But if you can earn 10 percent return, the money grows to $174,494, more than three times as much. You have to learn to love (some) risk.

Unfortunately, many investments do not have a predictable return. So that although you know that a CD may have a set return of, say, 4 percent for 1 year, it is impossible to predict what return you may get from, say, a stock or a piece of real estate. The challenge, therefore, is in trying to predict how you will have a reasonable chance at getting a decent return. If history is an indicator, the stock market has provided better long-term returns than many other types of investment. The figures in Table 12.1

Table 12.1   Market Returns 1926 to End of 2001

	Excluding Inflation %	Including Inflation %
U.S. Treasury Bills	0.73	3.81
U.S. Government Bonds	2.18	5.30
U.S. Corporate Bonds	2.63	5.77
U.S. Inflation	N/A	3.06
Total U.S. stock market	7.04	10.32
Small cap stocks	8.41	11.73
Large cap stocks	6.83	10.09

Source: Data from Ibbotson Associates.

show that after inflation, stocks have returned more than a 7 percent annualized return 1926 through the end of 2001. Compare that to government bonds, which returned just over 2 percent.

Returns on real estate investment trusts (REITs) over the past 30 years averaged 7.16 percent excluding inflation and international stocks averaged 5.88 percent. The bottom line is that it pays to be a confident investor who can find the right balance of risk and return, and the more you learn about investing, the more confident you are likely to be.

Compounding Returns

Getting your money to work for you involves not only investing it so you get a decent return, but also leaving it alone for long enough that you start getting a return on your past earnings. Let's say you have $100 getting a 10 percent return. At the end of year one you have $110, so you have earned $10. However, at the end of year two you have $121 and have earned $11 that year because not only does the initial $100 you invested earn its $10, the $10 interest you earned in the first year earns an additional dollar of interest. Over time this effect, called compounding, makes a huge difference. The takeaway: invest early and invest often.

Diversification

Diversification is the art of not putting all your eggs in one basket. You may diversify between categories (A percent in stocks and B percent in bonds) as well as within categories (of your stocks: X percent in large cap stocks, Y percent in small cap stocks, and Z percent in international stocks). Diversification spreads the risk, so that if one of your investments does very poorly, it doesn't harm your total investment portfolio too much.

Another way to think about diversification is in terms of which industries you invest in. A portfolio with shares in companies of different sizes is not diversified well if all of those stocks happen to be in one sector, such as high tech.

It is easy to turn a blind eye to diversification if your employer offers you discounted stock in its company through its retirement savings program, bonus system, or directly. You can not only end up with too much of your portfolio in a single company, but also you are putting your investment eggs in the same basket with your employment eggs. When energy trader Enron declared bankruptcy in December 2001, employees found themselves unemployed, as well as reeling from the loss of value of their retirement portfolios. Many had a significant slice of their retirement portfolios locked up in Enron stock, which plummeted in value. Buying some stock is fine, but resist having more than 5 percent of your total portfolio in your employer's stock.

Dollar Cost Averaging

Another important concept is dollar cost averaging. As I write this, the stock market is floundering after a major sell-off. The market pundits speculate whether this is the bottom. The answer is . . . who knows? Last time most pundits agreed that we had reached the bottom, we hadn't. Next time there is agreement, the market may have already picked itself up and brushed itself off from the tough times it currently faces. Dollar cost averaging helps us manage our inability to predict what will happen. Instead of trying to time the market—buy when you think it is at the bottom, sell when you think it is at the top, and be wrong a whole lot of the time—dollar cost averaging simply acknowledges that there is a bumpy road to ride and good shock absorbers are needed. By investing at a regular pace, you ignore the ups and downs, stops and spurts, of the market. In many ways it is the no-think approach. No "Will I/Won't I?" debates when the price goes up, no gnashing of teeth and tearing of hair when the market dips.

The math behind dollar cost averaging is explained in Chapter 10, Skill 3: Getting into Good Habits, because investing regularly is one of the best habits you can get into. Although investing a certain amount regularly is great, remember to also invest a little more when you have a little extra.

The Range of Investments

But what to invest in? Disney shares? Government bonds? The money market? Swampland in Florida? Here is a high-level overview of the different investments.

Stocks

Buying a stock means you are buying a (very small) slice of a company. You own part of the company, and so you get privileges: you receive dividends if the company pays them, you receive the annual report, you can vote on key issues, you can attend annual meetings, and you can drop its name at cocktail parties. The total value of the company, that is, the total number of shares multiplied by the market price of the shares, is called the *market capitalization* and terms such as "large cap" and "small cap" refer to whether the company has a large market capitalization (such as Coca-Cola or ExxonMobil) or a small market capitalization (such as those little high-tech companies that your brother-in-law lost his shirt on). Stocks are also classified by sector (transportation, pharmaceuticals), and whether they are seen as undervalued compared to the market (value stocks) or growing their revenue or earnings faster than the market (growth stocks).

You can make money on stocks in two ways: by a capital gain, which is the amount that the stock rises in value, and by the dividend, which is the portion of profit that a company pays out to its investors. Not all companies pay dividends because they reinvest their profits in the company or they don't make a profit. For investments outside your retirement portfolio, you may prefer stocks that don't pay dividends because they are taxable income.

Fixed Income

Fixed-income investments include treasury notes, bonds, and CDs. They are investments where you lend money to an institution and it pays you interest. They are for a set period, such as a 10-year bond although you can buy and sell it during its term.

Most pay interest along the way, though zero coupon bonds pay it only at the end. The amount of interest paid to you will depend on two things: (1) the duration of the underlying investment (10-year bond versus 3-month CD versus 30-day treasury bill); (2) the quality of the organization you are lending to (government bonds versus corporate bonds). The relation between interest rates and duration changes over time is known as the yield curve. As we saw above, risk and return are inversely related, so a government bond will pay less interest than a bond issued by a company. Bonds are rated by their quality, ranging from AAA to DDD or lower. The value of fixed-income investments changes over time as market interest rates rise and fall.

Cash or Money Market

When people refer to cash or money market, they mean money that is invested one day at a time. It's not actual cash stuffed under some banker's mattress; it earns interest but you don't know in advance exactly how much.

Mutual Funds

People get confused about mutual funds, because often they are spoken about as if they are separate from stocks and fixed-income investments. A better way to think of mutual funds is that they are simply different packaging of the same investments we have already discussed. So while buying stock is like selecting a type of snack—say, M&Ms—buying a mutual fund is like choosing trail mix—say, the one with nuts, raisins, M&Ms, and sunflower seeds. When you buy a mutual fund, you are paying a fund manager to choose the right mix of goodies for your investment trail mix, as opposed to buying a whole lot of separate items and creating your own mix.

Types of Funds

Mutual funds can focus on a specific type of investment or hold a range of investments within them. Some mutual funds primarily hold stocks, with the balance held in cash. Others may primarily invest in bonds. Still others hold a mix of assets, say, some stocks, some bonds, and some cash.

Most mutual funds have clear objectives that define what type of investments that they seek to hold in their fund. Stock funds may focus on companies that are:

- A certain size (e.g., a large cap stock fund).
- Similar in their investment outlook (e.g., a growth fund).
- In a particular market index (e.g., S&P 500 index fund).
- In a specific sector (e.g., a transportation industry fund).
- Overseas or based in a specific region (e.g., an international or an Asia Pacific fund).
- Based in certain types of countries (e.g., an emerging markets fund).

Bond funds may focus on bonds that are:

- Of a specific duration (e.g., long-term bonds).
- Issued by certain types of organizations (e.g., municipal "muni" bond fund).
- Have specific tax advantages (e.g., California tax-exempt bond fund).
- Have similar expected returns (e.g., high-yield bond fund).

Mixed stock and bond funds, sometimes called balanced funds, may focus on:

- Investments that generate good dividend or interest income (e.g., income funds).
- Investments aimed to meet a certain investment goal (e.g., a "life cycle" fund aimed to have the mix of investments that a person 20 years from retirement would need).

Another thing to know is the difference between closed-end and open-end funds. Closed-end funds issue a limited number of shares and, when all are sold, are closed to new investors. Shares in the fund are then traded on the market like a stock. Most funds are open-ended and will continue to accept investors' money.

Fees and Expenses

Another key consideration is how the fund charges its clients. Funds require different amounts of management. Some have teams of experts constantly scouring the market for good companies to buy and assessing the value of companies they already hold. Others are essentially run by a computer that adjusts the shares in the fund to mirror a certain index. Also, some firms have large teams of salespeople, all needing to earn a commission, whereas others sell their funds through other companies. The result is that companies have different sales and management costs that they need to cover. Some funds charge a sales load (essentially a commission) up front and others don't. Some variations exist; for example, some funds charge a load up front that is eliminated if you hold the fund for a certain period, or some funds charge a redemption fee when you sell the fund. Should you pay a load? There seems to be no reason to. A load eats away at the amount you invest, and if you are choosing your own funds, then you will be able to find plenty of no-load funds that perform as well as load funds. The one exception is if you are using a commission-based advisor who is choosing funds for you. The load is their income.

In addition to the fees at the time of purchase or sale, there are management expenses that range from 0.2 percent to about 2.0 percent a year and are taken out of the fund's earnings. These decrease the return a fund gets, and the long-term impact of a percent or two in expenses a year can be significant, so, all else being equal, go for funds with low management fees. In addition, there may be fees covering marketing and distribution costs called 12(b)-1 fees. Look at all the fees and expenses before choosing a fund.

Mutual Funds and Taxes

Mutual funds differ in their tax effectiveness. This is not important for mutual funds that are in a tax-advantaged retirement account; however, it is critical for the rest of your portfolio. A mutual fund that buys and sells its investments a lot may generate capital gains that the owners of the mutual fund have to pay tax on, effectively reducing their long-term return. Check the tax effectiveness before you buy a fund.

Mutual Fundlike Investments

Some products are similar to mutual funds, but are traded more like stocks. These include unit investment trusts. Some replicate market indexes, providing a simple way to invest in a market, for example, the stock traded as SPY ("spiders") tracks the S&P 500 index.

Another mutual fundlike investment is the REIT. REITs own properties or parts of properties. They may focus on commercial, industrial, or residential property or a mix of different types. The good thing about investing in REITs is that they offer diversification, as real estate often moves in different patterns than does the stock market.

Other Investments

There are many other types of investments that you can consider putting your money in, including options, futures, and commodities. Be careful of the many organizations marketing complex investment products as if they can easily be mastered using their exclusive 10-step program. There are scams a-plenty, and there are even more people who make their money selling classes that offer misleading advice. If you are ready for advanced investing strategies and complex products, skip the infomercial kings and take classes through industry organizations such as the

Chicago Board Options Exchange, which offers great (and free) on-line lessons.

A Simple Strategy for Starting Out

If you have never invested before, it can be overwhelming. I hope that within your relationship at least one of you has a little investment experience and can help the other learn. However, investing can be daunting even to very experienced people—after all, a lot of market professionals lost substantial amounts of their client's money in the recent downturn, proving that no one can tell what the market will do.

First Plan Your Diversification

The first step in your investment strategy is to work out what you want your total investment portfolio to look like. Think of your portfolio as a pie you need to slice. As you plan your allocation of assets, keep two things in mind: (1) how long your time frame is; and (2) how comfortable you are with risk. If you have a long time frame and are comfortable with sensible risk, aim for an aggressive portfolio. If you need to start accessing the money within 5 years and tend to be very risk averse, choose a more conservative asset allocation plan.

Table 12.2 shows examples of asset allocations for different degrees of risk taking, but note that the conservative allocations are designed for people who are preretirement. A conservative asset allocation model for a person who is retired and in his mid-seventies would look substantially more conservative than this, with higher percentages of bonds and cash.

Note that these asset allocations are based on the widely held assumption that stocks perform better than other investments over the long term. There are some academics who believe that this will not be the case given the massive rise in the stock market over the last decade. They recommend lower holdings of stocks, and, given

Table 12.2   Investment Strategy

Asset class	Aggressive	Somewhat Aggressive	Somewhat Conservative	Conservative
Stocks				
Large cap	40%	35%	30%	25%
Small cap	22.5	20	17.5	15
International	25	22.5	20	20
REITs	7.5	7.5	5	5
Bonds	0	10	20	25
Cash	5	5	7.5	10
Total	100%	100%	100%	100%

the lack of a crystal ball, you are left to decide whose assumptions you believe. The next thing to do is to think about your total investment portfolio.

Action Item: Design Your Portfolio
. . . .

First, determine which investment strategy is appropriate. Sit down together and answer these questions:

- How long will it be before we need to access our invested money?
- How many years until one or both of us retires?
- Are we willing to have short-term losses if they may lead to higher longer-term returns?
- Given our ages, personalities, and need for good returns, what investment strategy best meets our needs?

Determine the total amount of money you have to invest by filling out the first portion of the work sheet presented as Figure 12.1. Exclude any money that is earmarked for short-term goals, such as buying a house within 5 years. Then use

1. List money available for investing.

   Retirement accounts at employer   _____

   Other retirement accounts   _____

   Current nonretirement investments   _____

   Other available money to invest   _____

       Total available to invest   _____

2. Multiply the total available to invest by the percentage you plan to invest in each category of assets.

ASSET CLASS	ASSET ALLOCATION	PLANNED INVESTMENT
Stocks	%	$
Large cap	_____	_____
Small cap	_____	_____
International	_____	_____
REITs	_____	_____
Bonds	_____	_____
Cash	_____	_____
Total	100%	$_____

Figure 12.1   Investment allocation work sheet.

the second part of the work sheet to design your portfolio allocations.

. . . .

Then Invest Your Money

Start with investing your retirement savings. If your company has a retirement plan, chances are that it offers a limited range of investments. The lack of choice is a great way to wet your feet if you have never invested before. Look at the funds offered within your company's plan and see which can be used to meet part or all of your asset allocation plan. If all of your investments are within a retirement plan, then simply replicate the allocations you determined in Figure 12.1. If some of your investments are outside your retirement plan, then use the nonretirement part of your portfolio for the most conservative assets: cash and bonds. Why? In case you need to tap the cash and because you want to minimize the taxable earnings. Because retirement accounts cannot be combined—that is, you will always have "his and hers" accounts—make sure you reflect the appropriate asset allocation in both portfolios.

If you already have some money invested, you will need to determine what category of asset it is in and determine what changes you will need to make to rebalance your portfolio so that it reflects the strategy you developed in Figure 12.1.

Choosing a Fund

As you begin investing, you may want to invest in mutual funds to ensure diversification. Even though the number of mutual funds outnumbers the number of companies listed on the U.S. stock exchanges—making choosing a fund almost as tough as choosing an individual stock—when you buy a fund, you spread your risk around all the investments in the fund.

Within your employer-sponsored retirement account, you probably have a relatively limited number of funds to choose from. Look through the list for the ones that seem to best match your investment strategy. There may be a series of separate funds, or they may even have funds that replicate an entire asset allocation strategy within a single choice.

For the rest of your investments, look at three things: (1) what sort of fund you want; (2) which funds have a good performance record; and (3) who manages the funds. You already know what proportion of your portfolio you want in, say, a large cap fund. There are hundreds of those funds alone, so how do you choose which one to invest in? Fortunately, there is a company that wades through all the data and compares the funds using a rating system based on stars. The company is called Morningstar,[2] and the cheater's way to choose a fund is to simply assume that if it has a four- or five-start rating by Morningstar, it must be reasonably good. Of course, the ratings are based on past performance, and funds that did well for the last 5 years won't necessarily do well for the next 5 years, but the Morningstar rating system does cut the list down considerably.

Another even easier way to choose is to simply invest in index funds or index tracking stocks. Index funds are mutual funds that are designed to replicate the movements of a market index, such as the S&P 500. Index tracking stocks are a special type of stock that also tracks the movements of a market index, but are managed and traded differently than an index fund. These investments have some tax advantages over actively managed mutual funds (i.e., where the manager is trying to pick stocks that will grow faster than the market as a whole) because there is less trading of stocks within the portfolio; therefore, you are going to delay receiving and paying tax on the capital gains until you sell the fund, leaving more money to compound in the meantime. Index funds also have significant advantages because they have much lower management fees. Although some in the market are not fans of index funds (particularly advisors who profit from selling other funds with higher commissions), academic studies have found that the chances of a manager who is picking stocks outperforming the index over time is less than 25 percent. Of course, index funds should slightly underperform the index due to fees, but you might still be better off. Index tracking stocks are not available for all parts of your portfolio; however, index funds are available for almost all of your portfolio.

If you buy an actively managed fund, look at who manages the fund: both the company that manages the fund (Strong, Fidelity, Baron), and the person who manages it. If the fund has a good

---

[2]www.morningstar.com.

track record, it is important to see whether the people who created the track record are still running the fund. The fund write-up should mention who manages the fund and how long that person has been the manager. Morningstar reports on changes in fund managers.

You do not have to buy mutual funds directly from the fund manager. You can go through a financial institution that offers a range of funds from various firms. Keep Skill 2: Simplifying Your Structure in mind. To stay competitive, many firms that used to sell just their own funds now offer a comprehensive range of products. They know investors like one-stop shopping and to have all their funds in a single account.

If you are choosing funds other than index funds, be aware that because funds own a basket of underlying shares, you need to take into account the overlap of investments within your portfolio. In the large run-up in high tech stocks in the late nineties, many people found themselves with investment portfolios that were very heavily weighted toward high tech stocks because so many funds put so much money in the fashionable technology companies. It was not only the high tech stock funds that were investing in companies such as Cisco and JDS Uniphase, but also many small, mid, and large cap stock funds. Of course, index funds also had plenty of tech stocks. It wasn't until the market started correcting that many people realized how heavily weighted their total portfolio was toward a single sector. Understanding your real portfolio requires looking under the covers of the mutual fund to what companies they invest in.

Tax and Investments

For investments outside your retirement portfolio, you will be required to pay tax on dividends as you earn them and capital gains when you or your mutual fund sell an investment. However, each year you can deduct net losses of up to $3,000, and carry losses above that amount forward to future years.

Owning mutual funds can expose you to additional tax burdens. Because the portfolio manager is making decisions on when to buy or sell stocks on your behalf, you may incur capital gains even though you did not sell the mutual fund. The taxable gain that occurs from trading within the portfolio is spread among everyone invested in the mutual fund. The catch is that the taxable gain is calculated based on the price at which the mutual fund first bought a stock, even if it was years before you bought into the fund. This scenario was particularly painful in 2000 when many funds had large taxable gains from profits taken, yet the value of the mutual funds declined significantly throughout the year. People who were new to the funds found themselves paying a tax burden related to purchases made before the high tech stocks took off. This tax burden is why it is important to seek funds that are either index funds or tax-effective funds for the nonretirement part of your portfolio.

Next Steps

This is a very general introduction to investing. As you start building your investments and becoming a financially Conscious Couple, you will probably want to know much more. There are many great books on investing (I particularly like the *Wall Street Journal* series) and many investment firms offer free on-line education or live investment seminars. Of course, they would love you to be their customer, so there may be a sales pitch within the class; however, it is a good way to learn more.

Another thing that you might want to do is to form an investment club and use that as a way of learning more about investing in individual stocks, if you want to try your hand at that. I'd recommend skipping all the structure and paperwork for the first 6 months to a year and simply doing paper trades, that is, don't use real money. It gives you a chance to see how you work as a team, how well you pick stocks, and whether all the members share a commitment to the group before you create the membership agreements and other such time-consuming things. If, like many clubs, it doesn't last the first year, then you have nothing to disband.

Finally, consider never learning much more! That sounds heretical coming from a personal finance writer; however, the more studies I read about the performance of individual stock pickers versus mutual funds versus index funds, the more convinced I am becoming that we may all be better off going for the lowest fee, simplest forms of investments: index tracking stocks and index funds. There are simply no crystal balls that work reliably over time.

CHAPTER 13

Skill 6: Creating a Safety Net for Two

FOR BETTER, FOR WORSE. FOR RICHER, FOR POORER. IN SICKNESS and in health. Till death do you part. In the glow of a wedding day, the dark side of the wedding vows are easily ignored, mere fine print on a contract of love. But what about worse, poorer, sickness, death? They do happen, to couples who are strong and to couples whose relationships won't survive the strain. It is unproductive to live life in fear of events that you may not be able to predict or control in any way, but it is necessary to do the occasional bit of worst-case scenario planning. A happy ending after a bad or sad event may not always be possible; however, with some planning, you can lessen the chance of financial pain compounding the emotional pain.

Preventive Pessimism

As a couple, it is important to create a safety net big enough for the two of you. Too often couples fail to take an inventory of the risks they face, putting off the awkward conversations, the "what ifs," the acknowledgments of mortality. Yet, caring for each other involves making sure that you protect each other as well as any children or dependents you may have.

It's an investment: Protecting your assets and your loved ones is not cheap. However, it far outweighs the cost of not having the protection, when you need it. For example, your home insurance is a large expense. If your home never gets robbed, burns to the ground, or falls into a sinkhole, did you waste your money? Yes and no. Yes, in retrospect, you could have been uninsured. But the answer is really no: none of us has perfect insight into the future (if so, we would have made a fortune in the stock market and retired by now). Your insurance is a necessary expense because your home *could* have been robbed, burned to the ground, or fallen into a sinkhole. You just got lucky.

What about those who aren't so lucky? Even small events can add up. A few seconds of distraction (and I wasn't even using a cell phone or my cordless curling iron at the time!) on a traffic-clogged Los Angeles freeway 8 years ago resulted in my rear-ending the car in front of me. We were going less than 20 miles an hour and the damage did not look significant. Yet, my front panels needed to be replaced and the car I hit required some bodywork too. The damage from a very minor fender bender added up to several thousand dollars. Fortunately, I was insured. Even so, my deductible was $500 and my insurance premiums rose by a few hundred dollars a year for 5 years. On the scale of life disasters, that minor accident rated maybe a 2 out of 10. Fortunately, I have never had an event that I would rate as more than a 3.

Unfortunately, it takes little effort to find people who have suffered through emotionally and potentially financially devastating events. A self-employed woman I met found out she had breast cancer shortly after accidentally letting her health insurance expire. An immigrant from North Africa who helped me paint my home saw his entire family murdered and his family home confiscated in a civil war. My mother was widowed at age thirty-one, left to bring up three children alone. My colleague lost her house and all its possessions in the 1991 Northridge earthquake. A mountaineer died and two of his team were critically injured on Mt. Baker the day before my mountaineering class successfully reached the summit. Dozens of friends have started life again after divorce ripped their hearts in two and doubled their household living costs. Thousands of families lost someone they loved in a deliberate act of terror in New York City.

Preparing for the worst does not mean dwelling on everything awful that could happen. It simply involves taking an occasional inventory of the protection you have in place and making sure you take care of yourself and those you love. I am talking about prudence, not paranoia.

This chapter looks at some of the most common events you may face as a couple. I outline the actions you can take to prevent the event from happening, and the protection available to stop it from resulting in financial ruin. Not surprisingly, most of the protective actions require buying insurance or getting your legal house in order. Specifically, I discuss unemployment, accidents, divorce, illness or disability, and death.

Unemployment

Downsizing, cutbacks, letting go, outplacement, laying off, severance, early retirement—the range of synonyms that pussyfoot around firing an employee or group of employees reflects companies' discomfort with the event. For the person being fired, there are bigger discomforts: loss of income, perhaps loss of face, and uncertainty about the future.

Unemployment may be the result of personal, business, or economic factors. You may be fired due to low performance, insufficient skills, changing job roles, internal politics, or a personality clash. A business may fire a number of people as it deals with poor management, increased competition, declining sales, bankruptcy, or product life cycles. And a whole industry may cut back as it deals with business cycles, a recession, political changes, technological developments, or international competition.

If you are a one-income household, you are especially vulnerable and need to protect yourself against the financial impact of losing your job or being laid off temporarily.

Preventive Measures

The first way to lessen the impact of unemployment is to build skills that will help you quickly gain alternative employment. If you have strong communication and personal skills, along with state-of-the-art job skills in your field, you will stand a better chance of being employed quickly after losing a job. Still, the more senior you are or the worse the economy is, the longer the transition may take. Therefore, the second way to lessen the chance of a lost job becoming a long-term financial disaster is to have a strong network among people in your field who work with other companies. Many of the best jobs are never advertised, so having a good network before you need it is a good investment in time.

Another good habit is to watch business cycles. Many industrial workers found their jobs going overseas in the 1980s. The move didn't happen overnight, yet many workers did not begin to think about gaining skills in alternate fields until after they were laid off. The smart ones were learning skills that would be valued in a growing sector while they were still working full time. Keep your eyes open to trends and ensure that you are not the last buggy wheel maker collecting unemployment insurance.

Another thing to keep your eyes open for is the interpersonal landscape at work. As much as I would rather work be apolitical, the simple fact is that unless you are a sole proprietor, politics is happening all around you. Manage your risk by being aware of interactions in your workplace, by staying clear of power struggles that may leave you standing alone, and by keeping good relationships with a number of people senior to you.

Low Cost of Living

The first way that you can protect your finances from the damage unemployment can wreak is to keep your cost of living down so that you can comfortably get by on one salary, should the need arise.

· ·

Jo and Charlie made a smart decision when they moved in together. Jo's condo was big enough for two, so their cost of living fell substantially. "We decided to keep one salary aside for savings—retirement, the kids' college, a cash cushion, and for some of our dreams—and live on the other," Charlie said. Jo was thinking ahead when she agreed to see if they could manage on one salary alone. "I knew that it would give me the freedom to stay at home if we have kids. I've seen too many friends take a massive drop in their standard of living when they go from two salaries and two mouths to feed to one salary and three mouths. If we don't, we can loosen up a bit and know our future is well on the way to being taken care of." Yet it also gave them the side benefit of being able to deal with an unexpected turn in life. "When Charlie's company went under, we assumed he would get a new job in no time; he's good at what he does and respected in the field. But all of his colleagues were suddenly on the market, too, and it took him 5 months to find a similar position." Charlie saw some of his former colleagues really struggling to get by in that time. "One family had to sell their home. I was so grateful for the decision we had made earlier. It really took the pressure off and in the long run, we have only lost 5 months of savings. No debt, no foreclosure . . . nothing serious."

· ·

Even if you cannot live on one salary alone, keeping your cost of living down does increase your ability to deal with an unexpected loss of income.

Cash Cushion

Another component of your financial protection against unemployment is to have a good cash cushion that will cover your basic living costs, plus some extras that may arise, for at least 3 months. Many people skip having a good cash cushion because they know they can draw on their credit cards if they need access to emergency funds; however, that is a risky strategy. Not only does it raise stress—who wants to be interviewing for a new job while feeling there is a loudly ticking clock—but it can backfire if you are out of a job for a longer period than expected and find your cost of living *rising* as you struggle to make the interest payments on the growing debt. A cash cushion covers your cost of living—and the more modest your cost of living, the smaller your cushion can be—as well as extra costs such as a new outfit for interviewing.[1]

Unemployment Insurance

State governments have unemployment insurance programs for workers who are laid off "through no fault of their own," which is defined differently in every state. Unemployment insurance is not a substitute for having a good cash cushion because it is not sufficient to cover your costs, and many state plans have caveats that limit your ability to draw on it, but it may help a bit. Most states offer a percentage of your income for a period of up to 26 weeks. Links to your state's program can be found at http://workforce security.doleta.gov/map.asp.

Accidents and Loss

Accidents happen: car accidents, household accidents, random tripping-on-the-sidewalk accidents. Loss also happens: theft, vandalism, and those mysterious and often terrible "acts of God." Sometimes the damage is tangible (a car to replace, a medical bill to pay) and other times intangible (the trauma resulting in lost nights of sleep). The challenge with managing the risk of accidents

---

[1]For more details on calculating how large your cash cushion needs to be, see my previous book, *The Ms. Spent Money Guide: Get More of What You Want with What You Earn* (New York: John Wiley & Sons, 2001), 81.

is that you may suffer both damage and loss yourself, as well as cause damage and loss to others. And if you harm others, there is a reasonable chance that they will look to you for compensation.

· ·

Recently I went hiking along a rocky riverside trail near Washington, D.C. It was a sunny day in early fall, and people were out in droves, resulting in logjams where the trail narrowed to thin boulder-strewn scrambles. The trail is not particularly difficult; however, there are plenty of opportunities to turn an ankle, slip and fall on hard rock, or even fall off a cliff overlooking the Potomac River. For a few minutes, my friend and I trailed behind a group of 10 or so young kids supervised by two men who were constantly hollering commands. "Peter, slow down." "Wendall, stay on the trail." "Jen, use you hands to balance." I carried one kid's soda bottle, filled with muddy water and tadpoles, to free up his hands as he scrambled down a narrow ledge and listened to my friend talk to one of the men in charge. It turned out to be a birthday hike for his son's eighth birthday. Once the kid herders were out of earshot, we laughed as we both realized that our first thought had been that the father was brave to risk litigation if one of the kids was hurt while under his care.

· ·

In this litigious society, it is important to minimize the financial risks that you and your family face both by aiming to prevent accidents and by having the insurance you need to protect your assets in the case of an accident.

Preventive Measures

The best option is, of course, to prevent accidents and loss in any reasonable way that you can. You can't eliminate every risk. However, you can cut risk. At home, you can ensure that dangerous environments are fixed up, the home is childproofed adequately, smoke and radon or CO_2 detectors are installed and working, the home is well lit, hard to break into, and perhaps has an alarm system. On the street, you can drive a car with a good safety rating and equipment such as airbags and antilock brakes, improve your driving skills, and drive safely. In your family, you can teach your kids to act safely, think twice before buying a dog whose breed is known for violence, and make sure you never fall in love with a professional stuntman.

The key is to understand risk factors and do as much as is reasonable to manage risks. This advice is being given, however, by someone who has gone skydiving, climbed a mountain, and worked with dangerous power tools despite her reputation for being clumsy . . . so I am not suggesting that you avoid doing anything that you truly enjoy. Simply be careful.

Car Insurance

Even if your car is an old clunker not worth insuring itself, you should be insured against the damage that your car can do to other people and property. Chapter 16, Decision 2: What You Drive, summarizes ways to manage the cost of car insurance while still maintaining enough coverage.

Home Owner's Insurance

When you insure your home, you are insuring four things: the structure itself, the contents, liability for damage to people or property that happen on the property or are caused by a family member even when not on the property, and the cost of living elsewhere if your home is being repaired or rebuilt after an insured event. Most mortgage lenders require that you have a home owner's policy great enough to cover the cost of your structure. If you own a condo, the home owner's insurance covers the parts of the structure that you are responsible for.

A well-protected home costs less to insure, according to the Insurance Information Institute. "You can usually get discounts of at least 5 percent for a smoke detector, burglar alarm, or dead-bolt locks. Some companies may cut your premiums by as much as 15 percent or 20 percent if you install a sophisticated sprinkler system and a fire and burglar alarm that rings at the police, fire or other monitoring stations."[2] Further savings can be gained by insuring your home and auto through a single insurer.

The fine print of any insurance contract is significant and worth reading to ensure that you know what is excluded from coverage. Damage arising from floods or earthquakes is usually excluded, but many other potentially catastrophic events such as fire or hail are usually covered. Note that you are not covered for poor maintenance of your home, so don't expect the insurance company to come to your rescue if your roof falls in due to old age and a stiff wind. Loss or damage to some high-priced possessions, such as jewelry or computers, may be limited and supplemental insurance is required to cover them fully.

As with other insurance, raising your deductible will save you money. However, do this only if you have enough of a cash cushion to easily cover the additional out-of-pocket expense you will face if you make a claim.

To aid future insurance claims, periodically do a thorough inventory of your home's contents. Some of the optional coverages that you can purchase are outlined below.

Replacement Cost

Think about something you bought a few years ago for a reasonable amount of money. Let's say it's a coat or piece of electronic equipment that cost you around $400. If you had to sell it today on eBay, what would it be worth? $100? $20? Anything? It is critical that your home owner's (or renter's) insurance covers your goods for the replacement cost, not the actual cost less depreciation.

A higher level of coverage is guaranteed (or extended) replacement cost. This coverage ensures that your property will be rebuilt

---

[2]www.iii.org.

and possessions fully replaced even if the total is greater than your insurance limits. Also ask your insurer about inflation guard, which protects your home at a constant level as prices rise, and code guarantee, which ensures that your home will be repaired or replaced to current code requirements even if they change.

Natural Disasters

In the early 1990s, I lived in Los Angeles. A large earthquake struck, snapping freeways, eroding mountainsides, and damaging homes and offices. Surprisingly, that was the first time many people stopped to ask whether they were insured for earthquake damage. Unfortunately, many were not covered—earthquakes, like floods, are not usually covered under a standard policy—and since then, earthquake coverage has been next to impossible to purchase in Los Angeles.

Talk to your insurance agent *today* about what you are covered for, and get the price on any optional coverage you may have skipped over that you feel you need. If your house is in a flood zone, you may be required to take out supplemental flood insurance. Sometimes, however, the coverage you need may simply be unavailable at a reasonable price. Since September 11, 2001, there has been a significant revision of the risk businesses face from terrorist attacks. Not surprisingly, it has the insurance industry taking a long, hard look at what coverage it can afford to offer.

Renter's Insurance

If you do not own a home, you still need insurance. Your landlord's insurance covers the structure you live in, and she has liability for damage that may befall you or your possessions if she is negligent; however, she is not responsible for insuring your possessions. Renter's insurance protects the value of your personal property: furniture, clothes, electronics, and other possessions. It protects them from theft and damage from most causes. It is not particularly expensive, depending on how valuable your possessions are and whether there are any specific possessions that you need to insure separately, such as valuable jewelry or an expensive computer. And like home owner's insurance, it is important to get insurance that covers your goods for the replacement value.

Umbrella Liability

Your home owner's and auto insurance cover you for a certain level of liability for damage to people or property that is your or your family's fault; however, the coverage is often limited to $300,000 or less, depending on your policies. Umbrella liability increases your coverage and protects your assets. It protects you in the case that your other insurances do not have enough coverage. It can be used for incidents ranging from your dog biting a child (even if not on your property) to someone falling and injuring himself in your yard, to a car accident where you cause significant damage or injury. It generally runs a couple of hundred dollars a year for a $1 million policy, and it is well worth considering in this litigious age.

Illness or Disability

If you are young and healthy, your chances of becoming sick or disabled are higher than of dying. For example, a 35-year-old has more than a 40 percent chance of having a disability that causes a loss of work for 3 or more months before he reaches age 65, according to insurance industry statistics. And of those who become disabled at, say, age 35, 5 years later more than 50 percent will still be disabled and 12 percent will have died. One in seven people will become disabled for 5 years or more before he or she reaches 65.

Preventive Measures

The most important way that you can manage the risk of having your family crippled by illness or disability is to lower the risk of getting ill. Not all illness is preventable, of course. Many illnesses from the common cold to heart disease are less likely to harm people who are fit, are at an appropriate weight, and are healthy eaters. Cutting out clearly unhealthy habits—smoking, drinking excessively, eating foods high in fat—can also cut the cost of health care in the long run. Of course, healthy living is easier said than done. It's a cruel joke that so many things that are bad for you taste so good.

Another preventative measure that will lower the cost of health care and the chance of lost income due to illness or disability is to manage the risks that you expose yourself to. This advice is not an excuse to ignore the advice above—being a couch potato to avoid life's risks is pretty lame reasoning—but rather to take the extra moment to take basic precautions, such as buying a helmet for your scooter-riding kids. If you do take up a sport or activity that is known to be dangerous, take the time to learn it well so you can manage the risks. Also be aware that some jobs have inherently more risk than others.

Health Insurance

Health insurance comes in two flavors: fee for care, which allows users to choose their providers, and managed care. The latter, provided through health maintenance organizations (HMOs), preferred provider organizations (PPOs), and point-of-service (POS) plans, has been getting a bad rap of late. In the movie *John Q*, Denzel Washington plays a father who finds out his insurance won't pay for the life-saving heart transplant his child needs. His solution: hold the hospital hostage. My solution: read the fine print before you need to.

No matter what type of insurance you have, it is important to understand what is covered and how it works so you can minimize the total cost of your health care. For example, recently a doctor's bill arrived for the amount of $110. I was expecting a bill for a $10 copayment. A phone call to the doctor's office explained the discrepancy. I had called the office before making the appointment to specifically ask whether the doctor was part of my health insurance plan. They said yes, and I made the appointment. It turned out that they were a participant, not a listed provider; therefore, while I would pay less than if they had not participated in the plan at all, I was still stuck with an extra $100. They assumed I knew the jargon of my insurer. I assumed "yes" means yes.

Generally, you will receive or buy your health insurance through your employer. If both of you are employed by companies offering insurance, compare plans and choose the one with the best benefits. Some health insurance coverage may be optional, and your insurer may offer dental, optical, prescriptions, alternative medicine, and so on either in the main policy, for an additional fee, or not at all. If you are laid off, you can continue your insurance for 18 months under federal law (called COBRA); however, you may be charged for up to 102 percent of the cost of the insurance. If you are not offered insurance through an employer, you can usually buy it directly from an insurer or a managed care organization. Sometimes it pays to join a trade organization or group that offers group coverage.

Ask your employer if she offers a way for you to put pretax dollars aside for your out-of-pocket medical costs. The money needs to be used in the year it was put away; however, it is a good way to lower costs.

Disability Insurance

While worker's compensation will cover you against workplace accidents and your employer may even offer short-term disability benefits, you need to protect your income from illness or disability that prevents you from working for a long period. Social Security offers some coverage, but not enough for most families to live on comfortably. Some employers offer long-term disability insurance, or allow you to buy it through them; however, many people are not covered. Aim for coverage that is noncancelable and is guaranteed renewable, but understand that if it is offered through your employer, you may lose the insurance if you change jobs.

Aim to cover about two-thirds of your income. If the price is prohibitive, see if you can extend the amount of time it takes for the insurance to kick in, or cover for a short period, especially if you have already saved a decent amount for retirement and can draw on those funds when you hit 59½.

Long-Term Care Insurance

Long-term care (LTC) insurance provides for at home or nursing home care for an extended period. If you are 60 or older, this is an essential insurance and the later in life you buy it, the more it will cost. Start pricing policies at age 50 or 55. A friend's elderly mother required nursing home care for the last few years of her life. The bill? In a major city, close to $90,000 a year. Not convinced? Here are some sobering statistics: "The chances of using your homeowners insurance are about 1 in 88. The odds of using your auto insurance at about 1 in 47. The chances of using your LTC insurance is about 2 in 5," according to the insurance industry.[3] Make sure you buy coverage from a company that is large and stable: you want it to still be in business when you are very old and very gray.

Death

Deaths that make the news range from the tragic to the ridiculous. The Darwin Awards, which "commemorate those who improve our gene pool by removing themselves from it in really stupid ways,"[4] document some of the most unusual ways to die. Last year's batch included a Croatian student who died when he dropped a live grenade he was juggling at a party, an Italian woman who burned to death after apparently dousing anthills

---

[3]From the *Journal of the American Society of CLU*, 1996 as quoted on www.efmoody.com/insurance/disabilitystatistics.html.
[4]www.darwinawards.com.

with flammable liquid while she was smoking, and an American student who jumped down the laundry chute at a campus library, only to discover that libraries don't have laundries, but they do have trash compactors. It is hoped that none of us will ever make the cut.

Most people die of much more dull causes: heart disease, cancer, stroke, chronic lower respiratory disease, and unintentional injuries are the top five causes.[5] If you need cheering up, the government also reported that life expectancy is at a new high—76.9 years.

Preventive Measures

The sad thing is that for many people, death comes much earlier than it needs to come because they fail to take fairly basic preventive action. Staying fit, keeping your weight down, and eating a well-balanced diet go a long way toward living longer. And giving up the obvious bad habits of smoking, drinking too much too often, and driving like a bat out of hell would help too.

Now, I'm not advocating choosing a dull life; however, I am advocating having a healthy lifestyle if you want to live longer. Of course, if you haven't saved much for retirement, that heart attack you are headed for may be just the answer . . . .

Anyone who is on a fitness kick is bound to hear stories about the superathlete who died of a heart attack or got run over the day after finishing a marathon . . . usually recited by a flabby friend with a remote control in one hand and a fistful of Doritos in the other. Your friend is right—even the best prevention is not a cure for death. Therefore, at any age, it is worth thinking through some of the ways that you need to manage your money just in case the worst happens.

---

[5]"Deaths: Preliminary Data for 2000," *National Vital Statistics Report* 49, no. 123 (October 9, 2001): 2–3. Published by the National Center for Health Statistics and Centers for Disease Control.

Estate Planning

The most important part of planning for the worst is creating an estate plan. Depending on your net worth and your family situation, you may be able to get away with a fairly simple will. However, if your estate is significant, you need a more thorough estate plan. The threshold changes every year at the moment, so if you suspect that you may be a millionaire, you need a good will.

Estate planning attorneys say that one of the biggest mistakes people make is failing to know their net worth.[6] The Internal Revenue Service (IRS) taxes inheritances by as much as 55 percent, so a well-developed estate plan can save a small fortune in taxes or prevent a large fortune from being shrunk to a small fortune. Another classic error is to leave all of your assets to your surviving spouse, which can cost a fortune in avoidable taxes if your estate is large.

An estate plan is not just a will. It can include:

- *Will* stating how you wish your assets to be distributed on your death.
- *Living Trust*, instead of a will, offering a greater degree of control, asset protection, and privacy.
- *Pour-Over Will* ensuring that assets outside the Living Trust get included in the Trust on your death.
- *Durable Power of Attorney* allowing a named person to make financial and legal transactions on your behalf if you are disabled and unable to do so.
- *Health Care Power of Attorney* authorizing another person to make medical decisions on your behalf if you are incapacitated.
- *Living Will* determining your wishes if you are terminally injured or ill and on life support. It is also known as a physician's directive.

---

[6]Robert A. Esperti, Renno L. Peterson, and Edward L. Weidenfeld, *Generations: Planning Your Legacy—Practical Answers from America's Foremost Estate Planning Attorneys* (Denver, CO: Esperti Peterson Institute, 1999).

- *Personal Effects Statement* outlining items that you wish to give to a particular recipient that are not already specified in your will or trust.
- *Anatomical Gift Form* specifying if you wish to donate your organs.
- *Memorial Instructions* directing whether you want to be cremated or buried, and if you have specific requests for memorial service arrangements.

As you can see, a comprehensive estate plan involves some pretty grim things that you would probably rather not think about while you are healthy. The bottom line is that it can save your family so much financial and emotional stress that it is worth doing well. Note to control freaks: the aim of a good estate plan is to make it easier on your loved ones, not to play mind games from the grave. I'm sure everyone knows one horror story of a will that pulled the people left behind into a heart-wrenching squabble.

Chapter 14 covers how to choose an estate planner. If your needs are fairly simple, however, you may be able to create your own documents by using software such as *Quicken Lawyer*, *Kiplinger's Willpower*, or *Family Lawyer* by Broderbund.

Life Insurance

Life insurance is important for those years when you have financial obligations such as taking care of children, parents, or even your business. It pays a lump sum and, as a rule of thumb, you probably need five to eight times your annual salary, depending on your net worth and the likely expenses that would be faced by your family if you were not around to earn an income.

A mistake many couples make is to buy coverage only for the main earner in the household. However, if you have children, your family may be equally financially devastated by the loss of the primary caregiver. Similarly, couples without dependents often skip life insurance, when the surviving partner could not afford to keep the house on her income alone. In that case, buy enough insurance to pay some or all of the outstanding mortgage. Make sure both of you have appropriate coverage so that your standard of living would not drop substantially if one of you was not around.

Life insurance comes in two flavors:

1. *Term insurance* covers a certain period of time. Useful if you just need coverage while your kids are young or your mortgage is being paid. The premiums are lower than permanent insurance, but may increase if you renew the policy. If you want to continue the insurance after the selected period, a medical exam may be required.

2. *Permanent insurance* covers you for as long as you pay premiums, and the rate is locked in when the policy is written. It is more expensive than term insurance; however, it accrues value, so you will get money back if you cash it in before your death. You can also borrow against the cash value. The variations include universal, whole life, variable life, and variable universal, which offer differing degrees of flexibility.

Shop around for your life insurance; however, make sure that you are with a company that you feel sure will be around as long as you are.[7]

Passing on Assets Before Death

If you know that your estate will be significant, it may be wise to begin to hand on your money while you are alive so you can experience the joy that it can bring to your heirs or the charities that you support. U.S. tax law allows you and your partner to give $11,000 each to each person to whom you want to give money; however, there may be reason to hold back. For example, if you

---

[7]Check insurers' ratings at www.embest.com, www.standardandpoor.com, www.moodys.com, or www.weissratings.com.

have children or grandchildren who have not yet finished college, your gifts may decrease their ability to get financial aid, so it may make sense to hold back until they have been graduated before beginning to give them money.

Action Item: Audit Your Safety Net

Take at least one hour to sit down together and discuss your preparedness for each of the following:

- Unemployment
- Accident and loss
- Illness or disability
- Death

Make a list of what you want to do to sew up any holes in your safety net. Next to each item, designate a completion date, a person to take primary responsibility, and the next step. Revisit the list every two weeks until you have a well-structured safety net.

CHAPTER 14
....

Skill 7: Getting Help When You Need It

JUST AS A GOOD MANAGER SURROUNDS HERSELF WITH EXPERTS, A good financial relationship is supported by a variety of experts. Some professionals provide occasional advice or offer products that are best bought person-to-person, others play an ongoing role in your financial life.

Great advice may not come cheap. The first time I paid hundreds of dollars an hour for an expert's time, it hurt. However, the pain was much less than if I had not received the advice and instead made a mistake that could have cost me thousands.

"Hiring help does not mean giving up on doing it yourself; it means shoring up the areas in which you lack the confidence to make decisions," says Charles Jaffe, author of *The Right Way to Hire Financial Help*.[1] I'd take it further. Even in areas where you have the confidence to make decisions, an outside opinion can help. When at least one half of a couple is financially savvy, it's

---

[1]Charles A. Jaffe, *The Right Way to Hire Financial Help: A Complete Guide to Choosing and Managing Brokers, Financial Planners, Insurance Agents, Lawyers, Tax Preparers, Bankers, and Real Estate Agents* (Cambridge, MA: The MIT Press, 2001), 9–11. I strongly recommend this book for people looking to start their team—it goes into more detail than I have space for here, and is a well-written and thorough resource.

tempting to skip getting outside help. However, even the fittest people get physicals, and a financially fit couple should occasionally get an outside opinion just to make sure that their plans are on track. Recently investment firms have started offering an annual checkup for do-it-yourself investors—not trying to convert them into full-service clients, but recognizing that everyone can benefit from an expert's opinion once in a while. If being good at personal finance meant you didn't need help, the very wealthy would not have whole teams of accountants, lawyers, and investment advisors behind them. The opposite is true: wealthy people usually have great teams helping them grow and protect their wealth.

This chapter looks at experts ranging from financial planners to marriage counselors. What if you can't afford an expert's help or feel that you are just starting out? There are a lot of low-cost alternatives. For example, if you need a simple will, there is excellent low-cost software on the market. If you are a new investor, there are some great books, Web sites, and classes. If you can afford to use experts, educate yourself on the basics. It will help you to know what questions to ask and to determine if the advisor you are talking to has the background and approach that will work well for you.

Choosing Your Team

Once you decide to turn to an advisor for help, the question is, to whom? Do you do business with a friend or family member? Do you rely on recommendations? Do you work with the first person who approaches you? Do you figure it is all a crapshoot anyway and pick a name from the Yellow Pages? Each section below talks about some specific things to look for, but here are a few general rules. First, think hard before doing business with a friend or family member. Even if he or she is an expert in the field, it can be a bad move. When the service you are getting is great, there is no problem. However, if you have a concern or complaint, want to change advisors, or simply do not like his or her style, your relationship can create an awkwardness that may mean you do not ask for what you need. Unless it is a friendship that you would sacrifice for the sake of getting the service you need, keep business relationships strictly business.

Referrals are a good starting point, but not the only way to find someone. For example, when I first sought an investment advisor, I asked my tax accountant for names. Fearing my portfolio was too small for most people to take seriously, I went with the first person I spoke with because he knew what he was talking about (and I knew enough about investing to feel sure about that) and was willing to take on my fairly small retirement portfolio. Within a year, its value had shrunk by nearly 50 percent. Was he a bad choice? Well, the market declined substantially in that time, so I can't blame him entirely. However, I should have asked more questions and watched more closely to ensure that he was appropriately conservative during a market decline. He didn't sell stocks as they started to slide and we both sat there like deer in the headlights as many of the tech stocks he recommended declined 80 percent in value. It's understandable that I was scared, but he should have cut the losses well before the stocks declined that far. Use recommendations as a way to get a short list of good candidates, then interview them to find the best person for you to work with.

As far as advisors who approach you . . . never, *ever* buy a stock from someone who cold calls you by phone. There are too many horror stories, and a reputable advisor doesn't have to build business that way. It's also probably a bad idea to buy insurance and other financial products over the phone. Same goes for Internet solicitations touting a fabulous deal on life insurance, a great way to refinance debt, or a must-buy stock. It is hard for a good, new financial professional to build business, so while some of the people fishing for new clients may be very good, most are simply not experienced enough for you to trust your financial future to. No one sits at home waiting for a door-to-door salesman to sell her a vacuum cleaner—she goes to a large store and compares what's on the market. Same goes for financial and professional services. You have to shop around.

One other source for candidates to interview that you may want to try: newspapers and magazines. At the moment, I am compiling a list of the best financial advisors, estate planners, and so forth for the *Washingtonian*, a monthly magazine in the D.C. area. Such a list is a good source simply because the people on it have been recommended by their peers.

As for the Yellow Pages: They may be a good source for compiling a list for straightforward services such as insurance. For more complex services such as estate planning, the Yellow Pages should not be your first choice. However, they may help you build your list of potential candidates, if you cannot find people through word-of-mouth recommendations.

Once you have a list of potential candidates, the key is to interview them carefully. Most will not charge for a preliminary meeting—though you should check before you set up the meeting—and the remainder of this chapter helps you to know what to ask once you are talking with candidates. My old boss, Mark, used to chant the mantra "screen for competence, hire for chemistry." He's right: If you find several good candidates, the final decision should be based on how well you interact with the person. Charles Jaffe says: "It is a subjective decision in which your gut will determine a lot but your brain has to know enough to figure out what makes your stomach queasy. It can be a daunting task."[2]

Deciphering the Alphabet Soup

You will come across many "impressive" credentials when you hire an expert. It's important to know what they mean and whether they are valuable. The reason that this list in Table 14.1 is being presented up front is that you may come across people with the various designations in different fields. For example, a financial planner may have qualifications that have to do with selling investments, even though he or she is not primarily an investment advisor.

---

[2]Ibid., 9–11.

Table 14.1   Financial Service Industry Qualifications

ATA	Accredited Tax Advisor	Trained in tax advising, including tax planning for the highly compensated and owners of a closely held business, qualified retirement plans, and estate planning. At least 2 years experience and ongoing education requirements.
ATP	Accredited Tax Preparer	Trained in tax preparation for individuals. At least 1 year experience and ongoing education requirements.
CFA	Chartered Financial Analyst	Trained in securities and portfolio management and investment valuation and agreeing to certain ethical standard. References and work experience required. Over 26,000 CFAs.
CFP	Certified Financial Planner	Has passed extensive exams, has at least 3 years of client experience, and does continuing education focusing on financial planning. Ethical code of conduct. Over 55,000 worldwide.
CFS	Certified Fund Specialist	Trained in mutual funds. Short course of study and 2-hour exam. Continuing education and code of ethics requirements. About 10,000 have this designation.
ChFC	Chartered Financial Consultant	Financial planning, investment, and insurance qualification requiring a degree or experience. Continuing education and code of ethics require ments. Over 34,000 people have this designation.
CIMA	Certified Investment Management Analyst	Taken advanced week-long program in invest- ment management and theory. Has at least 3 years of experience. Continuing education requirements.
CIMC	Certified Investment Management Consultant	Passed two levels of National Association of Securities Dealers (NASD)-administered courses in investment theory and investment consulting. Continuing education and code of ethics requirements.
CIS	Certified Investment Strategist	Advanced training following completion of CIMA, covering advanced concepts and strategies in asset analysis, tax planning, and legal issues pertaining to investment consultants.

Table 14.1   *(continued)*

CLU	Chartered Life Underwriter	Trained in life and health insurance. Also has at least 3 years experience. Continuing education and code of ethics requirements. Over 88,000 people have this designation.
CPA	Certified Public Accountant	Extensive training in accounting. Completed degree and passed state exams. Ongoing education and ethical code. Can gain personal finance designation (see PFS). More than 600,000 CPAs.
CPCU	Chartered Property Casualty Underwriter	Trained in property and liability insurance, met experience requirements, and subject to a code of ethics. There are more than 49,000 CPCUs.
EA	Enrolled Agent	Tax preparer licensed by the federal government. Only EAs, attorneys, and CPAs may represent taxpayers before the IRS. Worked at IRS 5 years or passed exam including taxation of individuals, corporations, partnerships, estates, and trusts. Background check by IRS, ongoing education, and ethical standards.
ELS	Estate Law Specialist	New designation offered by the American Bar Association to lawyers who have taken advanced training in estate planning.
JD	Juris Doctor (Law degree)	Degree in law. Check to ensure that lawyers are licensed to practice in your state. May be a member of state or national bar association sections related to estate planning.
MBA	Masters of Business Administration	Has a masters degree in business that may not have included any classes in personal finance.
PFS	Personal Financial Specialist	Designation offered by the American Institute of Certified Public Accountants to CPAs who have completed additional training and have experience in personal finance. More than 2,500 awarded.

(continued)

Table 14.1   (*continued*)

RIA or RR	Registered Investment Advisor or Representative	Not an actual designation, but often used by people trained in trading securities and registered by the NASD. Check which series exams they have passed to determine what securities they are trained in. There are over 670,000 registered representatives in the United States. See also Series X.
RFC	Registered Financial Consultant	Trained in financial planning. Experience and ongoing education requirements. Ethical code. More than 1,600.
RHU	Registered Health Underwriter	Trained in disability, health, medical, and long-term care insurance. Experience, continuing education, and ethics standards. More than 6,000.
Series X	See also RIA/RR	Passed exams sponsored by the NASD that allows them to sell and advise about particular securities. There are a number of different series exams, the most common are listed below: Series 6: mutual funds, variable annuities, variable life insurance and unit investment trusts. Series 7: general securities, including stocks, REITS, options, government securities, and securities in Series 6. Series 11: limited to processing unsolicited orders.
Other		All sorts of credentials and certificates, degrees, masters, or even doctorates are offered in subjects related to personal finances. One good place to check on various credentials is www.advisorsdirectory.com/addi/designations.asp.

Financial Planner

Once upon a time, I visited a financial planner to get a second opinion on my plan and to double check that I was using appropriately conservative numbers. Although she was well qualified and associated with a high-profile financial planning expert, what I got back was a canned plan that ignored all the information I gave her about the age I expected to retire, the age that I would like the plan to last to, and so on. I should have invested more time in finding a planner who didn't have to rely on her boss's reputation.

A good financial planner is like an air traffic controller. He or she looks not only at your current financial life, but also at upcoming events and potential dangers. The result is a plan that encompasses most aspects of your financial life. If you have only one expert help you with your financial life, it should be a financial planner.

When to Get a Financial Planner

Don't wait until you are wealthy. A financial planner can help you *become* wealthy. Just as preventive medicine is better than waiting until you are sick, financial planning while you are starting out is better than waiting until you are so close to retirement that you cannot change the outcome in time. Unless you are deep in debt, *now* is a good time to start working with a financial planner. What if you are young, just starting out, and have no money? You will walk away with a plan that tells you how much you will need to save for retirement, and looks at other issues you need to think about, such as saving for a house or having children. If you have a more complex financial life and some assets already built, your financial plan will tell you if you are on track and highlight other issues to think about. Seeing a financial planner is a particularly good move if you have significant financial questions to answer, such as whether you should pay off a mortgage or invest in a rental property.

How to Choose a Financial Planner

Financial planning is confusing because there are planners who focus on creating a thorough plan for your financial life, and there are others who use a brief plan as a foot in the door for selling you products from insurance to investments. My goal in this section is to focus on pure planning: giving your financial life a good once-over and determining what you need to do today to reach your future goals. I talk about investment advisors and insurance sales agents later.

Any person can claim to be a financial planner, so it is very important to know what qualifications to look for. The Certified Financial Planners Board did a survey that found that more than half of the people they surveyed "feel that it's hard to know who's really qualified."[3] It's not surprising, because the range of qualifications that people have is an alphabet soup, as we saw in Table 14.1.

The first thing to look for is professional training. Seek a planner with the most respected qualifications: CFP, ChFC, or CPA with PFS specialization. There are good financial planners out there without these qualifications, but unless you are sure that they have a substantial base of clients, have significant training and experience in financial planning, and are up to date on the latest developments in the industry, keep looking.

Financial planners are compensated in different ways. Some are "fee only," that is, they charge by the hour or a set fee for the thinking they do for you. Others are partially or wholly compensated by commissions earned from products they sell, such as insurance or investments. Under the code of ethics that financial planners agree to, they should base their recommendations on what is best for the client, not the potential commissions they earn. However, there is an inherent conflict of interest if they sell you anything that earns them a commission or bonus of any kind. You have the right to ask if they earn or receive anything for the products they recommend to you. You are under no obligation to buy products through the planner, and you should shop around for the best price on insurance.

Some financial planners also hope that you will invest through them. However, my bias is toward finding a separate investment

---

[3] CFP Board national consumer survey of 897 upper-quartile households of all ages, December 1999.

advisor to manage your money. Why? Simply because there are not enough hours in the day for a financial planner to stay on top of developments in financial planning *and* research good investments. In addition, many base their recommendations on a relatively limited number of funds that their company has agreed to distribute. If you use a financial planner who is also an investment advisor, see the section on investment advisors to find out more about checking up on his or her qualifications.

Questions to Ask

- What does your practice involve? Do you sell investments as well as create financial plans?
- What are your qualifications?
- How do you charge clients?
- Do you offer a preliminary interview at no charge?
- Can you show me a sample financial plan?

Resources

- www.cfp-board.org/cons_main.html allows you to check up on financial planners who say they are a CFP, and offers information on choosing a planner and your rights as a client.
- www.napfa.org offers referrals to fee-only planners and a brochure on how to choose a financial planner.
- www.fpanet.org offers referrals to its members, who are all CFPs.
- www.financialfinesse.com offers referrals to rigorously screened financial planners throughout the country.

Investment Advisor

Managing money can be a time-consuming second job if you invest in individual stocks or try to select the best mutual funds. There's simply so much to track unless you buy and hold investments for long periods (which, of course, you should do, but it's hard to keep your resolve when markets jump about). The first time I considered getting an investment advisor was when I realized that I was logging on daily to check the status of the stocks I owned. I was spending too much time second-guessing my own guesses. However, you are never handing over full responsibility for your portfolio. Even if you give an investment advisor the right to make trades on your behalf (discretionary trading, which is usually not a good idea), it is still your money. Your broker is not the one who will go hungry if he loses all your money.

When to Get an Investment Advisor

Nobody needs an investment advisor, and the markets are becoming more democratic, thanks to the Web, as individuals get access to top quality research and fast simple charting. However, once your assets have reached a certain level, say, at least $50,000 to $100,000, you may want to outsource the decision-making process to an investment advisor, sometimes also called a money manager, stockbroker, or broker. Some financial planners offer investment advice; however, you are likely to be better served by someone who regards watching investments as her full-time job. How much money is enough? Often people put off getting help, fearing that they are the small fish in a big pond, and have to wait until they are wealthy. However, Jaffe advises that it is simply a case of choosing the right person for your financial stage. "You can bet that the hotshot broker with the $100,000 minimum account is not interested in placing your first-ever $500 purchase of stocks. But there are plenty of established advisers out there who take on small clients at reasonable prices."[4]

You don't *need* an investment adviser to buy stocks or funds, though some funds are sold only through advisors. If your portfolio is $10,000 or less, you may be better off simply opening an on-line trading account and buying some index funds. Do-it-yourself investors can pay for a portfolio checkup every so often,

---

[4]Jaffe, *The Right Way to Hire Financial Help*, 13.

getting a professional to check their diversification and to watch for overlapping mutual funds.

How to Choose an Investment Advisor

In *The Millionaire Next Door*, Thomas J. Stanley and William D. Danko emphasize the importance of investing time in the search for the right advisor. "The more intellect, time, and energy you spend in hiring a financial advisor, the more likely you will be to find a suitable one."[5]

The first thing to look for is professional qualifications—a Series 6 or 7 license—and a clean record. The Series 6 or 7 license merely gives the broker a right to buy and sell investments. You may even find that a financial planner who deals with your investments does not have those licenses because another person in his firm recommends and implements investment strategies. Table 14.1 should help you sort through the range of acronyms, but particularly look for CFA, one of the hardest qualifications to get, CFP, CFS, or CMFC.

Your money is on the line in this relationship more than any other, so be dogged about getting all the information you need to be comfortable that the broker is good at her job and good to work with. You can ask for clients who can give references, ask if the firm is a member of the Securities Investor Protection Corporation (SIPC), which guarantees some of your investments if the company goes bust, and check for a clean record through state regulatory arms of the NASD if you have the broker's Central Registration Depository (CRD) number. In addition, ask to see parts one and two of her "form ADV," an annual regulatory report. Any broker who gets defensive about giving you her CRD number or both parts of form ADV is not someone you want to do business with.

---

[5]Thomas J. Stanley and William D. Danko, *The Millionaire Next Door* (New York: Pocket Books, 1996), 129.

Investment advisors tend to charge in one of two ways: a percentage of the total portfolio value that they manage for you or a commission per transaction. The problem with the second way of being compensated is that it creates a conflict of interest because the advisor doesn't get paid if you are not buying and selling stocks. Many manage that challenge well, but there are stories of advisors who "churn" their clients' portfolios, that is, they recommend excessive buying and selling in order to generate greater commissions. Some firms charge account management fees on top of commissions. My preference is to work with people who charge a percentage of the portfolio because there are no conflicting interests.

Questions to Ask

- What are your qualifications?
- What is your CRD number?
- What is the size of the minimum and average portfolio you manage?
- How do you charge your clients?
- What range of investment products do you work with?
- How will you choose what investments to recommend?
- How will you interact with us when you have a change you want to make in the portfolio?
- What are your criteria for recommending a stock or fund?
- What are your criteria for selling one?
- Can we see parts one and two of your form ADV?

Resources

- www.nasdr.com/investors.asp allows you to check up on a registered representative in your state.
- www.sipc.org allows you to check whether the financial institution you are thinking of doing business with is a member of the SIPC.

Accountant or Tax Advisor

The U.S. tax code is a complex and confusing creature. It entangles the minds of legislators, regulators, professionals, and regular little taxpayers like you and me. Even full-time professional tax experts can't agree on the meaning of every part of the tax code. One personal finance magazine gave a fictitious household's information to several top accountants and wrote an article highlighting how each professional's understanding of the tax law and calculations differed. How does the government expect us to manage on our own?

The aim of the game is to pay only the tax that you are legally obliged to pay—not a cent more or a cent less. Sometimes we need help working out how much that is. Software and well-written tax guides help many couples who have straightforward taxes to prepare their own returns; however, sometimes professional advice is needed. Accountants and tax preparers can help you manage your taxes proactively, by advising you on actions that can help or harm your tax situation, and reactively, by preparing your tax return.

When to Get an Accountant or Tax Advisor

The main reason to use an accountant or tax advisor is to manage a complicated tax return. The times when I have turned to an expert include starting out in my own business, buying my first home, selling an investment property, managing my first ever profits and losses from shares, and relocating for work. Could I have figured the return out for myself? Probably. However, even the accountant found some of the challenges I threw at him tough, so I'm glad I chose to let an expert handle it. A good accountant will leave you enough of a paper trail that you can try it on your own the next year, if you want to.

Another way accountants or tax advisors can help is when you are planning your financial moves. They can give you a heads up about the complications that you are creating *before* you create them. They can also meet with you before the end of the tax year to help you take the actions you need to lower your tax obligation.

Some people use an accountant or tax advisor because they are simply disorganized or lazy. Hey, if you would rather just take a shoebox full of receipts in and dump it on someone's desk and say "handle it," that's fine. But the bigger the mess, the bigger the bill. Also, if you have failed to keep receipts and records, your accountant can't help you find all the deductions you may be eligible for.

If you have a straightforward tax return—income from your employer and some investments, fairly normal deductions, perhaps a mortgage or two—then you should be able to manage your own tax return. There are some great software packages, including some that interact directly with personal finance packages such as *TaxCut* from H&R Block and Quicken's *TurboTax*.

How to Choose an Accountant or Tax Advisor

If your neighbor's cousin brags about an accountant that gets every possible deduction "including every vacation I have taken in the last year," steer clear. You want to get every legal deduction you are entitled to, but beware of the tax preparer who tries to stretch the truth.

Anyone can call him or herself an accountant or tax preparer. I'd prefer to use great software than rely on someone whose background I was unsure of, so look for a tax planner or preparer with solid qualifications. The best qualification for an accountant is a Certified Public Accountant (CPA), which means the person has a degree in accounting, has passed a national test, and has maintained his qualification through continuing education. Another type of professional is an Enrolled Agent (EA). EAs are certified by the IRS and can represent you before the IRS if you are audited. Two other qualifications to look for: Accredited Tax Planner or Accredited Tax Advisor (ATP or ATA). Both are tax specialists.

Questions to Ask

- What are your qualifications?
- What does your practice involve?
- What percentage of your work is with individual tax returns?
- What is your approach toward getting deductions?
- How do you charge for your services?

Resources

- www.aicpa.org/yellow/ypascpa.htm offers links to each state's CPA society, many of which have a referral service. In my area, however, the referral service listed only a few local firms.
- www.acatcredentials.org has a listing of professionals with ATA and ATP qualifications.
- www.naea.org lists qualified enrolled agents.
- www.irs.gov has tax forms and a slew of information about the tax code. Also offers advice on specific situations, though just because the IRS tells you something does not guarantee that the information is correct (gotta wonder about a tax code that is that confusing!).

Estate Planner

An estate planner is a lawyer who helps you prepare for life events you never want to think about: death, disability, and someone else getting to enjoy the spoils of all your hard work. The financial and legal impact of your death or disability can be managed ahead of time in a way that the emotional impact cannot be.

When to Get an Estate Planner

A good estate plan makes sure that your assets go to your loved ones (the beneficiaries you choose), not your unloved ones (exes, evil stepchildren, the IRS). Of course, the less money you have, the less likely estate planning is an issue. As I write this, a law has been passed in the United States that changes the amount that can be handed on to your beneficiaries without being hit by a estate tax every year until 2010. As a rough rule of thumb, if you have assets of $1 million or more, you should talk to an estate planner. However, even if your assets are not that large, an estate plan may be important. Some of the circumstances an estate planner can help you manage are: caring for elderly parents, caring for a disabled child, and complex wills or trusts with beneficiaries such as stepchildren, half children, same sex partners, or animal companions. They can help you manage your assets not only in the case of death, but also if you are disabled.

If your financial and personal life are pretty straightforward and your assets not significant, you can probably get away with a will and other documentation created by a software package.[6] If you have children, however, be sure the plan you create doesn't hand over all your assets when they are young (under 21) in the case of both parents' death.

Once you have an estate plan, you need to revisit it when life circumstances change: divorce, death of a spouse, change of beneficiaries, relocation to another state (different states have different laws, meaning some changes to your estate may be needed).

How to Choose an Estate Planner

Any lawyer can whip up a will for you, but estate planning is a very specialized area and a good advisor has a depth of knowledge that your local all-purpose attorney will not have. Washington, D.C., estate planner and author Ed Weidenfeld recommends that you choose someone who specializes in estate planning because it is a complex, rapidly changing field. Ideally he should be a member of the Tax Section or Real Property, Probate, and Trust Law Section of the American Bar Association or the Trust, Estate, and Probate section of the state bar association. Make sure that he is licensed to practice in your state. Also find out what his philosophy is: You should seek someone who aims to preserve and manage your assets through death as well as disability.

Estate planners will charge either an hourly fee or a set fee to create your estate plan, which they can only determine after get-

---

[6]For more about estate planning software, see Chapter 13, Skill 6: Creating a Safety Net for Two.

ting to know enough about your situation to determine whether your estate will be particularly complex. My preference is a set fee simply because it is very hard for a layperson to guess how long it will take a lawyer to draft all the documents.

You can find an estate planner through, in order of preference, referrals (preferably from a lawyer, accountant, or financial planner), your local bar association, and the Yellow Pages. Once you have a couple of leads, call to ask questions about the planner's qualifications and memberships, his fee structure, his approach, and how he works with people. Although it's nice to get someone you feel comfortable working with—you will, after all, be covering some sensitive topics—this is not someone you will meet with often, so it is more important to find someone who is very competent.

Questions to Ask

- What does your practice involve?
- What percentage of your practice deals with estate and trusts?
- What sections of the state and American Bar Association are you a member of?
- Are you a member of the local estate planning council?
- What is your philosophy toward estate planning?
- How do you charge clients?
- Do you offer a preliminary interview at no charge?

Resources

- www.abanet.org/rppt/public/home.html provides a good overview of wills and trusts.
- www.findlegalhelp.com is a directory of lawyers run by the American Bar Association.
- www.lawyers.com is a directory of lawyers managed by Martindale-Hubble that has detailed descriptions of lawyers' training and specialties.

Insurance Agent

Every time I get my car serviced, I feel like I am at the mercy of a bunch of guys who use a language I don't understand to sell me a fix I don't necessarily need for a cost I would rather not pay. Buying insurance can feel the same way. It can involve profit through obfuscation: Lots of big clauses, little add-ons, and really fine writing means that it is hard for a layperson to understand exactly what she is buying and whether she is paying a fair price. A good insurance agent will cut through confusion. A bad one will use it to his advantage.

When to Get an Insurance Agent

As more people shop for insurance on-line, there seems to be less need for insurance agents. However, I am still a big fan of having an agent for a number of reasons: First is that you will have one person who can look at the range of your insurance needs and help make sure you are not over- or underinsured. The second is so you have a name and face to deal with at a large organization where it is easy to feel overlooked. In addition, if you have a number of different policies with one organization (house, car, liability), an agent can ensure that you are getting all the discounts offered. But the biggest reason to go through an agent is that you will have someone on your side if you have made a number of claims and the insurance company is considering dropping your coverage.

The times most people talk to an insurance agent is when they buy or sell a car or house, gain a spouse or dependent, or change their work situation. However, it is usually better to think about insurance before you take action. For example, an agent can help you winnow down the list of cars you are considering buying by letting you know if any of them are substantially more expensive to insure.

When it comes to life insurance and disability insurance, as soon as you have financial obligations that cannot be met by one of your incomes alone, you need to talk with someone about having life and disability insurance. Another important time is when you have dependents, especially children.

How to Choose an Insurance Agent

Insurance agents come in two flavors: independent or exclusive. Independents shop around a number of providers to get you the best coverage, whereas exclusive agents sell one company's insurance. Often you will need more than one agent as many exclusive agents work with companies that do not offer a full range of products. For example, my insurer offers auto, home, umbrella liability, and life, but not health or disability.

Just as with every commission-based sales person, an insurance agent has an incentive to sell you as much of her product as possible or, in the case of an independent agent, the insurance that garners her the greatest commission. However, a good agent will help you understand what products you need and how to get discounts. Agents can earn very large commissions the year they write a policy, yet you want an agent who will provide good service for years to come, so get referrals from friends or colleagues who have been in your area for a while and have made at least one claim.

Agents selling life insurance may hold a CLU or ChFC designation. States also provide licenses and log complaints against trouble agents. Another critical thing to look for is the financial stability of the underlying insurer. Otherwise, the most important thing to look for from any agency is a history of doing business in your community and membership in industry organizations with meaningful standards of ethics.

If in doubt, get a second opinion. You are shopping not only for price, but also for service.

Questions to Ask

- What is your training and do you have any professional credentials?

- What types of insurance do you offer?
- Do you carry the insurance products of one or multiple insurance firms? Which firms?
- How long have you been in insurance? How long with this company?
- How can you help me get the cost of my insurance down?
- What is your insurance license number?

Resources

- www.iii.org has about all the information you could want on any type of insurance. A great resource.
- www.insweb.com and www.quotesmith.com are two good Internet sites for getting insurance quotes.
- www.naic.org/1regulator/usamap.htm provides a list of insurance regulators.
- Check insurers' ratings at www.standardandpoor.com, www.embest.com, www.moodys.com, or www.weissratings.com.

Debt Counselor

Debt counseling can be viewed as bankruptcy intervention. Debt counselors help you before your house of credit cards comes tumbling down. Although they cannot help you manage all debt—secured debt, such as a mortgage or car loan, is off limits—they can create a strategy for digging yourself out. They may consolidate your loans into a single payment and negotiate lower payments.

When to Get a Debt Counselor

Do you dread opening the mail for fear of more overdue notices? Get phone calls from creditors at dinnertime? Wake up screaming from nightmares about drowning? It's time for a debt counselor. It's best to see a debt counselor as soon as you realize that you are having trouble meeting your obligations. Even if your financial life is falling apart before your eyes, a debt counselor is a better place to start than a bankruptcy specialist. The difference is that a debt counselor tries to keep you out of bankruptcy, a bankruptcy lawyer is paid to get you into it. Bankruptcy is not something to be taken lightly; it takes years to regain your good financial name. It affects your ability to borrow money, rent apartments, or get a job. Bankruptcy is truly a last resort.

If you are in minor financial difficulty, just beginning to feel the pressure of juggling loan payments, your bank may be able to help you manage your debt by consolidating your credit card loans into a home equity loan. It's a good place to start if you are not sure that you are in bad enough shape for debt counseling.

How to Choose a Debt Counselor

The Federal Trade Commission warns consumers to read between the lines when companies advertise that they can consolidate your loans into one easy payment: Often they are not selling debt counseling, but bankruptcy. "You'll find out later that such phrases often involve bankruptcy proceedings, which can hurt your credit and cost you attorneys' fees."[7] There are other shady operators out there charging high monthly fees or hiding a large upfront fee in the small print. Skip the chance of getting ripped off by finding a credit counselor through either the National Foundation for Credit Counseling (NFCC) or the Association of Independent Consumer Credit Counseling Agencies (AICCCA). They represent ethical, nonprofit debt counselors. Fees run from $0 to $75 for the initial counseling, with monthly charges of $0 to $20 (or up to $50 for independent agencies) if you pay your bills through them. The service is largely funded by the creditors receiving the money, not by the debtor paying the debt off.

---

[7]Advertisements Promising Debt Relief May Be Offering Bankruptcy. On www.ftc.gov/bcp/conline/pubs/alerts/bankrupt.htm.

Questions to Ask

- Are you a member of the NFCC or AICCCA? (If not, run!)
- What charges will I be expected to pay?
- What is included in the counseling?

Resources

- www.debtadvice.org is the NFCC's consumer help page, offering links to well-screened credit counseling services.
- www.aiccca.org offers links to well-screened independent debt counselors.
- www.ftc.gov is the Federal Trade Commission's site with excellent materials on credit issues in its consumer protection section.
- www.debtorsanonymous.org offers 12-step style group meetings for people who have trouble getting a handle on their spending.

Therapist or Marriage Counselor

This book was written because financial and emotional issues get muddled at times. Sometimes the solution to marital bickering about money involves getting financial expertise on board, whereas at other times all the money savvy in the world isn't going to change the destructive pattern.

Couples fight about money because couples fight. A therapist or marriage counselor can, at the very least, help you learn how to fight fair. At best, he can help you heal the emotional patterns that lead you into a frenzy of overspending, a deep fear of not having enough, a strong need to control your partner's actions, or other emotional drama underlying your financial tragedy.

When to Get a Therapist or Marriage Counselor

If money issues have become a major source of tension in your relationship and you are unable to find a way of talking through the money issues without setting off a larger number of emotional issues, then it is time to get some help.

Marriage counseling isn't only for marriages that are on the rocks. It can help you learn how to communicate about money without spiraling into a fight, how to discuss money without dredging up old issues, and how to put the past hurts behind you so you can move to a more positive relationship.

First, decide whether you need counseling together or separately. If you agree that there is a problem that is potentially damaging to your relationship, starting out together is a great idea. Even if you find that the underlying problem is an emotional issue that just one of you has to deal with, it is valuable to learn how the other partner can support the change that one is trying to make. You can always cut back to being counseled alone. What if you think it is an issue that needs to be dealt with as a couple but your partner doesn't agree? It is better to start alone and get some tools for talking about the issues you face than not to start at all.

How to Choose a Therapist or Marriage Counselor

Some therapists or marriage counselors shy away from financial issues because they are not aware of or willing to explore the emotional issues lurking below. "Marriage and family therapists are trained to serve families who present a diverse range of problems. However, there seems to be a glaring deficiency in training marriage and family therapists to deal with married couples who are experiencing financial conflicts."[8]

In my life I have seen therapists for a range of reasons. They come in all shapes and sizes. There was one who had overly strong opinions about choices I should make. There was another who barely grunted and felt I would find all my own answers if I floundered out loud in his office for long enough (at $150 an hour!). It

---

[8]Stanley W. Koutstaal, "What's Money Got to Do with It: How Financial Issues Relate to Marital Satisfaction" (Ph.D. diss., Texas Tech University, 1998), 1.

is only by trying different people with different training and styles that I have found what works for me. Don't be afraid to give a few therapists a test drive: If you feel uncomfortable talking with him or her or feel there is nothing useful to work with after a couple of sessions, move on. That is not to say that you should look for a quick fix, but you do need someone you feel you can trust and who is helping you move forward.

Just as with financial experts, the counseling world has a smorgasbord of acronyms to sort through. Seek a well-qualified therapist with a master's degree or well-respected credentials.

Many people find it hard to ask for referrals to a therapist or counselor for fear of letting the world know that they're having a problem. You can ask for suggestions from friends who have been through rough times, your doctor, a minister or rabbi, or another trusted source. Check whether your health insurance covers counseling for you and your spouse and if it does, see if its list of providers includes any therapists. You can even resort to the Yellow Pages and simply ask a series of questions.

You are looking for the content of their answers, as well as whether you feel comfortable asking questions and are comfortable with their style of interacting with you.

Questions to Ask

- What training do you have and where did you get it?
- What credentials do you hold?
- Did you do a clinical residency?
- How long have you been in practice?
- Do you work with couples and individuals?
- How would you describe your style of interacting with clients?
- What are your fees?

Resources

- The American Psychological Association's national referral center is at 1-800-924-6000 and can put you in touch with a local referral center.

- www.aamft.org/therapistlocator is the American Association of Marriage and Family Therapy's referral service.
- www.find-a-therapist.com has a listing that includes all qualified therapists who apply, as well as a selective list (only 5 percent of applicants are accepted) of "e-therapists" who practice therapy on line and are screened.
- www.4therapy.com is another on-line listing that seems to attract well-qualified professionals.

Other Experts

Throughout your relationship, there may be times when you need to call on other experts. Other specialists out there include:

- *Lawyer.* There are many reasons that you may call on lawyers. If one or both of you are self-employed or own a business, if you have a dispute with a neighbor or service provider, if one of your kids decides to impress her friends by shoplifting . . . each circumstance will probably need a lawyer with a different specialty. It is good, however, to have a general family lawyer who can be a first point of contact and who will be able to refer you to a specialist when you need one.
- *Mortgage broker.* Unlike a bank, which offers you only its own mortgage products, a mortgage broker shops around a variety of lenders to find the most appropriate loan at the best price. She is paid a commission by the lender so that does not make the loan any more expensive for you. I have found that these brokers often get a better deal for me than if I go through a bank directly.
- *Forensic accountant.* If you are getting divorced and don't believe that you are seeing all of your spouse's assets, a forensic accountant can track down your partner's assets and help you substantiate your claim on those assets.
- *Private banker.* Many banks target wealthy families and offer a greater level of service, hoping, of course, that the family

keeps more of its assets and gets more of its loans through the bank. A private banker offers the sort of personalized service that any good customer got from his friendly bank manager a generation ago. Generally, if you are wealthy enough to be a candidate for such services, financial institutions will already be wooing you.

Four Lifestyle Decisions That Make or Break Your Finances

Becoming a Conscious Couple, at least as far as your finances are concerned, takes more than just fiscal discipline. As we have seen, working together as a couple, communicating well with each other, and having the services of a good team can be critical as you create a shared financial life. Yet even with the best set of skills, your financial life will create friction if you live beyond your means. Part Four looks at the biggest financial decisions you will make as a couple and how to manage them.

Four decisions can make or break your finances. Although these are not the only important decisions you will make, they have the most lasting impact on your personal finances. They are significant because each is a lifestyle decision that has a substantial impact on your cost of living year after year after year.

The first decision is where you live: what type of house, what neighborhood, and how often you change your housing. The second decision is what you drive: what sort of vehicle, whether you own one car or two, how you insure your car, and whether you let your kids drive it. The third decision is whether you have children. Having children is not traditionally a financial decision, but it has massive financial implications. The fourth decision concerns retirement. When you retire makes a big difference on how much you need to save and how much financial freedom you will have in later life. It is possible to make smart decisions in these areas—home, car, kids, and retirement—and still go broke by making silly choices for the rest of your spending. However, the numbers are on your side. The average U.S. household spends close to half of its after-tax income on housing and vehicles alone. Managing those two expenditures gets you well on the way to financial fitness. Having a child will cost almost as much as buying a home, possibly much more, and the child doesn't come with a guarantee of accommodation for the rest of your lifetime! Understanding the magnitude of your decisions about your family structure is important. Finally, the dream of early retirement clashes with the financial truism of compounding returns. The earlier you start dipping into your retirement savings, the less chance it will have had to grow to a significant nest egg. We look at the math behind making your retirement dreams come true.

If you make the right decisions as a couple in these four areas (there is no objective answer about what is right, simply what is right for the two of you and your financial situation), your financial relationship is likely to be much more blissful over the years.

CHAPTER 15

Decision 1: Where You Live

HOUSING IS THE SINGLE LARGEST EXPENSE FOR MOST HOUSEHOLDS. Your decision about where you live will influence almost one-third of all your spending. The decision not only has a large price tag, it has a long shelf life: most people live with—or, rather, in—their decision for several years at least. If you overspend on housing, you are likely to have to carry that mistake for years. Where you live, therefore, deserves your best thinking.

Housing is taking an ever larger slice of the spending pie for most households. Why? Because people are living in larger and larger homes with amenities regarded as luxuries only a generation ago, and also because banks and financial institutions are egging them on by granting larger mortgages. They are lending more compared not only to the income a household earns, but also to the value of the property. A generation ago a bank would lend you only 28 percent of your gross income and would expect you to put a 20 percent down payment on the house. Today, banks are stretching the percentage of income they will lend and only expecting a deposit of 10 percent, 5 percent, or even zero.

This chapter is about where you live, whether you should buy or rent, whether you should move or stay put, and how to manage the cost of this major expense.

How Much House Do You Need?

You have a lot of control over the cost of your housing. You probably can't negotiate your rent or mortgage where you currently live, but you can make very conscious decisions about how much you want to spend on housing today and in the future.

A little frugality goes a very long way in housing. I don't expect you to stay in a studio apartment while stashing away a heap of cash; however, keeping your housing costs lower than your income would suggest can buy you long-term financial freedom. I have always chosen to live in much less of a home than I could afford, and the result has been that I have had money to spare for saving aggressively, traveling to over 40 countries, and trying my hand as a writer.

Many couples get on the bigger-better-bigger-better treadmill without thinking. First comes love, then comes marriage, then comes a moving van full of fancy china. I challenge you to think very consciously about your decision regarding housing because even a hundred dollars a month variation in your housing costs can add up to substantial amounts over time.

As renters, couples are often conscious about keeping their spending down. However, many couples fall into the trap of buying as much as they can afford, aspiring to a big new house in the best neighborhood. And if they can't afford the lifestyle they want now, they buy anyway (simply because they can afford something) and upgrade a few years down the track. That striving for more and more house can keep couples struggling for a lifetime. The size, age, and location of your house can have a substantial impact on your spending.

Big Versus Small

Size costs. A large house will have you opening your wallet more often than a smaller house even if the purchase price is similar. More rooms to furnish, more windows to dress, more yard to take care of, more space to heat or cool, and more contents to insure.

Yet many people with minimansions, McMansions, or starter cas-
tles, as social scientists have nicknamed them, still spend most of
their time in three rooms: the kitchen/family room, the bedroom,
and the bathroom.

. . . .

Recently I chatted with a young couple in New York, who live in a
small apartment, ridiculously expensive for its size, but typical in
Manhattan. The husband commented that having such a small
apartment forced them to be smart. "We simply don't buy books.
Furniture shopping is out unless we have to replace something. We
don't have the room to accumulate stuff. We can't have dinner par-
ties, but we didn't have many in our big old house in Michigan ei-
ther. It's surprising to find how much a small space disciplines our
spending."

. . . .

How much space do you really need? How will your needs
change as your family situation changes? If you want extra space
so you can entertain occasionally and have guests rarely, think
twice about how much being hospitable is costing you. That extra
space may eat up so much of your disposable income that overall
you end up with a lower quality of life, despite a higher quality of
living. Buy a home large enough for current and easily anticipated
future needs, but don't buy more space than you need just because you can afford it.

Here Versus There

The single biggest influence on the amount you will spend on housing over time is the location in which you live. Location can be
looked at on several levels: country, state, city, and neighborhood.

Most people don't consider moving to another country in
order to lower the cost of housing; however, more retirees are
looking to countries with lower costs of living. In Costa Rica, I saw

billboards for beach communities featuring on-site medical care, high-speed Internet access, airport proximity, and golf courses designed by famous players. Their target market is clear: American retirees.

Another alternative is to live in another country as an expatriate for a multinational employer. A friend was recently moved to Hong Kong by his employer. He not only had his move paid for, he also receives a substantial housing allowance.

· ·

Steve drives 45 minutes to work every day. "I hate the commute, but it simply makes sense." He works on the outskirts of Chicago, Illinois, but lives in the neighboring state of Indiana with his wife who is a stay-at-home Mom and their three kids. "Taxes are lower, schools are better, and houses cheaper. In Illinois, we would have a much higher cost of living to live in an area with comparable schools. I figure the time I spend in the car is a good investment in our standard of living and our kid's future." Another bonus of choosing to live in another state: Steve and Suzannah's children will qualify for in-state tuition at the University of Indiana, Suzannah's alma mater, which is less than one-third what nonresidents pay. "I loved it there: a good school at a great price. We will save a lot if the kids buy my sales pitch about what a great school it is."

· ·

Although your career and family are likely to be the main factors behind which state you live in, the cost of living may be another factor to consider in your choice. You may be better off taking a job—even at lower pay—in or near a city or state with cheaper housing, good tax rates, or top quality state colleges.[1] A small difference in tax rates can add up to a very significant amount over a lifetime.

------

[1]A cost-of-living calculator showing average numbers for everything from car insurance to health care can be found at www.bestplaces.net, along with tools to search for areas with good schools, great weather, low crime, and so on.

As you look around neighborhoods, take into account the variety of financial and other factors that add up to a smart decision: cost of houses, quality of schools, amenities of area, crime, access to public transportation, commute to work, and so on. Let's take a quick look at two of the most pertinent.

Schools

If you are parents, a major factor to consider is the schools. Throughout your children's younger years, the school district your home is in can make the difference between a good or bad education. I used to live on the border of Maryland and Washington, D.C., and housing prices jumped more than $30,000 as buyers crossed the road. Why? Tax rates are lower in Maryland, and schools are known to be significantly better. The bigger demand for Maryland properties drove the prices higher. Becki, a Texas attorney with three teens, warns that schools in a high-end district can bring a lot of hidden costs to parents. "If you live in a very rich district, most children over 16 will have cars, and children without cars will be at a social disadvantage. Kids are much pickier about their cars than they were when I was a kid—old beaters may actually increase the likelihood of ostracism. There can be issues with clothing, too, since children from rich districts usually have no concept of money, and can and will ostracize children who don't wear generally perfect clothing (not necessarily designer, but that does help)." State and city policies on school vouchers may also impact the amount your family spends on education.

Commute

Another key factor to consider is the transportation infrastructure. What is are the time and cost involved in commuting to your work? If you travel out of town regularly, how easily can you get to the airport or the freeway out of town?

Inner-city neighborhoods in many areas are undergoing a renaissance as people who are tired of spending hours in the car or on public transportation choose to move closer to downtown jobs. Not only is their commute shorter, they often can get by with only one car. A good inner-city home may be more expensive than a home of equal size in the suburbs, but the lifestyle change and transportation savings may make it worthwhile. If you have young children, however, an urban lifestyle is quite different from a suburban lifestyle. As we saw with Steve and Suzannah, there may be a very good reason to spend more time in the car once kids and schools are taken into account. Of course, many couples have two careers to juggle with jobs that change every so often, so choosing a home one year to reduce the commute may turn out to be a bad choice in the long run if you change jobs or your employer relocates.

New Versus Old

Another question is whether you want to live in an old or new home, an established or new neighborhood. Recent construction has its advantages, as anyone who has dealt with drafty windows, failing electrical systems, antique plumbing, and an old roof knows. However, there is plenty of range between one year old and a hundred years old. Older homes, when well renovated, have a charm that new homes cannot reproduce (though they try very hard!). Buying a brand new, never-lived-in home requires paying a premium, and initially, you may not realize as much of a capital gain as you would be buying a similar home that is a few years older because the people likely to buy your home are probably comparing it to the new construction down the street. Another thing to note about new home construction is that the houses are much bigger, in general, with larger closets, bathrooms, and casual living spaces, all requiring extra furniture and inviting extra clutter.

Between areas full of the beautifully historic and the cutting-edge modern, there are plenty of neighborhoods with homes of a certain age that are neither run-down nor trendy. If all other factors make sense—good schools, right location, safe streets, and solid transportation infrastructure—there is a chance that you may find a deal. Families that build wealth over time are more likely to buy homes in established neighborhoods and live in them for a long time, according to *The Millionaire Mind*. "There is nothing flashy or even modern about the style of houses in these neighborhoods. . . . [Millionaires] typically don't live in large mansions."[2]

Should You Rent or Buy?

Ah, the American dream: a home of your own and two cars in the driveway. The dream can be a nightmare, however, if the home keeps you cash poor, results in a loss when you go to sell it, or demands a never-ending stream of unexpected maintenance. Many couples buy a home as soon as they can afford a down payment. Most banks and real estate agents push people to buy the most expensive house they can afford. But just because you *can* does not mean you *should*.

There are many reasons to wait before buying a house. Don't buy if you cannot afford a home you would want to live in 5 years from now, a home large enough for the family you are planning to have in the near future, or a home that is in good enough condition for you to live with or renovate without overspending. Wait, also, if you think that there is a reasonable chance that you will change locations within a couple of years, want to upgrade as soon as you can afford it, or will be dropping back to one income without the ability to manage the mortgage on that income alone.

Although owning a home is undoubtedly an important emotional decision, it is also a massive financial decision. The math behind the rent-versus-buy decision is not as straightforward as it seems. Unlike many countries, U.S. tax laws make owning a home a fairly attractive proposition: mortgage interest is tax deductible[3] and up to $500,000 of the capital gain is tax free, depending on

---

[2]Thomas J. Stanley, *The Millionaire Mind* (Kansas City, MI: Andrews McMeel, 2000), 306–308.

[3]Up to a limit of $1,000,000 or $500,000 married filing separately. J. K. Lasser, *Your Income Tax 2002* (New York: John Wiley & Sons, 2001), 302.

when and why you sell.[4] The tax deductible interest means that your out-of-pocket expenses may drop when you go from renting to buying a home of similar value. However, many people want to buy a larger home than they rent, which usually means more money out of pocket every month.

It is possible for your home to turn out to be a good investment because of leverage. Leverage means that changes in the value of the house are significant compared to the amount you actually invested. For example, you may only need to put $10,000 down to buy a $200,000 home. Your investment will *double* if you get $210,000 after costs when you sell. That is, while your house has only gained 5 percent, the return on your investment is actually 100 percent because you only put a fraction of the value of the house down to begin with.

If the market rises, you get a great return on the money you put into the house; however, the opposite is also true. Housing markets don't always rise. After years of a strong market, it is easy to forget about periods such as 1989 when housing prices sat still in some areas and plunged 40 percent in other areas, tying people to homes they could not afford to sell. If your $200,000 home is not worth a penny more when you go to sell, you will lose the transaction costs, eroding all of the $10,000 equity you initially put into the house and more.

How Much House Can You Afford?

Home owners are borrowing more than ever before for their homes. As observed in *Fortune* magazine: "The rule of thumb used to be that a household spent at most 20% of income on rent or a mortgage. Now one in five two-income families is spending more than half its income on housing."[5] This rise is partially due, as I mentioned earlier, to banks being willing to lend larger amounts.

---

[4]Ibid., 474–482.
[5]Anna Bernasek, "Honey, Can We Afford It?" *Fortune* (September 3, 2001): 129–132.

When you buy a home or refinance your existing home, you must understand how much you can borrow based not only on your ability to pay, but also on the value of the property you are interested in. Work out how much house you qualify for before you begin looking: after all, why spend weekends test-driving a Porsche if you are on a Beetle budget?

To understand what you can afford, you need to look at what you will be allowed to borrow, as well as what you need to bring to the table at closing.

What You Can Borrow

No one wants to lend money to someone who cannot afford to pay it back. Each financial institution has formulas for how much it will lend and what interest rate it will charge. These calculations take into account your income, your credit rating, the amount that you want to borrow, and the value of the property you want to finance. The first two calculations give a rough estimation of what you can afford.

- *Debt to Income.* The debt-to-income ratio is one measure banks and mortgage brokers use to determine how much they are willing to lend you. Many banks are willing to lend the amount that results in a total debt-service payment equal to 36 percent of income, and some have figures a little higher or lower than that.
- *Income to Mortgage.* Another key ratio that lenders look at is your mortgage expense as a percent of your gross income. Generally, lenders will allow your mortgage expense to be equal to 28 percent of your gross income.

Note that these ratios calculate the amount that you can afford for a total mortgage payment, that is, not only the principal and interest, but also the property tax, property insurance, and mortgage insurance, where applicable.

Action Item: Determine How Much You Can Borrow
. . . .

These two calculations are just a starting point. Until you talk to lenders, you cannot know how much they will qualify you for. As a start, take a minute to fill out the work sheet shown as Figure 15.1. Note that the example shows that

1. Calculate your potential mortgage payment based on the debt-to-income ratio.

	EXAMPLE	YOUR FIGURES	
Monthly gross income	$5,000	_____	
Multiplied by .36	1,800	_____	
less car loan (monthly)	380	_____	
less student loan	0	_____	
less credit card debt	120	_____	
less other debt	0	_____	
Potential mortgage payment	$1,300	_____	(A)

2. Calculate your potential mortgage payment based on the income-to-mortgage expense ratio.

	EXAMPLE	YOUR FIGURES	
Monthly gross income	$5,000	_____	
Multiplied by .28	1,400	_____	(B)

3. Determine the likely maximum monthly payment.

	EXAMPLE	YOUR FIGURES
Line (A)	$1,300	_____
Line (B)	$1,400	_____
Lowest of (A) and (B)	$1,300	_____

Figure 15.1   Borrowing qualification work sheet with example.

lenders would probably cap the mortgage expense at $1,300 due to the debt-to-income ratio; however, if some of the non-mortgage debt is paid off, it may raise that amount to $1,400.

....

Once a financial institution calculates how much of a monthly payment you are qualified for, it will then work out how much it can lend you, based on the terms of the loan, including its length, the interest rate, whether it is a fixed or adjustable rate, and so on. Some of those factors will be affected by your credit record, so if you are planning to buy a home in the next couple of years, take a look at how to clean up your credit record in Chapter 10.

How Much Money You Need

The second constraint many couples face when buying their first home is having enough saved. Most people think only of the down payment; however, there are other costs you need to think of as well.

Down Payment

The biggest amount you will need is the actual down payment on the house. Back in our parents' day, people used to save for years before buying a home because most banks would require a 20 percent down payment. Today, many lending institutions are willing to lend 90 percent, 95 percent, or even 100 percent of a home's value. This percentage is called the loan-to-value ratio, or LTV. Some lenders offer loans of greater value than the house you want to purchase. There is, of course, a catch. The more they lend you, the greater the risk that they will lose their money. Thus, the higher the LTV, the higher the interest rate you are likely to pay. In addition, many lenders will try to make you pay Private Mortgage Insurance (PMI) if you put down less than 20 percent of the house's value; however, some lenders will structure the loan so that you do not need to pay it.[6]

Does this mean that you should aim for an LTV of 80 percent? No. Most couples who are buying their first home have little cash lying about, and it is unwise to put all of your available cash into the home you are buying because you don't know what other costs you will be facing. It is much wiser to borrow a little more, increasing your monthly payment by a bit, than to find yourself cash strapped and without a cash cushion.[7] Another advantage of a higher mortgage is that mortgage interest is tax deductible, and there is a very good chance that you are paying less to borrow the money than you could typically earn on a long-term investment. Therefore, you are better off in the long run to leave some of your investments untouched and to aim for a 90 percent or 95 percent LTV. Remember to check with your lender first about whether the loan can be structured without PMI and whether the interest rate will go up substantially.

Closing Costs and Prepayments

You will have to pay a myriad of closing costs, ranging from bank and legal charges to government fees and taxes, on the day you settle on your house purchase. Some of the fees are fairly standard, such as the settlement attorney's fee or the inspection cost, but others vary greatly by city, such as recordation tax. When you are serious about buying a home, ask your mortgage lender to prepare a good-faith estimate early in the process that shows all the

---

[6]Some financial institutions will structure a loan in a way that will save you a lot of money in PMI. If, for example, you are putting down 10 percent of the property's value, you can either get one loan for 90 percent of the property's value and pay PMI, or you can get two loans (a first mortgage of 80 percent and a second mortgage of 10 percent of the property value) and avoid the PMI. The second loan structure may save you hundreds of dollars a month. Ask your lender how you can avoid PMI. If your lender does not offer such a structure, find a lender that does.
[7]A cash cushion is explained in detail in Chapter 13.

fees that you are likely to face if you purchase a house at the top end of the range you can afford. Some fees are negotiable; be sure to raise questions if these increase substantially prior to closing.

Prepayments are another category of costs. They are not extra costs; they are simply expenses that you pay in advance. Prepayments may include several months' worth of house insurance and property tax, as well as enough interest in advance to pay the mortgage from the date of closing (also known as the settlement date) to the first official mortgage payment. Even though the prepayments are amounts you would spend anyway, the collection of them at the time of closing can come as a bit of a surprise the first time you buy a home as they can add up to thousands of dollars. Some lenders will allow you to fund some or all of your prepayments by taking out a larger mortgage.

Moving Costs

Once you purchase the house, don't forget that it will cost you time and money to move your worldly possessions into the house, hook up the utilities (some of which may require a deposit), and possibly do some maintenance before you move in. Also, don't forget to allow for expenses once you move in: curtains for the windows, appliances that do not come with the house, basic tools for the everyday care and maintenance of your home. Don't spend every last cent buying a home and find yourself running up credit card debt to move into it.

How Much You Will Pay Monthly

Your monthly payment will include several components: the principal and interest of the actual mortgage, PMI, if you are being charged for it, property insurance (sometimes called hazard insurance), and property taxes. The amount of principal and interest you pay will depend on the length and interest rate of your loan, as well as whether there is a balloon payment. The interest paid on most mortgages, home equity loans, or home equity lines of credit is tax deductible, subject to certain limits.[8]

Types of Mortgages

A number of types of mortgages are available. Your lender or mortgage broker can help you assess the benefits of each in your situation. To approximate the amount you may be able to borrow at current rates using the different types of loans, use an on-line calculator such as those you'll find in the home loan section of www.quicken.com.

- *Fixed-rate mortgage*. This is the most common mortgage. The interest rate is fixed for the entire period of the loan, and usually the loans are for 30 years, though 15-, 25- and 40-year fixed-rate mortgages are available.
- *Adjustable-rate mortgage*. An adjustable-rate mortgage (ARM) has an interest rate that can change over time. Generally, there is a period at the start of the loan when the rate is fixed, usually 3 or 5 years, and then the loan's interest rate can be adjusted periodically, based on a formula set in advance (usually based on the prime lending rate). For example, a 5/1 ARM means that the rate is fixed for the first 5 years and potentially adjusted every year after that. The adjustment is usually limited to a certain percentage. The advantage of an ARM is that the interest rates are lower to begin with, allowing borrowers to qualify for larger loans or to keep their loan payments down. The disadvantage is that you cannot tell what interest rates will do in the future, so you may find yourself 3 or 5 years down the track having to pay more than you paid when the loan began. When mortgage rates rise substantially, people with ARMs feel the pain while their neighbors who have fixed rates do not.

---

[8]Up to $1 million of debt ($500,000 filing separately) for first and second homes, if mortgage was obtained after October 14, 1987. Lasser, *Your Income Tax 2002*, 301–304. See a tax advisor for information regarding your specific circumstances.

- *Balloon mortgage.* Like ARMs, these mortgages may allow you to borrow more than you might qualify for under a fixed 30-year mortgage. In this case, at the end of the mortgage, you have not paid off the entire principal, and have a "balloon" amount that you need to pay. Chances are that you will refinance or sell the home before the end of the mortgage, so it is unlikely that you will need to come up with the balloon payment. Also, you can simply refinance when the balloon is due. It lowers your monthly payment because your principal payments will be lower.

- *Specialized loans.* Ask your lender or broker about special loan programs that are available that may allow you to either borrow more or have a lower interest rate than you would otherwise qualify for. Some of these programs are designed for first-time buyers, low-income buyers, military personnel, and people in other special circumstances. The specialized loans include Acorn, FHA, VA, and other loans.

- *Home equity loan.* A home equity loan is not a mortgage, but does allow you to borrow against your home. If you need to borrow some additional money, it may be cheaper to get a home equity loan (or line of credit) than to refinance your whole mortgage because the transaction costs are lower. Like a mortgage, the interest is tax deductible to a certain degree, depending on how much you borrow, what your home is valued at when you take out the home equity loan, and what the proceeds are used for. Generally, the deduction is limited to the lesser of $100,000 (or $50,000 married filing separately) or the fair market value of your home less the outstanding principal on mortgages secured by the house.[9]

- *Home equity line of credit.* This is similar to a home equity loan and has the same advantages, however it offers even greater flexibility because you are able to draw down the money when you need it, rather than borrow the whole

---

[9]Lasser, *Your Income Tax 2002*, 303. Seek tax advice to determine whether the interest on a home equity loan or line of credit you are considering will be tax deductible.

amount for a set period. It allows you to access the equity in your home without incurring interest payments when you do not need access to the funds.

- *Reverse mortgage.* These specialized mortgages are used to draw out the equity of your home and are generally used by retirees who want to tap the value of their homes to fund their retirement. They're complicated beasts with potential downsides, and AARP's Web site does the best job of demystifying them. See www.aarp.org/revmort.

Escrow

Lenders like to know that their borrowers are going to pay all of their expenses on the house, particularly insurance and property tax, on time. Although your loan contract requires you to keep the property insured and the taxes paid, many lenders offer—or demand—to pay those critical bills on your behalf. The lender will notify your insurer and the local property tax authorities and will receive a copy of your bill and will pay it directly on your behalf. The lender collects some of the money from you every month along with the mortgage payment, puts it in an escrow account (which just means that it is held by them in your name), and pays those bills for you. They usually keep about 5 months' worth of insurance and tax in escrow so that they have enough to cover the bills when they arrive, which is usually every 6 months.

Sometimes lenders offer a lower interest rate to borrowers who use an escrow account because it lowers the lender's risk. It's a good thing: it saves you paperwork, ensures that you never forget a payment, levels out your payments throughout the year, and keeps your lender relaxed. Your prepayments at closing will fund the amount needed to establish your escrow account.

How Do You Buy Wisely?

For the past few years, the Washington, D.C., housing market has been hot. Really hot. Properties put on the market were sold the same day, and often bid above their asking price, sometimes by more than 10 percent. Buyers started panicking after losing a house they liked, discovering that five, six, even nine people outbid them. Several friends who were in the market quickly learned that if they wanted to win, they had to get aggressive, bidding high, adding escalation clauses to allow the amount to go even higher, waiving many of the usual cautious clauses in the contract, and putting large amounts of cash on the table. Some even resorted to emotional tactics, writing letters or sharing photos of their children. When markets get that hot, it is easy to forget that there have been times when markets have fallen in value, properties sat on the market for months, foreclosures flourished.

Selecting Potential Homes

The home-buying process used to start with legwork. Today, you can do a lot of basic research about neighborhoods on Web sites such as www.bestplaces.net, which has information on school districts, crime rates, and so on. Once you have selected a couple of neighborhoods that sound promising, time spent looking at homes on the market will give you the best education on prices in the area. The longer you can spend getting a good idea of the market, the better you will recognize a good deal when you see it. Finding a deal in an area may also include looking for foreclosed homes or fixer-uppers, if you don't mind the idea of some renovation.

Prequalification

If the market is competitive, it may be useful to go through a full prequalification, which ensures that you can get a loan up to a certain amount. Some banks will charge you the loan application fee to get prequalified. The advantage of being prequalified is that if other bidders on a property are not, the sellers may be more positively inclined toward your offer because they know your financing will go through.

Negotiating a Price

The more emotionally attached you are to buying a specific house, the more likely you are to overpay for it. The wealthy studied in *The Millionaire Mind* are generally willing to shop slowly for a home and walk away from any deal. What you are willing to pay should not be determined solely by what your mortgage lender says you can borrow. Your knowledge of the market, you and your real estate agent's read on how *motivated* the seller is, and the limits on borrowing that you have agreed on as a couple should all come into play when you make an offer. And never hold back on making a low bid for fear of offending the seller: This is a transaction, not a relationship.

Managing the Expense and Value of Your Home

Many expenses related to your home add up to thousands of dollars over the years. Managing the cost of both one-time expenses such as decorating and recurring expenses such as utility bills can free up money for something more fun than your average water bill. Protecting the value of your home not only involves making sure that you are carrying appropriate insurance and doing basic maintenance, but also may involve renovating the property and even improving the neighborhood.

Running Costs

The first place to look at managing expenses is in all those bills that arrive every month or quarter: electricity, gas, and water. Simple steps can cut costs significantly. Some quick fixes are:

- Fix drafty windows and doors and check that you have enough insulation.
- Install a programmable thermostat and only pay for heating and cooling during the hours you most use the house. Set the

temperature a few degrees lower in winter and higher in summer.
- Fix dripping faucets and install low-flow toilets.
- Use energy-efficient appliances and light bulbs.
- Replace filters regularly.
- Install drip watering in your garden.

The best time to think about the running costs is when you purchase a house. Larger houses have higher running costs—there's simply more to heat and cool—and older houses may have leaks and drips that new houses usually avoid.

Insurance

Your property and household contents need to be protected from accidents and disasters that can damage them. Carrying enough insurance is vital. Generally your mortgage lender will require that you carry insurance on the property, and most home owner's policies automatically cover contents as well. A detailed discussion of home insurance is in Chapter 13 on Skill Six: Creating a Safety Net for Two.

Maintenance

. . . .

Seth is an avid home handyman, always with a project on the boil. And with every new project, there is a new tool. "I had to paint a whole room, so it made sense to get a power painter." The simple task of redecorating a room could have cost $40 for a can of paint, drop cloth, roller, and brush. "I like doing these sorts of projects and it made sense to buy the power painter because I thought it would make it a lot faster. It turned out not to make much of a difference—most of the time-consuming part is the edges and corners anyway. It seemed like a good idea at the time." His simple room-painting project grew to $200. Seth's storage area is full of time-saving gadgets, *many of which aren't used that often, weren't as good as they were claimed to be, or were superseded by new, better gadgets. How often does the average home handyman need a tile cutter anyway?*

....

Another way to protect your investment is to ensure that you are conducting good basic maintenance. The amount of effort that basic maintenance requires depends on the age of your property, how well the previous owners cared for it, and how large and complex the systems are. Some simple steps, such as changing your air filters in your heat pump or air conditioner regularly, can keep your long-term costs down.

Old homes may be a lot more expensive to maintain, especially if they have been patched together in the past. The key question is to know when to maintain and when to replace. My rule of thumb is that if a problem begins occupying a corner of my mind on a regular basis, it is time to put the money into fixing it properly. For example, an old roof on a home I owned was prone to springing small leaks. After one serious series of storms had increased the frequency and size of the leaks, I patched them. Most held for a while; however, once I realized that I was holding my breath everytime a storm hit, I decided it was time to replace the roof.

The other rule of thumb is that if replacement is not much more expensive than repair, it simply may pay to replace. I had a noisy dishwasher that needed fixing. One quick fix by a workman who was at my home for another reason gave it 6 months of reasonably silent operation, but when the noise returned, it was time to fork out the money to replace the machine. Basic dishwashers cost a few hundred dollars on sale, plus installation. Repairmen charge around $70 an hour, plus the cost of parts and perhaps even travel time. The old saying "never throw good money after bad" applies as soon as you know that the good money spent on repairing has a reasonable chance of being wasted.

Another question is whether you should maintain your home yourself or pay others to do it. The answer depends not only on your skill level and whether you own the right equipment, but also on how much time you want to spend taking care of your home and how much you can afford. The problem is that many home maintenance jobs are too small to justify calling someone in for; however, most of us don't have the right equipment to deal with the myriad of small problems that arise. If the equipment is cheap and either of you enjoy taking care of small projects, by all means, maintain your home yourselves. If you don't enjoy maintenance work, however, and there is not a pressing need, it pays to simply get a list going of all the little repairs that need doing and handle a group of them at one time with an annual or semiannual visit from a handyman.

Decoration

At least one of the two of you is likely to have the nesting urge. Home decorating magazines tempt with the latest designs, catalogs tempt with the color of the moment. Home fashion is big business, and it is easy for it to be big bucks too. *Metropolitan Home* notes that spending on home fashion is rapidly catching up to that of clothing fashions. "According to the trade journals, consumer spending on home goods is poised to overtake apparel consumption. Since 1991, furnishings sales have grown 79 percent, 26 percent more than clothing sales (in 2000, that's $319.1 billion on clothes and $307.3 billion on home)."[10] The simplest way to manage home furnishing costs is to decorate once in a stylish way and resist the temptation to hop on home furnishing trends. Opting for less square footage and staying put in one home also keeps the cost of home decorating down. However, if lining your nest comfortably fits with your goals and values, then get creative about ways to manage the cost. It is more affordable to use a neutral backdrop and change the color of accessories than to have neutral accessories and replace the curtains or recover the furniture. Paint is a surprisingly cheap way to get a new look, particularly if you can do the painting yourself.

---

[10]Donna Warner, "Editorial," *Metropolitan Home* (March/April 2002): 26.

Renovation

. . . .

Susan and Ahmed spent more than $50,000 upgrading their kitchen and reconfiguring the adjoining sunroom to make it a breakfast nook and office. Their appliances are top of the line and their cabinets a beautiful cherry. "We know that this adds to the value of the home: They say you get back at least 90 percent of what you spend on a kitchen," Susan was quick to point out. Did I ask her to justify her spending? Ever the grinch, I simply smiled and commented, "I didn't know you were planning to sell."

. . . .

Let me debunk a myth here. Renovations of kitchens and bathrooms are *not a good investment if you do not have plans to sell.* After all, the bathroom or kitchen you are replacing were new once. If you spend a fortune today on a state-of-the-art kitchen, but don't sell the home for 10 or so years, you have not made an investment. You have simply spent good money on a nice kitchen for your own enjoyment. By the time you sell, your kitchen will look dated. It may add something to the value of your home—after all, at the time of sale the kitchen would be 10 years old, not 25—but probably not as much as you put into it. The next owners may even rip your precious new-but-now-not-so-new kitchen out and redo it. I am not saying that you shouldn't upgrade your home. Just stop hiding your spending behind false financial justifications.

Some renovations *do* add to the value of a home in the long run. Renovations that increase the square footage, improve the flow of rooms, add bathrooms, bring in modern amenities such as central air or indoor plumbing, or make unusable space useable do add to the value. Improving the structure is a very different matter from improving the décor, and a renovation of an existing kitchen or bathroom is largely a change in décor.

Another renovation that is a good investment is one that saves you from moving. If adding on space or improving the usability of existing space means that you will be happy staying put for a few more years, then by all means do it. After all, the transaction costs alone for selling and buying a home of similar value are about 10 percent of the home's market value. So spending $20,000 on improvements that make you happy to stay in your $200,000 home is a no-brainer, if you can afford or easily finance the changes.

One thing to be careful of is overcapitalizing. Overcapitalizing means that you have a home that costs more than you can ever sell it for. You never want to own the best house on a street, because the day you go to sell, the quality of your neighbor's homes will drag down the amount you can get for yours.

Financing Renovations

Regardless of whether you are renovating for investment purposes or simply because you enjoy living in a nice home, you may be able to finance the renovations through a home equity loan or line of credit, through refinancing your home with a larger mortgage, or through a home improvement loan. The advantage of loans that are secured by your home is that your interest may be tax deductible, as discussed earlier. Remember that there are limits to those tax deductions, but they usually do not apply until you have a million dollar property.[11] Keep track of the capital improvements you make on your home as you may need the information to calculate your capital gain on the sale of the property when you sell and eventually move on.

Community Commitment

Property values rise and fall not only with economic trends, but also with neighborhood trends. Although most of the value of our homes depends on national, regional, and local trends, we all can make a difference by becoming active in our neighborhoods.

---

[11]Lasser, *Your Income Tax 2002*, 304–306.

. . . .

Logan Circle in Washington, D.C., seemed to have everything it needed for gentrification: beautiful Victorian townhouses on large, tree-lined streets just waiting for some TLC, proximity to hip neighborhoods, a market full of home buyers forced out of nearby Dupont Circle by its escalating prices. Yet this inner-city neighborhood was ignored by the young, affluent home buyers. It was as if the neighborhood was waiting for the buyers as much as the buyers were waiting for the neighborhood. In the background, a group of local citizens were busy taking matters into their own hands. They had heard rumors that a Fresh Fields supermarket—an upscale grocery store larger and fancier than anything in neighboring Dupont—was to be built somewhere north of Logan Circle. In an unusual move, a group of home owners and property developers approached the parent company, Whole Foods Markets, Inc., and presented a compelling argument why the new store should be located in the heart of Logan Circle, at 14th and P Streets. Today, Logan Circle is thriving. Crack houses are snapped up and redeveloped into condos. Dupont residents drive the few extra blocks for the Fresh Fields market. And home prices are going through the roof.

. . . .

Activism can involve grand plans or small gestures. A friend of mine in a transitional neighborhood near downtown Chicago takes her kids to a nice new public park after becoming concerned that all the local kids were not using it enough and it would fall into disrepair. "I want this neighborhood to feel like a good place for other families to live, and having kids playing safely in a park helps project that image." Another friend meets monthly with a local group that is lobbying for an extra park for dog owners to use. "It's not just that I want more places to walk Jaxx. I want to live in the sort of neighborhood where residents feel connected to each other and there is no better way than to walk your dog and talk to your neighbors." Many others are active in local schools, knowing that good schools support good home prices. Taking care of your neighborhood, not just your home, is a good investment in the value of your largest asset.

Housing Decisions Throughout Your Lifetime

I'm an avid house hunter (it's my idea of window shopping), and every now and then I stumble across a home that has been lived in by a family for a generation or two. Sometimes they are meticulously kept period pieces, and other times they are murky dungeons redolent of days gone by. Having never lived anywhere for very long, even as a child, I marvel that a family can be so stable. I got my fixer-upper instinct from my stepfather who found diamonds in the rough, polished them into homes, and moved on. The longest I have ever lived anywhere is 6½ years, during elementary school. In these well-lived in and much loved homes, I picture the day that their mortgage was gone, finished, paid off in full. Now that's living happily ever after!

Today people are likely to move a number of times, depending on where they are in their lifecycle. Newlyweds often buy a starter home, then upgrade as their earnings rise or their family grows, perhaps expand to a vacation home, and then retreat to a smaller home in later years. Yet if we look at the housing habits of the very wealthy, we find that they tend to be stable, buying a decent home in a solid neighborhood and sticking with it for some time. Their buy-and-hold strategy helps them build wealth.

Refinancing

When should you refinance? Generally people refinance for one of two reasons: to lower their monthly mortgage payment or to get access to the equity they have built up. So the answer to our question should be when interest rates have fallen to the degree that you will save enough to cover the transaction costs of the refinancing within a couple of months, or when you have a pressing need that will be cheaper if financed through a mortgage than through other means. Often, however, the two reasons get muddled. A couple may start talking to their lender about refinancing because they know interest rates have lowered, and then the lender says: "Would you like to get some extra cash out? You can get an extra $35,000." Suddenly, visions of a new deck and some fancy kitchen appliances dance in their heads (it's house related, so it's an investment, isn't it? Isn't it?). It is not surprising to see couples who planned on lowering their monthly payment end up with a payment of exactly the same amount or even more, with some cash to splash on a new car, renovations, and so on.

Refinancing when rates are lower, however, can be a great idea. You lower your payments today, and you lock in a low interest rate for the next 30 years or so if you get a fixed-rate mortgage. It's been awhile since interest rates were high, so it's easy to forget how painful an 18 percent-plus mortgage—which was the going rate in 1981—can be. Also, a third reason to refinance may be to convert your adjustable-rate mortgage into a fixed-rate mortgage, so you can keep your payments steady in the long run.

There are several other factors to consider when you refinance. One is whether your current loan has any prepayment penalties. Lenders may offer lower interest rates in return for a prepayment clause that ties the borrower to the loan for several years. Before refinancing, check if you will have to pay a prepayment penalty and the date on which the prepayment penalty expires. Another factor to consider is transaction costs. Even if you don't change financial institutions when you refinance, you will face a number of costs, including a property appraisal, title insurance (though at a lower cost than when you originate a loan), the attorney's time, and various bank, state, and city fees and charges. Sometimes the lender wraps all of those costs into the new loan so you do not have to meet them up front. It doesn't mean that the refinancing was free, but that you borrowed a few extra thousand to pay for the refinancing, which works out to be a minor amount in the monthly payment.

If you are refinancing, the LTV may also be important. If, for example, you have had your home for a while and have built up equity in it (either because the house has gone up in value or you have paid off some of the loan), your lender may be willing to lend you more money when you go to refinance. For example, let's say you bought the home when it was worth $200,000 and its value has now risen to $250,000. If the original loan was 80 percent LTV, you would have borrowed $160,000. Today 80 percent LTV would give you $200,000, so you may be able to take cash out—that is, borrow additional money—when you go to refinance, without increasing the LTV. Of course, any cash out means that you are more in debt, so only borrow more if you really need the cash, have other debts to pay off, or intend to invest it for the long term and believe you can get a higher return than the mortgage costs.

Staying Put or Moving Up

Moving your household has significant transactions costs and should not be taken lightly. If your main complaint with your current home is its superbly seventies kitchen or insufficient bathrooms, improving your home may make more sense. However, sometimes it makes sense to sell.

If your house has increased substantially in value, selling could be the best thing you could do. A recent U.S. tax law has created a good reason to sell your home if you are sitting on a very large capital gain. The new rule allows a couple to take a tax-free capital gain of up to $500,000 *every 2 years* on their primary residence.[12] (Find me affordable houses that rise that quickly in price and I will be very happy indeed!) This capital gain exclusion used

---

[12]Ibid., 474–477. Note that you have to have lived in the property for at least 2 years out of the preceding 5, and there are specific rules if both partners in a marriage have not lived in the residence for 2 years or one of the two has taken the exemption within the preceding 2 years on another property.

to be a once-in-a-lifetime exclusion, but was recently changed. This means that if you have a home that has appreciated substantially, you may be better off selling your home once the capital gain approaches half a million dollars (or $250,000 for single taxpayers) and buying a new home of the same value as the one you just sold. This way, you get to lock in your gain tax free, and start the meter at zero again. You can take a prorated exclusion even sooner if you have to sell for specific reasons such as relocating for work, funding health care costs or "unforeseen circumstances."[13] If you are relocating for work, the good news is that your moving expenses[14] may be tax deductible and your employer may cover some or all of the costs if they initiate the move.

Lifestyle decisions such as opting into or out of the urban, suburban, or rural life for a different pace, changing family size, learning to live with a physical disability, or seeking a community that can offer the care required as you age may all prompt you to move. Or perhaps you simply have a passion for renovating. Given a spare weekend, I'd rather be ripping out walls on a renovator's delight than doing almost anything else. (And I have the scars to prove it.)

One House Versus Two

Another major lifestyle decision that can have a significant financial impact over your lifetime is whether you own a second home. It is critical to understand the total cost of owning a second home, not only in terms of money, but in terms of time and energy that you will spend managing the property and taking care of it from

---

[13]At the time of writing, the IRS had not defined what it means by "unforeseen circumstances." See your tax professional for advice if you are selling at a gain within 2 years of purchasing.

[14]This not only includes the cost of moving, but also the costs incurred while finding a new home. There are a number of limitations that may restrict your ability to claim moving expenses. See your tax professional for advice or read Lasser, *Your Income Tax 2002*, 268–271.

afar. Talk to others who own vacation homes before making your decision. If you decide to buy a second home, the ever-generous tax code allows you to deduct interest on the mortgage of the second home, as long as the two homes together are worth less than a million dollars.[15]

Downscaling for Empty Nesters and Retirees

As kids leave home, many couples find themselves rattling around a home that is larger than they need, except for the occasions when family come to visit. Moving to a smaller home or a property requiring lower maintenance may be very appealing. Although it may be hard to let go of the kids' old bedrooms, chances are that your grown children will be happy to stay at a local hotel if your guest room is taken during the holidays.

The ability to take a tax-free capital gain on your property makes a decision to live in a smaller, and probably cheaper, home even more attractive. Of course, some people make the opposite decision. Now that my parents are grandparents and they have time to explore their hobbies fully, they have moved to a home with extra guest rooms for the grandkids and a large garden so my mother can indulge her love of horticulture.

---

[15]As always, there is a lot of fine print about when you bought the home, whether you rent it out for part of each year, and so on, so get professional advice.

· ·

CHAPTER 16

Decision 2: What You Drive

WHAT SORT OF CAR ARE YOU? A SOLID CHEVROLET? A YOUNG, FUN Beetle? A Caravan soccer Mom? A worldly Saab? A salt of the earth Ford F-150? A midlife-crisis Maserati? And how about your spouse? The chances are, you can easily answer that question. Cars have personalities—or at least are marketed as such—and you probably know a few cars that fit your perception of your own personality. The marketing messages from the car companies so permeate our culture that we instantly spot a misfit between driver and driven. Whether your taste in cars is pick-up practical or Lexus luxury, there are ways to manage the cost of getting around.

The Cost of Cars

What do you think you spend annually on your cars? Without making any calculations, take a guess and jot your answer down. Also without doing any math, what percent of your after-tax income do you think is reasonable to spend on having a car or two?

I live in the inner city of Washington, D.C. where parking is at a premium, public transportation is plentiful, and most of my everyday activities are within walking distance. Lots of people living in D.C. get by without a car. Recently, a car-sharing service opened near my home, offering cars for a membership fee and a low hourly cost.[1] Although I am not planning to sell my car, I was curious about the math. I own my car outright, so I don't notice large amounts of cash flowing out of my pocket. Even though I own my car fully, I nearly fell over when I worked out how much it costs me a year. I added depreciation, parking (I own the space; however, I kicked out a $160/month renter to reclaim it, so I counted the income forgone), insurance (expensive in D.C.), gas (low, I don't drive much), maintenance (only one scheduled service and an oil change per year), plus a little in incidentals such as car washes, windshield fluid, and parking tickets. Overall, my car costs me close to $6,000 a year. I was stunned. Because parking and depreciation don't involve my opening my wallet, I had not thought about my car's full cost.

Most households spend close to $1 in $5 on transportation, most of which is on their car. That's one day a week of work simply to pay for getting around. However, most couples are probably unconscious about how much they are actually spending. Part of the reason that you may be unaware of the total cost is that one of the largest costs, depreciation, can be largely invisible if you buy rather than lease. It is only when you go to sell your car that you realize how much less it is worth than the day you bought it. If you lease, your monthly payments cover depreciation and financing.

Action Item: The Cost of Your Car

Trying to be as accurate as you can, spend 10 minutes working out how much your annual expenses are likely to be using the work sheet provided as Figure 16.1.

---

[1]There are a number of services, for example, www.zipcar.com operates in Boston, New York, and Washington, D.C., and plans to expand to more cities. Another service is www.flexcar.com in Seattle, Portland, and Washington, D.C.

	HIS CAR	HER CAR
Loan/lease payments	_____	_____
Depreciation (if car is bought, not leased)	_____	_____
Insurance	_____	_____
Gas	_____	_____
Maintenance	_____	_____
Parking	_____	_____
Parking and traffic violations	_____	_____
Car wash and incidentals	_____	_____
Total	_____	_____

Figure 16.1　　Annual expenses for a car.

How does the total compare to the estimate you made earlier? What percent of your after-tax income is this total equal to?

....

Now, that exercise was probably painful! Chances are, you spend a whole lot more than you realized. Trim your total car spending a little and you have a lot of extra cash. Another cost that most people don't include is the opportunity cost of having money tied up in a car that declines in value every time you look at it. For example, if you have a $20,000 car that is paid off in full, you are missing out on the income and capital gain that the $20,000 could generate if it were invested instead.

Should You Lease or Buy?

Simple answer: Buy, don't lease. Why? Because couples who lease get into a mind-set of getting a new car every couple of years. Because couples who lease consistently have cars for the period of the greatest depreciation and have nothing to show at the end of it. Because couples who lease are more likely to pay for expensive options and gadgets than if they were buying.[2]

You would never dream of automatically getting a brand new home every few years. Why do it with a car? Sure, new cars are nice, but as the second biggest expense that your household is likely to face, you could be sacrificing your financial future for the sake of the new-car smell every few years.

Leasing is a habit that costs many households dearly. Most people who lease don't think of paying off their lease and keeping the car at the end. And you can't lease a secondhand car, so you are paying top dollar to use something in its period of greatest depreciation. Add to that the fact that the lease assumes that you drive a certain number of miles per year. If you drive more, you pay more. If you drive less, it's money down the drain because the lessor is not going to write you a check for keeping the mileage down. And with any nicks, scratches, and dents beyond normal wear and tear, you pay. Yet about 85 percent of people who lease, lease again at the end of the lease's term.

Ever notice that car ads rarely mention the cost of the car? Instead they trumpet: *$369 a month*. Whatever the dollar amount, the implied exclamation mark begs you to respond: *What a bargain. Give me two!* They are training the public to think of cars as a monthly expense, not as a purchase that may require some short-term debt. The strategy appears to be working. The number of lessees is growing. In 1990, 5.7 percent of new cars were leased (excluding corporate and fleet vehicles). By 1998, that figure rose to 26.7 percent. That a large percentage represents a large number of people in the market for a new car who are tying themselves into perpetual payments . . . at least until they break the leasing habit.

Don't take my word for it—clearly this is a subject I am opinionated about—let's take a look at what the wealthy do. *The Millionaire Next Door* says: "How do millionaires go about acquiring

---

[2]Lessees are 50 percent more likely to load their cars with expensive options and gadgets, according to a survey quoted by General Car Leasing's Web site.

motor vehicles? About 81 percent purchase their vehicles."[3] These folks are rich because they're smart with money. Follow their footsteps and give up the leasing habit.

The bottom line is that if you lease, you are tying yourself into a lifetime of *$369 a month!* Each time you go to lease a new car, inflation ensures that the slice of your income spent on a car remains significant, and the temptation to get the latest and greatest options means that it may even grow. If you buy, you may have a monthly payment for a while; however, if you buy and hold, you can have years of payment-free living. After you have paid off the car, you get to bank the *$369 a month!* Keeping a car for, say, 8 years can save you a fortune. Let's look at three scenarios over 8 years:

1. Buy a new car and finance it for 5 years, trade it in after 8 years.
2. Lease a new car on a 3-year lease and renew with a similar car afterward.
3. Buy a 2-year-old car and finance it for 5 years, trade it in after 8 years.

For the example, I looked at a Toyota Camry LE four-door sedan. New, with taxes, title, and fees, this model runs about $20,000.[4] Two-year-old Camrys run about $17,500. At the end of 8 years, the 8-year-old Camry would bring about $3,450 as a trade in and the 10-year-old Camry would bring about $2,200. You might get more selling it yourself; however, one of the advantages of leasing is the sense of just handing the car over at the end, so the trade-in figure is the best comparison. I have assumed that inflation is zero so the costs can easily be compared across years.

For the example, the new and the used car that were purchased were financed for the full amount over 5 years. Just to give the

---

[3]Thomas J. Stanley and William D. Danko, *The Millionaire Next Door* (New York: Pocket Books, 1996), 139.
[4]New and 2-year-old car prices were taken from www.carmax.com. Trade-in prices were taken from the Kelly Blue Book site www.kbb.com.

lease a fighting chance, I assumed the loans were at 8 percent, though rates are currently 1 percent lower than that. The payments on the new car came out to $405 a month and the 2-year-old car came out to $355 a month. For the leasing scenario, I assumed a 3-year lease, a typical term. The lease required a security deposit of $375 and monthly payments of $353.

So how much does that new car smell every 3 years cost? Compared to buying a new car and keeping it for 8 years, you end up spending an extra $14,116 out of your pocket over the 8-year period, averaging $199 a month over the 8-year term. Compared to buying a 2-year-old car, you end up spending $15,907 more over the 8-year period, or an average of $218 a month. Is it worth $200 *a month* every month over your lifetime for the joy of smelling a new car every 3 years?

Lease-versus-buy worksheets usually conclude that if you want to buy a new car every couple of years, leasing makes more sense. What *I* am saying is that *neither* makes sense. The depreciation of a vehicle in the first couple of years and the transaction costs, as well as the time and effort spent researching and negotiating, simply make turning cars over that quickly a huge drain on your finances. Cars today are built to last. If you are too, you and the car can have a long, happy relationship.

This simplified example doesn't take into account other costs. Don't forget:

- Your insurance costs will get lower as the car declines in value. For example, the Camry would cost around $690 to insure if I bought it new today, yet that figure drops to $650 if I had a Camry that was a year or two old, and $560 if I had a 6- to 8-year old Camry.[5] Both the collision and the comprehensive components of the insurance fall by up to a third over the 8-year period. Once the car is worth less than 10 times the annual insurance premium, you may want to discontinue the comprehensive coverage.

---

[5]Approximate figure based on a 35-year-old, single female driver who lives in Washington, D.C.

- The day you stop your loan payments, you can start putting away that money every month and earning a return on it. It will compound nicely as you drive around and your nest egg at the end will be larger than the savings previously estimated. If you continue the buy-and-hold habit over a lifetime and save the difference, you will build a very significant nest egg.
- Maintenance costs may rise as the car ages. It is possible to purchase an extended warranty; however, a car with strong reliability ratings such as a Camry is unlikely to have significant maintenance costs in the first 8 to 10 years of driving.

Those who love leasing will argue that they really enjoy having a completely reliable new car every couple of years that they can hand back at the end of the lease term. Is that the most fun you could have with $200 a month for life? It is fine to lease if you are already saving enough for your retirement, well on the way to funding your kids' college, free of credit card debt, and sitting on a good little cash cushion. If you are not, then get over it. Don't let leasing become a habit that eats away your financial future or prevents you from paying for your dreams.

How Much Car Should You Buy?

The first place to look when you wonder why you spend so much on cars is the amount you initially pay for the car. In Stanley and Danko's research on how millionaires really live, they found that automobiles make up a small fraction of a millionaire's total wealth. If you look at your car's value in relation to your net worth, you will probably find it is a significant percentage. Millionaires buy relatively affordable cars. "The average American buyer of a new motor vehicle paid more than $21,000 for his most recent' acquisition. This is not much less than the $24,800 paid by millionaires!"[6] What was the price of your last car? If it was over

---

[6]Stanley and Danko, *The Millionaire Next Door*, 140.

$30,000, you are living better than many millionaires. "Fifty percent of the millionaires we surveyed never spent more than $29,000 in their entire lives for a motor vehicle."[7] Even if your car was under $19,500, you are still on par with 30 percent of millionaires.

How much should you spend on a car? Simply speaking, you should buy as little car as you need to safely and reliably get around in reasonable comfort and style. Reasonable is, of course, in the eye of the beholder. For me, a good compact disc player is reasonable and, given my willingness to hold a car for a long time, affordable. Sit down as a couple and work out what you regard as a reasonable amount to spend on a car, then work out the percent of your net worth that amount represents and the annual price tag it implies. As Conscious Spenders, understand clearly the impact of your car spending on your other financial plans. If you are putting having a nice car ahead of other key goals, then rethink your auto expenses.

Cut the Cost by Getting a Good Deal

Once you have decided that it is time to replace your car, the homework begins. What brand? What model? And, most of all, what price? Paying the right price requires homework. I *hate* buying a car through a dealer where negotiation is required. Yet, you'll overpay at most dealerships if you don't negotiate. Again, we can learn from the very wealthy: "Those who are not wealthy are less likely to shop, haggle, and negotiate than those who are millionaires."[8]

You can skip the dealer games altogether (as I now do) by buying through a set-price dealer, such as CarMax or Saturn, or by buying through a service that sets a standard markup over dealer invoice ahead of time, such as discount membership store Costco.

---

[7]Ibid.
[8]Ibid., 157–158.

However, even the no-haggling waters have been muddied of late as dealers have seen the popularity of set prices and started claiming to have no-haggle prices. Apparently, a good number keep the prices reasonable, but still dump a pile of mark-ups and extra fees on the end. The result: no haggling, but no great deal either.

Some things to remember as you buy a car:

- Begin your negotiations with the wholesale price in mind. The wholesale price is not the same as the invoice, and both are significantly below the manufacturer's suggested retail price (MSRP). It is becoming more popular to negotiate from the invoice price, yet car companies encompass some fees and charges into the invoice, so it does not really indicate what the dealer pays. The result is that you should try to negotiate from the dealer's wholesale cost, which is probably 5 percent to 10 percent below the invoice. You can buy an estimate of the wholesale price of the make and model in your area at www.consumerreports.com for $12.
- Understand the sales tactics that dealers use, from acting as if they are new on the job to "losing" your car keys as they appraise your potential trade-in. Such tactics range from standard negotiation to downright sneaky. Read more at www.edmunds.com.
- Negotiate the price, financing, and trade-in value separately, getting each in writing. Otherwise, it's like a balloon where you squeeze one end and merely inflate the other.
- Be willing to walk away without a car.
- Consider using a car buying service or purchasing through a warehouse club that can negotiate a set markup for you.
- Before you buy, shop around for financing. The auto finance company may offer you a great low rate, but make sure they aren't inflating the price to make up for it.
- If you can pay for the car in cash, that's the best deal of all. Otherwise, aim to hit the debt on the head quickly so you minimize the interest expense.

Cutting the Cost by Choosing Wisely

Makes and models vary greatly in their running and repair costs. To lower the long-run cost:

- Check the reliability ratings in the car magazines that do independent testing, especially if you plan to buy a used car or keep your car until it is 10 or more years old.
- Buy a model that thieves hate and safety testers love. It will keep your insurance rate down. Get information on different vehicle crash test ratings (complete with pictures of the famous crash test dummies in every brand of tested car) at www.iihs.org.
- Insurers love normal. Skip the sporty upgrades that drive up insurance costs, and get quotes for the makes and models you are considering before you buy. Buy the most boring, safe, slightly used car that is so dull that even thieves won't want it. What about the midlife-crisis convertible you are craving? You can have it as long as you can afford it without skimping on retirement savings and other essentials.
- Buy the safety and security features that may save your car, your insurance bill, and your life.
- Ask the dealer what the first few scheduled services will cost to get a general indication of the maintenance costs.
- Go for a car with good mileage to cut your gas bills, and keep the mileage up by keeping tires inflated as recommended by the manufacturer.
- Choose a car that runs well on regular gas and don't pay for premium gasoline.

Cutting the Cost by Buying Used

We all know that the period of greatest depreciation for a car is the 5 minutes it takes to drive it off the lot. Suddenly, it becomes a used car, and even with low miles and perfect maintenance, it is worth less than its sparkling sister still sitting on the car lot. Choosing to buy secondhand can cut the cost of owning a car. The average new car costs more than $22,000, and the average secondhand car less than half that. The first way that you save by buying secondhand is either spending less money up front or getting more car for the same money. However, the biggest saving is because someone else owned the car during the period of greatest depreciation. According to Edmund's, a leading car information company, "a well-maintained car—any car—will generally depreciate from its current value by about 50 percent every four years." Depreciation rates vary a lot between makes and models and there may be times when a new car is only a little more expensive than a similar used car. For example, when I priced a 2-year-old Camry as a comparison in the example above, it was only $2,500 less, that's 12.5 percent, than its new counterpart once taxes, fees, and so on were included.

Offsetting some of the long-term cost savings, you may have a tougher time financing a secondhand car and may pay a higher interest rate. Also, maintenance may be higher, because the car is older. You can mitigate those costs by buying a used car still under warranty and having it thoroughly checked out beforehand. Countering these potentially higher costs, older cars cost less to insure, though there may be a slight premium because you are not the first owner. Overall, however, the cost of ownership of a secondhand car will be lower than a comparable new car.

Tips for Buying a Used Car

- Never buy a used car without a thorough checkup and a vehicle history report. The only exception: dealer-authorized used cars being sold through a dealership with warranties as to their condition. Even then, make sure you have the warranty in writing.
- Order a CarFax vehicle history report from www.carfax.com on any vehicle you consider buying used. It will tell you about the history—number of owners, past accidents, odometer

readings, whether it has been a lease, rental, or fleet car, whether it has been written off and much more—so you can be pretty assured that there are no skeletons in the trunk.

- Don't rely solely on the Kelly Blue Book (www.kbb.com) to check the going market rate of the car. The Blue Book is based on asking prices, not actual sales prices. Also check the Edmund's True Market Value (www.edmunds.com), which tries to estimate the actual going price.
- Try to find a used car that is still within its warranty period. It is one extra layer of protection.
- As with new cars, everything's negotiable. Do your homework about what you should pay and be willing to walk away from a deal if you cannot reach what you feel is a fair market price. The exception: used-car superstores such as CarMax, where prices are set at a fair price and they profit from volume sales at lower margins.

Cut the Cost by Keeping Your Car

The final part of the equation is how long you keep the car. A lower-priced car kept for only a couple of years is going to end up costing as much as a higher-priced car kept for longer, though a lower priced car kept for a long time wins out over either of those options. Buy and hold, keep the car for as long as it is running well and meeting your needs. You may need to change cars when kids come along, or you may want to splurge on a convertible when they finally leave the nest. The rest of the time, however, resist the temptation to buy one car after another, with only a few years in between. Aim to own each car for 5 to 10 years so that you have years of payment-free transportation.

One Car or Two?

Unless you are high school sweethearts, you probably both had a car when you met. Chances are you still have two cars. The reality of modern relationships is that many couples need two cars. Between juggling careers, errands, meetings, life—not to mention soccer, PTA, baby-sitter ferrying, and an ever-increasing roster of school activities if you have children—one car often is not enough. Saving money is not about creating inconvenience; however, couples able to get by with one car can save a considerable amount of money compared to their two-car compatriots.

Where you live in relation to where you work makes a significant difference in your ability to cut back on car costs. Living near work or near good public transportation can eliminate the need for a second car, as can living in an urban neighborhood where most of life is in close proximity.

How you live also affects your ability to save money on car expenses. It amuses me to see my friends who live in Manhattan have a life that more closely resembles the suburban life of my childhood than most of my friends who live in neighborhoods full of homes on quarter acre lots. My friends walk their three children to childcare and school, the father listening to the eldest recite her multiplication tables as he walks eight blocks to her school. After school their children play in a local park, meeting kids from the neighborhood, with grown-ups looking on. The mother walks to local shops with her folding cart—the bag-lady accessory becomes high urban style in Manhattan—produce from one store, groceries from another.

As many cities go through urban renaissances, more couples are rediscovering the joy of living within walking distance of life, although mainly younger couples and empty nesters are populating the urban neighborhoods.

Insuring the Car

Automobile insurance can be a significant expense, especially if you have a sporty car, bad driving record, or history of accidents. But even for dull, safe drivers it can add up. Auto insurance covers more than just the vehicle. It can include:

- *Collision*, which covers damage to your car resulting from an accident or collision.
- *Comprehensive*, which covers damage or loss due to theft or something other than a collision with another car or object, such as a hailstorm or vandalism.
- *Property liability*, which reimburses others for damage your car inflicts on property, such as another car, light pole or building.
- *Uninsured and underinsured motorist*, which insures against injury if an underinsured or uninsured driver hits you, a designated driver, or a family member. It also covers you for pedestrian or hit-and-run accidents.
- *Medical/personal injury*, which covers injuries to the driver and passengers of your car, possibly also covering funeral costs, lost wages, and services normally performed by an injured person.
- *Bodily injury*, which covers injuries that you or a designated driver cause to others. It also covers injuries you and family members cause to others when you are driving another car with permission, including rental cars.

Few people read their policies at all, much less in detail. However, it can be instructive and a good way to pass a cold winter's night. The policy will include a jacket that describes the general policy, the declarations that describe exactly what you are buying, and the endorsements with amendments made since the policy was originally written. Check that you have the coverage you thought you had and are neither paying for anything you don't need nor missing out on anything essential. Don't pay for any optional coverage that you don't need, but make sure you get the ones that make sense. The optional coverage may include:

- *Rental reimbursement*, which covers some or all of the cost of a rental car if your car is stolen or in the shop as the result of an accident. Usually it costs $1 to $2 a month and can save hundreds. According to the National Safety Council, one in eight drivers will be in an accident this year and the car will be in the shop for an average of 10 to 12 days. So unless you have a spare car or can easily get by without one at all, it is worth buying.

- *Towing and roadside assistance*, which may be redundant if you are a member of AAA.
- *Auto replacement*, which guarantees that the car will be completely repaired or replaced even if it costs more than its depreciated value.
- *Gap coverage*, which may be required if you lease rather than buy. It covers the difference between what the insurance would pay if your car was written off and what the leasing company would need to come out even. Generally, the lease company arranges this coverage and wraps it into your lease cost.

Some factors in the insurance equation are beyond your control. Insurers make assumptions about individual drivers based on broad trends. Young drivers, male drivers, people with body piercings . . . if there is a statistically significant trend that doesn't violate antidiscrimination laws, you can be sure it is built into the insurance company's pricing models. Yet there are many choices you can make to keep your insurance cost low:

- Choose a make and model that is less expensive to insure.
- Consider raising your deductible if you have enough cash to cover yourself in case of an accident.
- Don't underinsure. The amount of physical and emotional damage an accident can wreak should not be underestimated. Consider raising the limits on the bodily injury coverage. Insufficient insurance can be very expensive in the long run.
- Don't overinsure. If you have an umbrella liability policy, you may not need as much auto insurance.

- Keep your mileage down. The more miles you drive in an average year, the greater your insurance bill.
- Drive safely. Don't cruise down hills in neutral (dangerous), accelerate at every yellow light (stupid), travel 10 miles an hour below the speed limit in the middle lane (dangerous and stupid). Safe drivers spend less on insurance and their cars last longer.
- Clean up your credit score (see Chapter 10). More and more insurers take your credit rating into account.
- Live in an area where it costs less to insure your car. A high-crime rate adds to insurance costs. Parking also has an effect on insurance costs: cars parked off the street are less likely to be stolen, and cars in garages are less likely to be damaged by a hailstorm.
- Shop for rates every few years, but know that staying with one company more than 3 to 5 years may result in additional discounts.
- Insure all your cars through one company, preferably through the company that also provides your home insurance.
- Take a defensive driving course. These courses teach you how to get your car out of a spin, how to stop on a proverbial dime, and just might save your life. You'll be a better driver, and you may get a discount on your insurance.
- Pay your bill all at once. Insurance companies often charge extra fees if you opt to spread your payments over 6 months.

Kids, Cars, and Cash

Uh oh. Little Johnny's turned sixteen! Try as you might, you can't stop your kids from growing older. Even if they are resisting maturity with every cell of their hormone-ravaged bodies, when they get to age sixteen, they will be craving the first sign of growing up: a driver's license. And probably a car to go with it.

Cars and kids can be a lethal combination. Teen drivers are more likely to speed and drive dangerously. The second you let a teen behind the wheel of you car your insurance premiums will go sky-high. If you have kids, should you let them drive you car?

As parents you have four options: let your kids drive your car, give your kids a car, help them save for their own car, or try to keep them off the road for as long as possible. As tempting as the last option sounds, not only will it create a huge amount of disharmony, it will also increase the chances of them being a passenger in a car driven by another teen, which is a very scary thought. New drivers are more likely to have huge, nasty accidents when their friends are in their cars. Whether it is passengers egging on or drivers showing off, teens drive less safely with passengers than when alone.

So let's look at the first approach: letting your kids drive your car. Many parents celebrate the day that they no longer have to play chauffeur to every after-school activity. However, letting your teen use your car can create scheduling conflicts.

The second option is to give your teen a car. Some families hand on one of their existing cars to their teen, whereas others purchase a car for them.

What about helping the kids buy their own car? Even if you don't help financially, you will likely help them find and choose the right car. Where I grew up, only the richest of parents bought their kids cars. Most of us worked summer jobs and weekends to save for our own cars and bought the cheapest cars that actually ran. My first car was a 10-year-old Corolla with a reconditioned (and souped up) motor and a horribly pocked paint job. It got me from A to B. The problem with this strategy, though, is that kids end up with cheap cars that are less safe and more likely to have high maintenance costs. A 10-year-old car today may be missing basic safety equipment such as air bags and anti-lock breaks that saves lives. If you encourage your children to save for a car, make sure they can afford a car you feel comfortable with.

You may choose a hybrid of these options to help teach your kids the value of a dollar and the need to save. For example, you may help them set a goal and then agree to match their savings dollar for dollar, give them a bonus when they reach their goal so that they can upgrade to a safer car, or pay for the car but insist they pay the running costs.

Insuring your teen can be very expensive. Even though your insurance company may offer the best rate if you include your teen on your auto policy, it is worth shopping around. If your teen has her own car, your insurance firm may still be the best bet, as you will receive multiple car discounts. Most insurers offer discounts for good students, and will give you a break on the premiums if your teen is at school more than 100 miles away, if the car stays put.

Apart from the additional insurance premiums, gas, maintenance, and cleaning are likely to rise too. With rights come responsibilities: You will need to work with your teen to reach an agreement about how costs are shared, along with rules about how and when the car is used, who has responsibility for refilling the tank and keeping it clean, and so on. While you're negotiating, you may want to have them do some of the chauffeuring for younger siblings. Creating limits is also important. You may choose to restrict his nighttime driving and insist that he not have teen passengers until he has proved that he is a responsible driver. And if your teen is caught violating any driving laws or has an accident, you can remove his driving privileges.

CHAPTER 17

···

Decision 3: Whether You Have Children

ONE OF THE MOST SIGNIFICANT FINANCIAL DECISIONS YOU WILL ever make is one that you probably do not consider financial at all: having children. Most couples think of having children as an emotional, personal, familial decision. However, while you will not—or did not—make the decision from a financial perspective, it is important to understand the financial implications of the decision. In addition, let's explore how to manage the cost of having children, especially the cost of college.

Kids cost. They cost a lot. Kids are as expensive as a house. Kids cost as much as retirement. If you choose to be childless, you can afford to be the rich aunt who spoils her nieces and nephews, the wealthy man in a sports car, the well-off couple who jet about the world each year. But having children has a value that cannot be measured in dollars. Think of the sweet smiles, the sticky kid kisses, the enthusiastic I love you's followed by heartfelt hugs. Sweet stuff. Then there are the resentful teenagers, embarrassed to be seen with you, breeding bacteria under the bed, brooding down hallways, and bickering with their siblings. Perhaps it's not all that sweet. I cannot put a dollar value on the intangibles of being a parent, and will leave that decision to you, but let's look at the financial implications of such a personal decision.

The Cost of Kids

The average cost of raising a child to age 17 is more than $165,000. That's an average income family—between $38,000 and $64,000 income in the year 2000—spending $8,740 to $9,860 per child each year, depending on the child's age.[1] This adds up to more than 20 percent of the after-tax income of the average family being spent per child. And that amount doesn't include nannies, private schools, or any kiddy luxuries. No wonder people have a tough time finding extra money to save for their kid's college education.

These figures assume that you did not have to spend thousands conceiving or adopting the child in the first place, which costs many couples unexpected thousands extra. One in six couples seeks some sort of fertility treatment, and the average cost of in vitro fertilization (IVF) is around $10,000 per treatment, with many couples requiring more than one cycle of treatment. Adoption can range from zero to over $30,000, depending on whether you adopt through a public or private agency, and whether you adopt a child from overseas.

Then, if you send your child through college, you will face substantial additional costs. Tuition, room, and board average $36,000 at a 4-year state college or $94,000 at a private college.[2] Babysitting for friends once in a while instead of having your own children looks more and more attractive.

How can an average family afford to raise children? Who knows, but most manage it somehow. Although childlessness is on the rise, 81 percent of women have had a child by the time they

---

[1] *USDA Estimates Child Rearing Costs.* U.S. Department of Agriculture News Release, June 11, 2001.
[2] The College Board, www.collegeboard.org.

reach age 40,[3] so it's reasonable to assume that the majority of couples choose to have kids. What is amazing is that the parents probably spent everything they earned before having kids—not many have $9,000 a year unaccounted for. Making it even tougher, some households decrease income sources at the same time they increase the number of family members, going from two incomes and two people to one (or one and a half) incomes and three or more mouths to feed. Yet somehow they flex their finances to make ends meet, I hope without running up significant debt in the process. The financial reality of this math hits home for some couples. In their Money and the American Family survey, AARP and *Modern Maturity* found that 14 percent of people postponed having children for financial reasons.[4]

Being a parent gets more expensive by the year. The cost is rising as our general standard of living rises, but also as our lives become busier. The more time-crunched parents are, the more willing they are to pay for a little extra convenience. And the more guilty parents feel about having less time with their kids, the more likely they are to assuage the guilt with little gifts and extra extravagances. Think back to when you were a kid. How different was your lifestyle from that of kids today? It's a different and more expensive time to be a parent for us than it was for our parents.

Managing the everyday costs of having children means becoming conscious of the myriad of ways you spend a few dollars here and a few dollars there.

Housing

Housing accounts for about one-third of the cost of raising a child. More people in the family require more space. However, houses are getting larger and larger all the time, even though household size is shrinking.

---

[3]*Fertility of American Women*. U.S. Census Bureau, June 2000.
[4]*The Allure of Money*. AARP/*Modern Maturity* Press Release, May 16, 2000.

One major way that you can manage the cost of having children is to choose to live in a more modest home. Hey, once you have kids and toys all over the place, even a mansion feels mini, so you might as well think twice before adding on to your existing home or moving to a larger home. Once you have a bedroom for you and each of the kids, and a family room to commune in, everything extra is gravy. And if staying put means sacrificing the guest rooms, then investigate local hotels where the grandparents can stay when they come to visit.

Food

Life as a parent gets incredibly busy. Spending on convenience food can skyrocket as you part with cash for a school lunch, for drive-through meals grabbed as kids are shipped from one event to another, for take-out or delivery on nights when cooking feels like one chore too many, and for the many packaged foods that save a little time here and there. Americans over 8 years old typically eat 4.3 commercially prepared meals a week, according to the National Restaurant Association.

Food accounts for 18 percent of the cost of raising a child. The challenge is to manage costs while still keeping convenience. Health is a factor too: Approximately 13 percent of kids are overweight[5] and convenience food too often means refined food high in fat and calories. A Happy Meal (cheeseburger, small fries, small Coke) has 690 calories and 24 grams of fat; that is over one-third of an *adult's* daily calorie requirements. Some ideas to lower food costs *and* to provide healthier snacks are:

- Kids graze, so always have food on hand. Stock the car with healthy snacks, such as whole-grain cereal bars. If the

------

[5]The 1999 National Health and Nutrition Examination Survey (NHANES), using measured heights and weights, indicate that an estimated 13 percent of children ages 6–11 years and 14 percent of adolescents ages 12–19 years are overweight.

weather permits, there's no reason why a bag of apples cannot take up permanent residence in the car.

- Stop the soda habit. A can of Coke has 39 grams, about 10 teaspoons, of sugar. Not to mention a good slug of caffeine. If kids never get into the soda habit, you'll save money—at the supermarket, the soda machine and the dentist. And if your kids are like I am and bounce off the walls with sugar and caffeine in their system, soda-free kids will probably be calmer, too.

- Have water—the greatest drink of all—on hand. Reuse plastic water bottles—lots of them—rather than throwing them out. Keep some in the fridge, some in lunchboxes, and some in the car. For flavor, add a squeeze of lemon juice (you can buy it by the bottle). If that doesn't satisfy them, try fruit juice or powdered drinks such as Kool Aid, but watch for excessive amounts of sugar.

- Fill the freezer and cupboards with convenience foods that can replace take-out or delivery meals. A frozen pizza costs a fraction of what a delivered pizza costs and takes little time to prepare. And there are plenty of healthier options available.

- Get to know the healthy, filling, fast-food places. A baked potato or small Subway sandwich has a fraction of the fat and calories of a Happy Meal, as long as you don't load it with high fat dressings.

- Join a warehouse food club. Most sell single-serve convenience foods at a great discount.

- Get an extra freezer if you have space so you can stock up and shop less often.

- Make preparing school lunches a chore for the kids. They do not have to be that old before lining up the bags, putting in fruit, juice boxes and cookies, and making sandwiches.

- Make planning and cooking a family meal a privilege and let the kids take over the kitchen one night a week. Even if they are putting a ready-made salad in a bowl and heating a frozen pizza, it can help share the load.

Transportation

Another expenditure when you're raising kids is transportation. It accounts for 15 percent of the cost of raising a child. The easiest way to keep this cost down is to live within walking distance of your child's school and major activities. Carpooling with other parents can also keep down the cost of shuttling kids around. Once kids hit driving age, watch out. Costs can skyrocket. Tips on managing the cost of a teen's car and other tips for keeping the cost of transportation down are included in Chapter 16 on Decision 2: What You Drive.

Clothes

Kids clothes are cute. It can be tempting to treat kids as big dolls or mini-me's. My nephew at age 6 months had wraparound sunglasses, and a tiny black denim jacket embroidered as if he were a big, bad biker. He looked like an adorable version of Jack Nicholson. How can you resist?

Whether you go for utilitarian or unbelievably cute, there is a constant battle between buying enough so you are not doing washing constantly and not spending a fortune on clothes that will fit for only a short time.

. . . .

"I've always shopped for quality, because quality lasts longer," Gina said. "But I realized that the kids were growing so quickly, and it really didn't matter if the clothes weren't designed to last 5 years." Her two kids are nicely dressed in basics bought on sale and at discount chains. Before they become fashion-conscious tweens, Gina is doing all she can to keep their clothing costs down. "Of course, I still want brands that don't shrink or run, but there seems like little value in spending top dollar on big name brands." Gina's kids look smart because her eye for color and clever buying means that the clothes they have mix and match stylishly. Her 10-year-old daughter is already starting to feel pressure to follow fashions. "One day I am going to

have to help my daughter understand that it costs a lot to follow trends. She will simply have to make choices within a limited budget. At least her school is not full of rich kids she would want to keep up with."

. . . .

Of course, the age-old way of managing the cost of kids' clothes is to use hand-me-downs, especially when they are young enough that the fashion police won't ostracize them for it. The key is to have friends or relatives with kids just a little older than your own; it pays to be one of the last in your circle to have kids. Whether you are the giver or receiver in the cycle of kids' clothes, it makes sense to pass them on. Kids simply don't fit in their clothes long enough for serious wear and tear to occur. Consignment stores are another source of preloved clothes (as well as other items). Another source of affordable clothes is discount stores. If you have not been into the clothes section of Target, Walmart, and the like for a while, you'll be pleasantly surprised. They offer well-made fashionable clothes at a great price. Of course, shopping the sales makes sense too. And if you have relatives who buy gifts for the kids and never know what to get, e-mail them the size that your children wear each year so they can add to the wardrobe, not the toy chest.

Toys and Hobbies

The range of kids' toys is overwhelming. Trends come and go faster than when I was young, and the merchandising of movie-related toys makes it harder to find toys that will stand the test of time. I remember when dimpled dolls that giggled when you moved their arms were *de rigueur* at Donvale, the elementary school I attended. A couple of kids had received them for their birthdays, and the rest of us waited with bated breath for Christmas. The next year the trend was dolls with extendable hair (you turned a dial in the middle of the doll's back to make the hair grow). Even though I was more likely to be found cruising the neighborhood on my bike or climbing trees, I wanted the latest, greatest doll because it was a sign of being part of the crowd. Between birthdays and Christmas, we had small treats: marbles or collectible cards.

The world has changed a lot, not only in how often kids get new possessions, but also in what those possessions are. Toy manufacturers are finding that kids are growing out of toys at a younger and younger age. Barbies are now the realm of the under eights, or even under sixes, and kids by age 10 are more interested in music, cell phones, and electronics than toys. How, as a parent, can you find the right balance between keeping up with the trends that your child feels are life and death needs, and not overspending on fads that come and go? When there are piles of toys barely played with, how can you know that the next toy bought will make its way to the top of the favorites list, at least for a while?

Along with the various possessions that kids and teens dream of, there are also many activities that they can get involved in, most of which come with hefty price tags. As a parent, you want your child to be active. However, some activities come with such a large price tag that a little encouragement toward lower-cost activities such as editing the school paper or playing sports with little equipment cost may be in order.

Kids' constant asking provides a great opportunity for you to help them learn to prioritize their wants and save for goals. You can also help them understand that limited resources means making considered trade-offs. But, the bottom line is that parents must learn to say the word that kids are so good at saying and so bad at hearing—"No."

Other Costs

Kids require an array of specialized equipment throughout their life, from baby seats and strollers, to computers for homework. For items that are used for just a while, hand-me-downs from friends or family can be great. There are many stores that sell secondhand equipment. However, do not root around in your parents' attic for the crib you used as a kid. The safety standards have changed so much over the last couple of decades that older is not better. Of course, you can help friends as they have kids by handing on or loaning out your kid gear once you no longer need it.

Whereas a cool pencil case was basic equipment for kids of my era (Josie and the Pussy Cats was the design of choice), a laptop is now required by some schools. As a parent, you can manage the technology costs by waiting until you know the standards that your child's school requires before spending money on a home system, seeing if after-school programs can give your kids the access to computers that they need to do their homework, or using an older computer until you know that a state-of-the-art system is worth buying. Also, many libraries and community centers have resources that families can use. The one thing that you can be sure of is that anything you buy will be surpassed in a few months, so going for the fastest, greatest machine you can afford only buys a small window of technological superiority. Given that, the close-out sale of the preceding model becomes more attractive.

Communication technology has also changed. My mother used to call out "Be home by sunset and don't slam the door" as we charged out of the house, grabbing our bikes and slamming the door behind us. The world is a more dangerous place today and the schedules of both parents and children overflowing. Increasingly, families are using pagers and cell phones to keep in touch between activities. Cell phone companies have seen the trend and now market family packages where each member can have a phone and the calls between family members have few costs. In addition, at home you may be paying for the main phone number, a second line or high-speed Internet connection, and perhaps a further separate line for the kids. It is no wonder that what used to be a minor expense for most families has ballooned into costs running into potentially hundreds a month. The key to keeping costs manageable is to avoid being at the very front of the technological trend. Wait until it is clear what you need and let the first wave of very high-priced technology pass.

Action Item: Plan for the Price of Parenting
· ·

Whether or not you have kids yet, spend 10 minutes looking at the cost of kids if you have, or plan to have, them. Discuss the following, skipping questions that are no longer relevant:

- When do you plan to have children? How many?
- What financial goals do you want to reach before having children?
- What lifestyle changes do you plan to make to afford the everyday costs of raising a child? Will you need a different house or car? Will you want to live in a different neighborhood?
- Do you plan to have a parent at home part-time or full-time? How will that affect your income?
- What sort of childcare do you expect to have in the early years?
- What type of college would you want your children to go to and how much can you put away each year to save for it?

Go back to the spending plan you created and see what changes you will need to make to include children's living costs and college savings in the plan.

· ·

Kids and Their Money

Sometimes the challenge of raising decent kids with reasonable grades seems overwhelming, yet parents are also on the frontline for teaching children about money management. Without any direct instruction, your children will learn plenty, from what you do well and what you don't do well. However, it is better to try to raise money-conscious kids from the beginning rather than to let them become unconscious spenders who have to buy my books a generation from now (even though I'll appreciate the royalties when I'm old and gray)!

Parents are often poor financial role models for their children. A study found that, although almost all parents say they understand financial matters very or fairly well and more than 80 percent think they do an excellent or good job of managing their money, a full 55 percent of parents are rolling over credit card debt from month to month.[6] When asked where they would advise their child to put $5,000 for a long-term goal, almost half named a low-return vehicle such as a savings bond, bank account, or CD.

Allowances

A child's allowance is his or her first interaction with real money. It is a perfect opportunity for parents to really teach their children how money works—a life skill not reinforced consistently in schools.

Kids are really sensitive about financial issues because no one wants to be the poor kid in class and everyone quickly learns that the kid with the largest allowance has more friends than his personality alone would buy. The big question for parents is how much should the allowance be? The Coinstar National Currency Poll found that kids were given an average of approximately $9 a week; however, other studies show that there is a lot more money than that passing through their hands. An Ohio State University study for the Department of Labor found that average teens receive $50 a week in disposable income and Teen Research Unlimited found that the average teen spends $84 a week. Knowing what is average doesn't help, however, if you don't have a sense of what is typical in your neighborhood. My friends, Martin and Susan, who have two boys under 10, find talking to the parents of their kids' friends is key because there is variation even within schools. Some PTAs even have Internet discussion groups where these topics can be discussed. Aside from the basic allowance, beware of the tendency to hand money out in between, muddying the meaning of the allowance.

---

[6]*2001 Parents, Youth and Money Survey* conducted by the American Savings Education Council and Employee Benefit Research Institute, www.asec.org.

How can you use an allowance as a teaching tool, not simply a whining-reduction tool? By using it to show how money is earned. Even better, extend the lessons to include tax, savings goals, debt, interest, and insurance. Although this can be complicated on a paper-based system, there is a software package called *KnowingMoney*,[7] which uses kids' comfort with computers to teach them financial basics. It requires parents and children to reach agreements about how allowances are earned, and offers a good replication of how money works for "big kids" without overcomplicating things.

Kids and Credit

If your kids don't have a debit or credit card by the time they leave high school, they will soon after. Every credit card company on earth is on college campuses trying to woo the freshly escaped youths and buy their brand loyalty. The average undergraduate student seeking a loan from student loan company Nellie Mae has $2,748 in credit card debt on three cards, a good start on the American consumer lifestyle. As a parent, teaching your kids basic real-world survival skills now includes teaching them to manage credit and all its temptations. Modeling financially responsible behavior and having your children involved in your household's financial process can be good ways for them to begin to get the idea. However, young adults need direct lessons on how to use credit cards responsibly.

It is relatively easy for parents to get their children credit cards. Children must be over age 18 before they can get their own cards, as they cannot enter a legal contract on their own before that age. Prior to age 18, a parent or other adult must cosign for the card and is legally responsible for the debt the young cardholder may accrue.[8] Parents can find lists of credit cards available for students

---

[7]The software can be purchased from www.knowingmoney.com. Disclosure: I help distribute the software in the U.S., but only because I was so impressed by how thorough it is.
[8]See at www.cardweb.com.

at www.cardweb.com or www.bankrate.com. The huge downside: If your cosigned teen goes wild with the card, your credit (as well as your teen's) suffers. To address this problem, credit card companies are offering cardlike products that give kids the feel of a credit card without the potential to wreak havoc. The best known is a product Visa offers called Visa Buxx, a prepaid, reloadable card that is accepted anywhere Visa can be used. Teens and their parents can check on-line where the money went, and parents choose how much money to give their teen when they reload the card.

The financial behavior of teens or young adults builds the foundation for their future credit record, so it is important that they understand the responsibility of credit. A spokesperson for the credit-reporting company TransUnion explains: "The first time a person applies for credit, or is named as a coborrower on a loan, a credit file is created for her at TransUnion or one of the other consumer-reporting companies." Their credit score follows not long after, according to a spokesperson for credit-score provider Fair, Isaac and Company. To create a credit-risk score, he says, "three conditions must be present on the consumer's credit file: 1) It must include at least one credit account that has been open for at least six months; 2) The file must show activity within the past six months on at least one credit account; and 3) There must be no 'deceased' indicator on the credit file."

Your teens can build a strong credit rating from day one by having at least one credit card, using it a little, and paying it off regularly. The best habit to teach them is to pay all their bills on time and pay off their credit cards in full every month.

Paying for College

If having kids is expensive, having them educated enough that they can support you in your old age is even more expensive! Is it parents' obligation to pay for their children's college education? Certainly in the current American culture, it is something many parents aim for. However there are plenty of caring parents who support their children's advanced education in other ways. Many successful Americans have worked their way through college, waiting tables, studying part time, joining the military, working summers, getting scholarships and grants, or getting into work-related programs. Another common way of funding part of the college bill is through student loans and other financial aid.

Put Yourself First

What if, when you do the numbers, you find you cannot save both for your retirement and your child's college education? As much as it may go against the grain as a parent, you should put your own retirement savings first. Why? First, because in most financial-aid calculations, your retirement savings will not be considered. Also, because you can borrow to put your kids through school, but you cannot borrow to put yourself through retirement. So, it makes sense to aim to fund your own retirement and to find a way of getting your kids through college with a combination of financial aid, student loans, part-time work, and so on. As a rule of thumb, max out your retirement contributions each year before you start saving for college, but aim to cut back in other areas if you cannot afford both.

Start Now to Save Enough

How much you need to put away depends on how early you start and your final goal. Let's say you want to save $100,000 per child and you want to reach that goal by the time each one turns 18. What is your best scenario? A lump sum on the day they are born, starting at birth, or starting later? Assuming an 8 percent return after all taxes and fees, Table 17.1 shows that a lump sum is clearly best. However, for many households, putting away that much money in a year is not feasible unless they started saving before their child was even conceived. The second best strategy is to start investing for their college at birth. Waiting to start costs you dearly. If you put off starting to save until your child is 5 years old, you have to put away 75 percent more per year than if you started

Table 17.1   Saving $100,000 by Age 18

Scenario	Amount of Investment	Total Contributions	Value at Age 18	
			8% Return	10% Return
Invest one lump sum at birth	25,025	25,025	100,000	139,137
Invest annually from birth	2,873	44,514	100,000	124,043
Invest annually from age 5	4,308	56,004	100,000	116,208
Invest annually from age 10	8,706	69,648	100,000	109,517

at birth. So instead of a $2,873 investment per year, you have to find an extra $1,835 each year that you contribute (totaling $4,308 per year) to make the same goal of $100,000 at age 18. If you put investing off until your child is 10, you have to put away an extra $6,233 a year (totaling $8,706), more than 3.5 times as much each year that you contribute than it would take starting at the child's birth.

Another thing to notice is that if the markets are kind to you and the earnings rate is higher than 8 percent, the difference between starting at birth and starting later becomes even more pronounced. You could either end up with more money than you planned—an extra $24,043 if you started saving regularly at birth—or stop saving a few years earlier.

These numbers are all based on a simple investment account. As soon as you add in tax advantages, the numbers get even more attractive.

Save in a Tax-Effective Way

When saving for college, parents face a difficult choice: By being a good, responsible saver, you may decrease the amount of financial aid you can access. Many families actively decrease their cash and income in the year before they apply for financial aid so they can qualify for more. For example, equity in your home doesn't count in the financial aid calculation for many schools, so families can increase the amount that they may qualify for by using cash to pay down their mortgage and any other loans. I leave questions about the ethics of bending your finances to increase your ability to qualify for financial aid to you; however, it goes to show that actions are influenced by what gets measured.

There are a number of tools that will help you save for your kids' education by giving you tax breaks. Because some of these programs have an impact on your ability to qualify for financial aid, talk to your tax advisor about what is best for your situation. The tools are:

- *Coverdell Education Savings Account.* An Education Savings Account (ESA) allows $2,000 a year to be put away to grow tax deferred, provided it is opened for a minor and used for qualified educational expenses by the time the beneficiary is age 30. The contributions to the account are not tax deductible, but the earnings accrue and the withdrawals are made tax free if they are used for qualified higher-education expenses. Anyone can contribute to a child's account, and a parent or guardian gets to choose the investments within the account, and can elect to retain control over the funds in the account. There are income limits on eligibility for these accounts (phasing out at adjusted gross incomes of more than $95,000 for single filers and $190,000 for married filers). ESAs used to be called Education IRAs.
- *529 College Savings Plan.* These state-sponsored plans can allow for very large amounts to be put away, with up to $110,000 per couple per year for each child ($55,000 per parent accounted for over five years to equal the $11,000 gift tax limit per parent per year). The contribution rules vary by state, so ask an investment advisor in your area. As with ESAs, the contributions are not tax deductible, but the earnings and withdrawals are tax free if they are used for qualified higher-education expenses. The state's plan administrator manages the investments, but the account owner may be able

to choose from different levels of risk for the portfolio, depending on the state. There is no age restriction on the beneficiary of the account and you are able to contribute to both an ESA and a 529 in the same year.

- *Prepaid State Tuition Plans.* Many states allow parents to prepay tuition, and sometimes it can be a good deal; however, such plans may restrict your child to going only to a state college in your state (though some states allow students to study in other states, whereas others allow parents from other states to set up plans). The advantage is that these plans lock in tuition at today's rates, even though tuition has been rising faster than inflation. Like the other savings plan, the earnings grow tax free. See www.collegesavings.org for more information.
- *Custodial Accounts.* Custodial accounts are regular investment accounts that are in the name of your child. The advantage is that earnings are taxed at the lower rate that your child faces; however, there are some major drawbacks. First, you cannot force your child to use the money for education once the control of the account goes to her at age 18 or 21 (depending on the state you live in). Second, assets owned by the child will affect the amount of financial aid she qualifies for much more than assets in your name, as a significant proportion of the child's assets are expected to be used for her education. Given the flexibility of 529 and ESA accounts, custodial accounts should be a last option.

What happens if you have saved for college and your teen decides to skip college or attend a school that does not charge tuition? All of the plans offer an out, although you may be subject to a tax penalty to make up for the tax not paid on income earned by the investment in the past.

Cut the Cost of College

The cost of college is rising faster than inflation, making quality education an ever-more difficult thing to afford. There are ways, however, to keep the cost of college down. Your teen can consider:

- Taking advanced placement courses while in high school to minimize the number of classes that he needs to take in college.
- Choosing a state, not private, college, especially one where he already qualifies for in-state tuition.
- Applying for financial aid. This topic is complex enough for a book on its own, and there is a lot that your teen can do to increase his chances of getting some aid to cover part of the cost of college. Be aware of those things that can hinder gaining financial aid. Well-meaning actions can have negative impacts. For example, grandparents who give money directly to their grandchild rather than holding off until after he graduates can negatively impact his chance of getting financial aid.
- Negotiating with the institutions that offer him a place to see if they can increase the amount of financial aid offered.
- Working part-time either on campus or off to cover some of his costs. For example, being a Resident Assistant in on-campus housing can offset the cost of room and board considerably.
- Looking into Pell Grants, awarded by the federal government based on need. The Pell Grant covers an ever-smaller percent of the cost of going to school, only 40 percent of the average public university.
- Going to a community college for the first year or two and then transferring the credits earned to a four-year college.

For your part, you can take all the tax benefits you are entitled to. Depending on your income, you may be able to take the Hope scholarship credit or Lifetime Learning credit to offset the cost of your child's tuition.

Borrow the Balance

After all the savings have been tapped, financial aid accessed, and cost corners cut, you may find you still do not have enough. Enter student loans. One of the rare examples of good debt, student loans allow your college-aged children to borrow today so that they earn more tomorrow. The College Board has found that student loans now represent 58 percent of financial aid, up from 41 percent in 1980–1981. Types of loans are:

- *Stafford loans.* The most common loans, Stafford loans are available to many students. Interest rates vary (but are generally low) as do the date at which repayment begins. If you qualify for financial aid, the government may pick up the interest payments while your child is in college. If not, interest can be deferred until graduation. If the graduate decides to teach in a low-income area school for 5 years, $5,000 of the amount owed may be waived.
- *Perkins loans.* Perkins loans are for low-income families and repayment is deferred until after graduation.
- *PLUS loans.* As parents, you may qualify for a PLUS loan, which is a government-backed loan for the shortfall after financial aid is received. The fees on these loans can be expensive, so other forms of borrowing, such as a home equity loan, may be a much better deal.
- *Other loans.* Either the student or parents may use other loans ranging from credit card loans to home equity lines of credit. Be sure to consider the after-tax cost of such loans when comparing your options.

CHAPTER 18

··

Decision 4: When
You Retire

THE DREAM OF RETIRING YOUNG IS APPEALING. THERE IS SOME-thing about not marching to someone else's pace that attracts many people. Finally, a chance to be the golfer I could never be professionally, to spend time with the friends and family I am too busy to see, to travel to the parts of the world that I have yearned to visit. . . . Perhaps if our lifestyles during our working years were more balanced, we would be less eager to escape the working world. But they aren't and we are. Very eager.

The trouble is that the dream of early retirement conflicts directly with the dream of a comfortable retirement. For many people, starting retirement 5 or 10 years early robs their retirement portfolio of the years critical to its growth, the years when compounding returns do their best. Early retirement breaks a critical investment rule: Money left alone for a very long time grows into a lot of money. Unfortunately, too many people do not save enough money early or leave it long enough to reach their dream of an early retirement. About 15 percent of people have to retire later than they desire because of financial needs.[1] An even larger number of people are worried about their ability to take care of

---

[1]Money and the American Family telephone survey, quoted in *The Allure of Money*. AARP/*Modern Maturity* Press Release, May 16, 2000.

themselves during retirement: 29 percent of men and 41 percent of women are not confident that they will have enough money to live comfortably throughout retirement.[2] The Consumer Federation of America says that over one-half of all people are behind in their retirement savings. Executive Director Stephen Brobeck warns: "The bad news is that most U.S. households will not be able to sustain their standard of living into retirement. The good news is that most of the unprepared households could get ready by taking advantage of the magic of interest compounding."[3]

Many people are retired for as many years as they worked. It takes a lot of money to fund a long retirement. The retirement age that you choose directly affects how much money you need to save every year that you work, so you are playing with the balance between your standard of living during your working years and your standard of living during retirement.

Is your goal of retiring young a pipe dream?

Time Is Money

Take a look at the shape of the graph shown in Figure 18.1. Depicted is a simple calculation of what $2,000 a year invested at 10 percent per annum looks like over time. Notice how the curve rises slowly before it takes off, and then at the end it *really* takes off. That growth is called compounding. Pretty sweet, isn't it? For a while, the rise in the curve is mainly because $2,000 a year is put in by the investor—the earnings on your investment are minimal—but by year nine and beyond, the amount earned by the investment is *greater than* the amount contributed by the investor. Why? Because the underlying investment is earning a return for you, earnings that are fully reinvested. The graph shows that after 40 years the investor has a nest egg of $885,185. In its last year, the

---

[2]2001 Retirement Confidence Survey conducted by the America Savings Education Council and the Employee Benefits Research Institute.
[3]*New Study: More Than Half of Americans Behind in Saving for Retirement*, Consumer Federation of America Press Release, April 26, 2000.

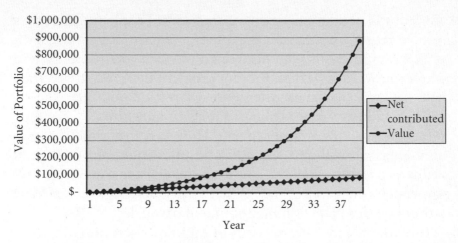

Figure 18.1   Growth of saving $2,000 a year at
10 percent return.

return on the investment is over $80,000—it took more than 16 years for the portfolio to reach $80,000 in total value in the first place. If, however, the investment was cut 5 years short, the total would be only $542,049. Ten years earlier, it is only $328,988.

Compounding is critical for two reasons. First, it means that the younger you start investing for retirement, the better off you will be. If you don't start saving for retirement until you are 40 or 50, you are in trouble. Second, the other end of the equation, the earlier you retire, the less time your money has to grow, especially if you started late.

Know When to Fold 'Em

We have all heard stories of the person retiring on a Friday and dying of a heart attack on the following Monday (did the thought of all that free time scare him to death?). We've also heard stories about people working productively into their eighties and then living decades more. Retirement is not about numbers. It is about making sure you get to pursue some of your life's passions while you are still able to enjoy them. And most people feel that they need to retire to do that.

To plan retirement, you need to know when you will retire, and when you will die. Hmm. Bit of a problem there. First, less than half of all workers know when they will retire.[4] And then, the insurance industry uses actuarial tables to guesstimate how long someone your age is likely to live. However, they don't tell you how long *you* will live. Complicating the equation, the age at which you retire influences how long you will live. People who retire earlier, die earlier. Maybe there's just so long we can hang around on this planet doing nothing in particular.

Buy yourself long-term peace of mind by overestimating how long you will live. It is better to have too much than too little, and it makes sense with the advances in medical technology to prepare for the possibility of living to 90, 100, or more.

While age is just a number, there are some key ages to remember when thinking about retirement:

50   The government figures you hit panic stations and contribution levels for many retirement savings tools are raised, allowing you to put away more money before retirement.

55   Discounts open up to you. Cheaper travel, discounts at museums . . . enjoy it. It's the first time you've been carded in a while.

59½   You can begin withdrawing money from your IRA accounts without facing a penalty. There are some limits; for example, the money in a Roth IRA has to have been in the account for 5 years.

62   Begin being able to claim Social Security benefits.

65–67   Full retirement age, as defined by Social Security. Your full retirement age is somewhere between 65 and 67,

---

[4]*Get Personal with Retirement Planning and Employees Will Stick with You.* Aon Consulting Press Release, July 17, 2000.

depending on your year of birth. Claiming Social Security before this age will reduce your payments.

70   You can delay claiming your Social Security benefits until age 70 and receive a greater benefit once you begin.

70½   You must begin taking payments from your IRA or pay a penalty.

100   You are wished a happy birthday on national TV. Now that's worth hanging on for.

122   That's how old the oldest recorded person lived to. Rumor is she took up bungee jumping at 107 because she was bored after all her friends died.

123   You get listed in the Guinness Book of Records.

How Much to Plan For

To work out how much you need to retire, you need not only to estimate when you will retire and how long you will be retired for, but also to guesstimate how much you will spend annually when you're retired.

Determining Your Cost of Living After Retirement

For years financial planners have assumed that couples need to replace somewhere between two-thirds and three-quarters of their past income to maintain their preretirement standard of living. The trouble is, that income-replacement ratio, as it is known, is simply too low. Why? Some expenses fall (clothes, commuting, housing, office lunches, and, of course, savings), while others are likely to rise (health care, travel, leisure and group activities, and utilities). However, researchers are finding that the decline in expenses is not as great as expected, especially at high-income levels.

Part of the problem is that retirees don't just sit about on rocking chairs exchanging tales with their neighbors. As retirees become more active, retirement becomes more expensive. People are using their retirement years to try all those hobbies they didn't try and travel to all those places they didn't see when they were younger. In Africa, I met a 78-year-old woman traveling alone on a group tour. She was as feisty as I expect someone 30 years younger to be, and said she wanted to get to Africa "before I get old." If you plan to be an old, bold retiree, then you need to plan for enough money.

A recent Aon Consulting/Georgia State University study[5] found that the income-replacement ratios should be more like 75 percent to 90 percent. The study found "only a relatively minor decrease in expenditure patterns after retirement." Higher earners should plan on using a replacement ratio of at least 85 percent. "Replacement ratios are higher at senior pay levels because, in relative terms, these individuals must pay higher post-retirement taxes than individuals at lower income levels."

One surprise in the study is that retirees spend about the same on transportation as do working families. Another factor that affects the rise in the replacement ratio is decreased savings. If you save, say, 10 percent of your income before retirement, then you are going to have no effective change in income if you only receive 90 percent of your income after retirement, simply because you no longer need to put money away. If, however, you were spending every penny before retirement, then you need to replace a larger amount of your income to sustain your standard of living. "Unfortunately, the study confirms that savings rates are shrinking, at least at the lower income levels."

The biggest wildcard in the equation is medical expenses. They are rising faster than inflation, and the scope of Medicare is slowly shrinking. Predicting your medical expenses, particularly if retirement is a long way off, is difficult. More than one-third of men

---

[5]*Benchmarking Retirement Income Needs: Latest Results.* Aon Consulting/Georgia State University Retirement Income Study, Georgia State University, March 2001 Forum.

and 45 percent of women are not confident about having enough money to take care of medical expenses in retirement.[6]

Saving Money for Retirement

The good news about saving for a long happy retirement is that the government wants you to do it. Not only does it have its own plan—Social Security—but also it gives a tax break on a number of plans that can help you either to save faster or to pay less tax when you retire. And the plans keep getting better. You can now put away more than ever before in tax-advantaged accounts, especially if you are over 50. This chapter gives you an overview of the many tools that you can use. Chapter 12 on Skill Five: Investing for Strong Returns discusses the specific investments you can use to grow your retirement savings. These investments include stocks, bonds, and mutual funds.

If your employer offers a retirement plan, be grateful and take advantage of it. An Aon Consulting Survey found that although only one-third of workers have a good idea of the amount of income their employers' plans will provide at retirement, employees still value the benefit highly. "Fifty-five percent would expect $10,000 or more in pay each year if their employer didn't offer a plan; 22 percent would expect $20,000 or more." When asked if they would rather have an increase in pay or benefits, 56 percent wanted more benefits.[7]

I discuss the main types of retirement plans that you may be able to invest in. Government employees, military personnel, and employees of some companies may be eligible for traditional pensions, also called defined-benefit plans. Most employers today, however, offer newer retirement savings plans, such as:

---

[6]2001 Retirement Confidence Survey conducted by the America Savings Education Council and the Employee Benefits Research Institute.
[7]*Get Personal with Retirement Planning and Employees Will Stick with You.* Aon Consulting Press Release, July 17, 2000.

- *401(k).* A widely-used employer-sponsored plan, where employees can contribute up to $11,000 of pretax earnings in 2002 ($12,000 if over 50, rising to $15,000 and $20,000, respectively, in 2006). Your contributions may be limited based on your earnings and whether colleagues contribute to the plan. Often the employer matches some of your contributions. It's free money! Don't miss out on it.
- *403(b).* Essentially the same as 401(k) but usually offered in the nonprofit and education sectors.
- *Regular IRA.* It allows you to save up to $3,000 a year in 2002 ($3,500 if you are over 50, rising to $5,000 and $6,000, respectively, by 2008), subject to limits based on income and other plans you contribute to.
- *Rollover IRA.* When you leave an employer, you can roll the money from plans such as a 401(k) or 403(b) into a Rollover IRA. This allows you to consolidate your accounts and manage your investments without the constraints of the employer's plan.
- *Roth IRA.* The Roth is a relatively new plan. The limit on a Roth IRA contribution is the same as for regular IRAs and is subject to income limits and other plans you contribute to. Most people who have an employer-sponsored plan can also contribute to a Roth IRA.
- *Simple IRA.* A plan offered in smaller companies. Employees can contribute up to $7,000 in 2002 ($7,500 if over 50, limits rise to $10,000 and $12,500, respectively, in 2006). The employer is required to make a contribution of up to 3 percent of employee compensation.
- *SEP IRA.* Designed for sole proprietors and very small firms, allows you to put away up to 15 percent of earnings to a maximum of $30,000. Funded by the employer.
- *Qualified Retirement Plans/Keogh.* Allows up to 25 percent of earnings to be put away and is usually used by individuals with relatively high stable incomes and few, if any, employees. It requires more administration and paperwork than other plans.

- *Variable annuities.* A tax/insurance hybrid that may be useful if you have contributed all you can to retirement plans or plan early retirement. Find a plan without excessive fees.
- *Regular savings and investments.* Useful if you plan to retire young and will need to draw on funds before you are able to access your retirement savings.

This outline is a very broad overview of the various tools. There are many more details that may affect you; for example, funds can be withdrawn from a regular IRA to pay for a home or education prior to age 59½. If your employer offers a plan and matches some of the contributions, that plan is the first place you should contribute funds. If not, then consider a Roth IRA as the first place to invest. Again, this is a topic you should discuss with a financial planner to ensure that you are taking advantage of all the retirement investment tools that are suitable for you.

The Tax Impact

When you are looking at retirement accounts, you need to think about how the contributions, earnings, and withdrawals are taxed. Generally, if the contributions are tax deductible, the earnings will accrue tax free, but distributions will be taxed on withdrawal. Examples of this type of account include most employer-sponsored plans, such as 401(k), 403(b), SEP IRA, Keogh, and Regular IRA. If the initial contribution is not tax deductible, the earnings and withdrawals may be tax free. An example of this type of plan is a Roth IRA. Of course, you can also save for retirement using a regular investment account, in which case there are no tax benefits.

If your retirement savings are tax deductible or come out of your income before you pay tax, putting, say, $5,000 in the plan will take less than $5,000 out of your after-tax income. The actual amount depends on your tax bracket and can be calculated by multiplying the amount by one minus your marginal tax rate. So if your state and federal taxes equal 32 percent, putting $5,000 into a 401(k) only takes $5,000 \times (1 - 0.32) = 5,000 \times 0.68 = $3,400 out of your pocket.

Reaching Your Retirement Goal

I started this chapter and intended to include detailed work sheets on how to calculate how much you will need based on your age, when you want to retire, how long you will live, how much you have put away already, how much Social Security you can expect, what return you will earn before and after retirement, whether your employer offers a pension, how much you have put away in Roth and after-tax savings, when the restaurants start offering early bird specials in your neighborhood and what the wind chill factor is in Chicago. Then I looked at an old reliable personal finance book and tried the retirement calculator, all seven pages of fine print and tables. I'd get bored writing such an exercise and you'd get repetitive strain injury in your calculator finger using it.

It's 2002 and the Internet has come to the rescue. If you don't have a computer, find a library or Internet café that does and let's go surfing. There are some very good retirement calculators on the Web. None are perfect, but most are good. The best allow you to tweak most assumptions: how long you will live, what return you will earn, whether Social Security will be scaled back. My biggest complaint is that most don't offer a simple printout of the assumptions and results. My suggestion is to run your numbers through two or three of these programs and take the most conservative results—better to save too much than too little. Sit down at the computer prepared to plug in:

- Your age today, at retirement, and perhaps expected life span.
- How much you have already saved.
- How much you can save each month.
- Income today and what you will need at retirement (see below).

Here is a review of some retirement calculators on the Web that are worth spending time on.

- www.usnews.com (look in the personal finance section under tools) is an extremely thorough calculator that takes into account the likelihood of Social Security and Medicare benefits being scaled back. It is the best I found, with most variables able to be adjusted, good explanations of the default settings, tables you can access on life expectancy, and other interesting topics. The weakness is it is hard to make changes in your assumptions without going back through a number of pages and it is not clear sometimes whether they are asking you to estimate some things before or after inflation; for example, pay raises. They have a slew of other financial calculators that are all well laid out and easy to use, including one that helps you adjust your savings plan if you expect to work part time for a while after retirement.
- www.kiplinger.com is a quick, back-of-the-cyber-envelope calculation that requires you to round your age and your years to retirement and so on to the nearest five. Does not differentiate between pretax and posttax retirement savings (e.g., 401(k) versus Roth IRA). Offers fewer ways to customize to your assumptions than some tools. It's great for checking how much results change if you adjust your retirement income up or down a bit. It's interesting to see how much less you will need to save if you cut your standard of living $5,000 a year in retirement, for example.
- www.money.com is a good retirement calculator that lies between U.S. News' complexity and Kiplinger's oversimplification. Nicely differentiates between types of current savings and allows you to calculate for employer matching.
- www.ssa.gov offers three calculators to determine what your Social Security benefit will be. One is a quick and dirty estimate based on current earnings, the second is more detailed and you input past earnings, and the final is a very detailed

calculation that requires downloading a program onto your computer.

The Tipping Point: Income for Life

As I run numbers to calculate retirement savings scenarios, I always get excited to find what I call the tipping point. Most retirement planning scenarios are shaped like a wave, with assets building up until retirement, then slowly dwindling down to nothing. The aim is to make sure that they do not hit zero before you hit the grave. However, there is a point in every scenario where the wave pattern suddenly breaks and looks more like a flight path. After retirement, instead of heading down, the total assets level off or continue to rise. The scenario never drops to zero. The fountain of youth is discovered; you cannot outlive your assets without choosing to increase your spending.

How? It's not that the retiree is not taking any money out, but rather that the amount withdrawn is less than the amount the portfolio earns each year by at least as much as is needed to cover the eroding effect of inflation. That is, the rate of return needs to be high enough both to give you the money you need and to cover the eroding effect of inflation. For example, $1,000,000 at an 8 percent return gives $80,000. If the income you need to live on is $60,000 and inflation is 2 percent, your portfolio will remain intact because $1,000,000 today will be worth $1,020,000 next year. Now if that math works year after year, your portfolio will remain steady or keep on growing while you live happily ever after.

There are a couple of catches with the tipping point. The first is that most investments do not generate a steady stream of income or grow at a steady rate. Therefore, if you have a good year in the market and your dividend income, capital gain, and interest income all add up to 15 percent one year, you may be able to live on your slice and reinvest the rest, but what if it is a slow year in the markets and your dividend income, capital gain, and interest income only add up to 4 percent and that is not enough to live on? You can either scale back your cost of living for a year or dip into your capital. The second catch is that the earlier you retire, the less likely you are to reach your tipping point.

Rethinking Retirement

If the numbers simply don't add up and your retirement dreams seem out of reach, redefine the dream. You can rethink both the standard of living you will have during retirement and the age at which and way that you will retire.

Managing Your Cost of Living After Retirement

One way to make retirement more comfortable is to lower your underlying cost of living. There are a number of ways to lower your cost of living without getting into extreme coupon clipping and hunting for early bird specials. The key is to find the balance between a good lifestyle—you retired so it would be more fun, not less—and an affordable cost of living.

You can change many factors in your lifestyle to lower your living expenses. Moving to a smaller home, moving to a lower-cost neighborhood, moving to a community where you can walk rather than drive everywhere, or moving to an area where taxes are lower (Florida is not only popular among retirees because of the weather) can make a significant difference. Another way to manage the cost of living after retirement is to get fit. Health care is a large slice of a retiree's expenses, and studies show that weight-bearing exercises and general fitness can lower the chances of your suffering from many common illnesses and injuries. And there are many other areas in your spending plan of the future where small trimming can add up to a big difference.

Semiretirement and Second Careers

Many people who retire find themselves surprised at how quickly they start climbing the walls with boredom. When life is too busy, the thought of uninterrupted days on the golf course may sound tempting. But when there is nothing to interrupt the days, the golf course can feel as oppressive as the office. Often, what people crave is not retirement, but choice. Choice about how they spend their days. Choice about what career or interests they follow. Choice about how much vacation to take a year.

It is possible to get that choice *without* leaving the workforce completely. If you extend the time that you are working, you give your retirement savings longer to grow. If staying in your current job a few extra years doesn't appeal to you, consider taking a break, changing what you do or how you do it. Even if you cut your income to the degree that you are not able to put away anything extra for retirement in those years, you will still give your investments time to grow, and as we have seen, those later years of growth are the most important. This strategy may also be good if you plan to retire earlier than your spouse.

Taking a Sabbatical

The first option is to take some time off to recharge. Sabbaticals are becoming increasingly popular as companies realize that their most experienced workers appreciate the opportunity to explore their dreams without cutting ties to the workforce. Even if you take leave without pay, if it means that you find the energy and enthusiasm to stay in the workforce for a few more years, it can be a very productive time. Sabbaticals, usually from 3 months to a year, can be used for anything from simply wandering the world to pursuing a dream project.

Working Part-Time

The second option is to cut the number of hours you work and cut your earnings commensurately. Even one extra day of leisure a week feels liberating if you have been working 5 days a week for years. Another big advantage is that you may be able to keep benefits such as health care and employer-sponsored retirement contributions while you work part-time.

Doing Consulting, Temporary, or Seasonal Work

Third, many people are asked to come back to work on a consulting or project basis after they leave the full-time workforce. The advantage of seasonal, temporary, or consulting work over part-time work is that it can leave large blocks of time for travel. Often, it is lucrative because consulting fees take into account your lack of benefits and uncertainty of workflow. Many people have found themselves earning as much consulting 4 to 6 months a year as they used to earn working a full year. However, it is less predictable than part-time work and may be harder to keep a stream of projects in the pipeline.

Finding a Second Career

The final option to extend your working years is to go and do whatever you dreamed of doing just for the fun of it. Many people retire so that they can pursue their true, heartfelt interests. Often those interests happen to earn money too. I have seen stockbrokers become school teachers, teachers become dive instructors, attorneys open jazz stores, reporters become academics. They all reached times in their lives where they could afford to decrease their income and they all had other passions that they wanted to pursue. Some even ended up earning as much or more in their second career as they did in their first career.

The Last Word About Love and Money

I started this book by talking about the complicated mix of love and money. It is a difficult, but far from impossible, combination to manage. I aimed to give you three financial rules to live by that can get you and your partner singing the same financial tune; seven skills to help you both manage your money better and manage your relationship around money better; and insights into the four biggest financial decisions you will make as a couple.

The challenge for you now is to take the lessons you need and start applying them every day. You may have to make a lot of little changes, such as getting into good habits and simplifying your structure, or you may have to make a substantial change in the way you reach financial decisions and talk about money as a couple. With some effort, you will work together to iron out the wrinkles that can arise where your emotional and financial worlds meet.

Money is a really awesome tool. It can buy you many things that can make your life more fun, comfortable, and fulfilling. However, your relationship is more valuable than any amount of money, and it is hoped that this book will give you tools to ensure that the way you manage money never weakens the strength of your relationship.

Bibliography

Books

Edelman, Ric. *Ordinary People, Extraordinary Wealth*. New York: HarperCollins, 2000.

Esperti, Robert A., Renno L. Peterson, and Edward L. Weidenfeld. *Generations: Planning Your Legacy—Practical Answers from America's Foremost Estate Planning Attorneys*. Denver, CO: Esperti Peterson Institute, 1999.

Gottman, John, with Nan Silver. *Why Marriages Succeed or Fail, and How You Can Make Yours Last*. New York: Fireside, 1994.

Gottman, John, and Nan Silver. *The Seven Principles for Making Marriage Work*. New York: Three Rivers Press, 1999.

Hendrix, Harville. *Getting the Love You Want: A Guide for Couples*. New York: Henry Holt, 1988.

Hertz, Rosanna. *More Equal Than Others: Women and Men in Dual Career Marriages*. Berkeley, CA: University of California Press, 1986.

Jaffe, Charles A. *The Right Way to Hire Financial Help: A Complete Guide to Choosing and Managing Brokers, Financial Planners, Insurance Agents, Lawyers, Tax Preparers, Bankers and Real Estate Agents*. Cambridge, MA: MIT Press, 2001.

Klebanow, Sheila, and Eugene L. Lowenkopf, eds. *Money and Mind*. New York: Plenum Press, 1991.

Lasser, J. K. *New Tax Law Simplified*. New York: John Wiley & Sons, 2001.

Lasser, J. K. *Your Income Tax 2002*. New York: John Wiley & Sons, 2001.

Millman, Marcia. *Warm Hearts and Cold Cash: The Intimate Dynamics of Families and Money*. New York: Free Press, 1991.

Pahl, Jan. *Money and Marriage*. New York: St. Martin's Press, 1989.

Stanley, Thomas J. *The Millionaire Mind*. Kansas City, MO: Andrews McMeel, 2000.

Stanley, Thomas J., and William D. Danko. *The Millionaire Next Door*. New York: Pocket Books, 1996.

Tannen, Deborah. *I Only Say This Because I Love You: How the Way We Talk Can Make or Break Family Relationships Throughout Our Lives*. New York: Random House, 2001.

Underhill, Paco. *Why We Buy: The Science of Shopping*. New York: Simon & Schuster, 1999.

Studies/Articles

Amato, Paul R., and Stacy J. Rogers. "A Longitudinal Study of Marital Problems and Subsequent Divorce." *Journal of Marriage and the Family* 59, no. 3 (August 1997): 612–624.

Atwood, Elizabeth Baker. "Money and Marriage: An Exploration of the Psychological Meanings of Money in the Couples Relationship." Ph.D. diss., Massachusetts School of Professional Psychology, 1998.

Berry, R. E., and F. L. Williams. "Assessing the Relationship Between Quality of Life and Marital Satisfaction: A Path Analytic Approach." *Journal of Marriage and the Family* 49 (1987): 107–116.

Ferber, Robert, and Lucy Chao-Lee. "Husband–Wife Influence in Family Purchasing Behavior." *Journal of Consumer Research* 1, no. 1 (June 1974): 43–50.

Gross, David B., and Nicholas S. Souleles. "Consumer Response to Changes in Credit Supply: Evidence from Credit Card Data." The Wharton Financial Institutions Center, University of Pennsylvania, February 2000.

Hira, Tahira, and Olive Mugenda. "Gender Differences in Financial Perceptions, Behaviors, and Satisfaction." *Journal of Financial Planning* 13, no. 2 (2000): 86–92.

Koutstaal, Stanley W. "What's Money Got to Do with It: How Financial Issues Relate to Marital Satisfaction." Ph.D. diss., Texas Tech University, 1998.

Lockard, Gail Ann. "Gender, Age, and Money: A Study of Confidence and Competence." Abstract in Ph.D. diss., University of Nebraska, Lincoln, 1992. *Dissertation Abstracts International* 53, no. 7-A (January 1993): 2301.

Lynn, Richard. "Sex Differences in Competitiveness and the Valuation of Money in Twenty Countries." *Journal of Social Psychology* 133, no. 4 (August 1993): 507–511.

Newcomb, Michael D., and Jerome Rabow. "Gender, Socialization, and Money." *Journal of Applied Social Psychology* 29, no. 4 (1999): 852–869.

Pahl, Jan. "The Allocation of Money and the Structuring of Inequality Within Marriage." *Sociological Review* 31 (1983): 237–262.

Prince, Melvin. "Women, Men, and Money Styles." *Journal of Economic Psychology* 14, no. 1 (March 1993): 175–182.

Singh, Supriya, and Jo Lindsay. "Money in Heterosexual Relationships." *Australian and New Zealand Journal of Sociology* 32, no. 3 (Nov 1996): 57–69.

Sternberg, Daniel P., and Ernst G. Beier. "Changing Patterns of Conflict." *Journal of Communication* 27, no. 3 (Summer 1977): 97–100.

Turkel, Ann Ruth. "Money as a Mirror of Marriage." *Journal of the American Academy of Psychoanalysis* 16, no. 4 (1988): 525–535.

Other Resources

Visit www.deborahknuckey.com for more information including:

- Lists of recommended reading.
- Links to useful resources on the Web.
- A downloadable spreadsheet for calculating your net worth and spending plan.
- Information on booking Deborah Knuckey for workshops, events and conferences.
- A schedule of upcoming events.

Deborah Knuckey's first book, *The Ms. Spent Money Guide: Get More of What You Want with What You Earn* is now available in paperback from John Wiley & Sons.

Index